EMPLOYMENT LAW

An Essential Guide for Colorado Employers

EMPLOYMENT LAW

An Essential Guide for Colorado Employers

KIMBERLIE K. RYAN, ESQ.

BRADFORD PUBLISHING COMPANY
Denver, Colorado

DISCLAIMER

This book is intended to provide general information with regard to the subject matter covered. It is not meant to provide legal opinions or to offer advice, nor to serve as a substitute for advice by licensed, legal or other professionals. This book is sold with the understanding that Bradford Publishing Company and the author(s), by virtue of its publication, are not engaged in rendering legal or other professional services to the reader.

Bradford Publishing Company and the author(s) do not warrant that the information contained in this book is complete or accurate, and do not assume and hereby disclaim any liability to any person for any loss or damage caused by errors, inaccuracies or omissions, or usage of this book.

Laws, and interpretations of those laws, change frequently, and the subject matter of this book can have important legal consequences that may vary from one individual to the next. It is therefore the responsibility of the reader to know whether, and to what extent, this information is applicable to his or her situation, and if necessary, to consult legal, tax, or other counsel.

Library of Congress Cataloging-in-Publication Data

Ryan, Kimberlie K.
  Employment law : an essential guide for Colorado employers / by
Kimberlie K. Ryan.
     p. cm.
  Includes index.
  ISBN 1-883726-93-X
  1. Labor laws and legislation--Colorado. I. Title.

KFC2131.Z9.R93 2004
344.78801--dc22

                        2003028048

Cover design by Cynthia Fonseca
Employment Law: An Essential Guide for Colorado Employers
ISBN: 1-883726-93-X

Published 2004 by Bradford Publishing Company
1743 Wazee Street, Denver, Colorado 80202
www.bradfordpublishing.com

ABOUT THE AUTHOR

Kimberlie K. Ryan, founder of The Ryan Law Firm, L.L.C., is a former "big-firm" attorney and Colorado native. Having represented companies of all sizes in employment matters, as well as individuals, she has a broad perspective from "both sides of the fence." As an attorney, speaker, and trainer for companies, Ms. Ryan knows the day-to-day issues facing employers in the ever-changing area of employment law. Because of this, she is in a unique position to help employers anticipate problems before they arise and to take action to help prevent them.

Ms. Ryan obtained her Juris Doctorate (J.D.), Master's of Public Administration (MPA), with an emphasis in Economic Development, and her Bachelor's of Arts (B.A.), cum laude, from Texas Tech University. She is licensed to practice law in Colorado and Texas, the Federal District Court of the District of Colorado, and the Tenth Circuit Court of Appeals. A prolific writer, Ms. Ryan has authored numerous articles for legal and business publications on cutting-edge issues in employment law, and she has facilitated training with companies, community groups, and individuals to help them understand their rights and responsibilities under the laws. Ms. Ryan is a member and active participant in many professional organizations, including the Denver Bar Association, Colorado Bar Association, and the Texas and Dallas Bar associations. She may be reached at (303) 355-0639, or via e-mail at kryan@ryanfirm.com.

ACKNOWLEDGEMENTS

I am indebted to Mr. Greg Smith and the wonderful people of Bradford Publishing (Reda, Lisa, Peter, Brent, and the entire organization) for recognizing the importance of employment law to our community, and for their immeasurable patience and staunch support for this project from start to finish.

To my fantastic teachers and professors, including Mr. Turner (Lt. Col., (Ret.)(Rampart High School, Colorado Springs); Dr. Robert M. Lawrence (Colorado State University, Political Science Department); Dr. Jerry Perkins, Dr. Kimberly-Farley Bernasky, and Dr. Evan Ringquist (formerly with Texas Tech University Center for Public Service); Professor Dean Pawlowic and Professor James Eissinger (Texas Tech University School of Law), I thank you for your thoughtful and excellent instruction in political science, public policy, and law, and for making it real in my life.

I could not have wished for more supportive colleagues and friends, who encouraged me and provided valuable insights as the book came to life, especially Ms. Julia Julian (HR Consultant, Translator, Trainer), Ms. Cynthia Wellbrock (Law Offices of Cynthia Wellbrock), Ms. Nora Nye (labor attorney and arbitrator), Ms. Brenda Ridgley, SPHR (HR Consultant, Business Owner, Saddleback Grapes & Grains), Mr. David Fine (Kelly, Haglund Garnsey & Kahn, LLC), Ms. Selena Solis (Mexican American Legal Defense and Educational Fund), Mr. Joseph Salazar, Esq., Ms. Heidi Van Huysen, Esq., and counsel at the Equal Employment Opportunity Commission, including Ms. Evangelina Hernandez, Ms. Nancy Weeks, Mr. Nelson Alston, and Ms. Ann Fuller.

Finally, and importantly, I could never have embarked on this journey without the inspiration, love, and support of my family, especially Kyle, Mom, Kellie, and Uncle Jim. Kyle, you are the light of my life, and you inspire me every day to continue fighting for equality for all. Mom, you taught me that we don't have to settle for roles others assign to us and that we can break the mold and make a difference in this world. Kellie, you have exemplified strength and perseverance and have taught me to reach for my dreams. Uncle Jim, you inspired my love of the law and encourage me to fight the good fight. To all of my friends, family, and Angels, thank you.

CONTENTS

CHAPTER 1:
The People Who Work For Employers

Employers Are Who They Hire

An employment relationship is one of the most significant relationships a person can have, outside of family and friends. Some people spend more time with their work colleagues than their own families. Like a marriage, an employment relationship can be joyous bliss or pure hell (or usually somewhere in between, depending on the day). Like some marriages, an employment relationship sometimes is entered into for the wrong reasons, lacking enough thought, or without much planning for the future. Yet, whether employers know it or not, "employers are who they hire," and that can have legal, financial, and personal consequences, for better or worse. To understand some of the legal aspects of hiring workers, it is helpful to review the concept of "employment at-will," the differences between independent contractors and employees, employer liability for workers' actions, and the implications of these issues for the employer.

The Low-Down on Employment At-Will

Colorado employers may understand that Colorado is an "at-will" state. But what exactly does employment at-will mean? The phrase "employment at-will" can be confusing, although at first glance it seems easy enough to some. In its simplest terms, employment at-will is a general rule that allows an employer to end an employee's employment at *any time* and for *any reason* or *no reason*. Likewise, it allows an employee to quit the employment at any time, without notice, for any reason or no reason. Easy, right? Wrong.

> ***WORDS OF WISDOM:*** Remember, "employment at-will" is different from a "right to work." Employment at-will allows the employment to end at any time, unless an exception applies. Right to work is a union term and involves the right to opt out of paying certain union dues.

Like many rules, the employment at-will rule has exceptions, and without an understanding of the exceptions, an employer applying the general employment at-will rule can easily run into difficult (and expensive) legal pitfalls. To understand the employment at-will rule, its exceptions, and ways to avoid legal difficulties, it is helpful to review the reason for the rule in the first place.

The Reason for the Employment At-Will Rule

Once upon a time, English law governed early Americans. Therefore, like many of the legal concepts in American law, the idea of employment at-will is the result of an English law transformed into something new.

English case law said that if an employer hired a worker without stating in advance the length of the employment time, the employer was required to keep the worker for one year. Imagine the difficulties this inflexible rule caused American employers. The only exception that allowed an employer to fire a worker before the end of one year arose when the employer could prove the worker had done something wrong (i.e., fired for "good cause").

Early American law changed the presumption of year-long employment, giving more flexibility to employers by stating that unless the employer and employee had agreed to a specific amount of time for the employment, the worker was hired for an indefinite period of time. Because the employment was for an indefinite period of time, either the employer or the worker could end the employment at any time for any reason or for no reason—even *without* good cause.

If that was the end of the story, employers could terminate workers' employment with little risk of lawsuits for improperly ending the employment relationship. But like many rules, over time the general rule of employment at-will has developed many exceptions. In fact, there are so many exceptions that the rule is almost meaningless, and employers who rely on the at-will rule too heavily, without looking at the exceptions, may be putting their businesses in jeopardy due to the risks of lawsuits.

But there is good news for employers. First, if a specific amount of employment time is not expressly stated during the hiring process, there is a presumption that the employment relationship is at-will. A presumption of at-will employment means that the *employee* has the *burden* to prove that he or she was not employed at-will or that one of the exceptions applies. Second, knowledge of employment at-will exceptions, and an awareness of how to apply them, can minimize the risks of lawsuits significantly.

WORDS OF WISDOM: Employers can minimize the risk of lawsuits by knowing and applying the exceptions to the employment at-will rule both before and after hiring.

The Many Exceptions to Employment At-Will

Since the late 1800s a number of exceptions to the employment at-will rule have evolved, giving employees some protection from the risk of losing their jobs. These exceptions fall into four broad categories:

1. Statutory exceptions;
2. Public policy exceptions;
3. Contract exception; and
4. Promissory estoppel exception.

Statutory Exceptions—All Those Laws!

WORDS OF WISDOM: Many state and federal laws impact the employment at-will rule.

While there are many laws protecting employers, Congress has also created laws to protect employees. Federal laws, and many state laws, limit the right of employers to terminate the employment of at-will employees. In general, a law may provide that an employee may qualify for *protected status* under the law if the employee meets specific criteria. If an employee qualifies for protected status and the employee is being fired because of employee's protected status, the employee cannot be terminated. In other words, an employee can not be fired *because* of his or her protected status.

For example, Congress passed a law prohibiting employers from firing women *because* they are pregnant. This law is called the Pregnancy Discrimination Act (PDA),[1] and it overrides the general rule of employment at-will. Although an employer *generally* has the right to fire a worker at any time for any or no reason the PDA forbids firing based on pregnancy. Thus, the PDA is an exception to employment at-will.

Similarly, in 1964, Congress passed the Civil Rights Act,[2] which prohibits employers from firing workers because of the workers' race, sex, national origin, color, or religion. Thus, the Civil Rights Act also overrides the general rule of employment at-will.

The legislators in the state of Colorado have also passed laws affecting employment. For example, the Colorado legislature passed a law, sometimes called the "smoker's law," designed to protect workers from being fired for engaging in lawful activities outside of work.[3] This law, with limited exceptions, prevents employers from firing a worker involved in legal activities while off-duty and off-premises, unless the conduct relates to job requirements, or to avoid a conflict of interest. Although the tobacco lobby originally proposed the law to protect smokers, the Colorado legislature expanded the law to encompass virtually every legal activity.

Colorado legislators also have passed a law protecting employees from discrimination based on the employee's marital status.[4] In the past, some companies preferred to employ single people rather than married individuals. For example, some airlines preferred to hire young, attractive, single flight attendants, and the airlines actually fired employees if they got married! However, because this Colorado law overrides the employment at-will rule, it limits the ability of employers to fire their employees based upon the marital status of the employee.

These state and federal laws clearly affect the employment at-will rule, and any time an employer considers terminating a worker, the employer should determine whether any of these laws could apply. The penalties for violating these laws could include back pay and benefits, damages for emotional distress, front pay, punitive damages, attorney fees, interest, and costs. Additionally, some of these laws provide for double or triple damages. These laws are discussed throughout this book, and a list of many laws employers should know is contained in Appendix 1.

Public Policy Exceptions—For the Common Good

WORDS OF WISDOM: Laws and rules sometimes advance important public goals and can alter the at-will employment relationship.

In addition to state and federal laws, employers also should be aware of public policy exceptions to employment at-will. Basically, public policy is a statement of what is good for the general population, such as issues that benefit public health, safety, or welfare. For example, the Colorado workers' compensation laws advance the important public policy of protecting workers who are injured on the job. To uphold this important public policy, Colorado courts have ruled that employers who fire workers because the workers file workers' compensation claims can be held liable for wrongful termination in violation of public policy.[5]

Sometimes, public policy is expressed through rules, such as the State Board of Accountancy Rules of Professional Conduct (ARPC). For example, ARPC Rule 7.3 directs accountants to refrain from knowingly misrepresenting facts. In one Colorado case, an accountant sued her employer for wrongful termination when the company fired her because she reported irregular accounting practices.[6] The accountant claimed that the company forced her to make a decision between loyalty to her employer and loyalty to her professional code of conduct, which required her to report accounting irregularities. The Colorado Supreme Court ruled that the employee could use a professional code of conduct to support her wrongful termination claim. Although the case ultimately settled out of court, the decision broadened workers' protections against wrongful termination in violation of public policy.

Additionally, Colorado courts have ruled that employers cannot terminate a worker's employment because of a worker's refusal to commit an illegal act. Thus, although an employer generally can end employment at-will, the public policy exception limits this ability.

WORDS OF WISDOM: Violations of the public policy exception can cost employers damages for the former employee's wage and benefit losses, economic losses (such as expenses for job searches), punitive amounts, and other losses. In Colorado the costs to

---

employers could be as much as $350,000 and over $700,000 in aggravated cases![7]

To avoid public policy wrongful discharge claims, an employer should consider at least two questions before firing an employee: (1) whether the employee is being terminated because he or she exercised a legal right or privilege (e.g. filing a workers' compensation claim); and (2) whether the employee is being terminated because he or she refused to commit an illegal act.

Contract Exception—"We Had an Agreement!"

WORDS OF WISDOM: Contracts can arise in many ways! In addition to written agreements, contracts can be found in offer letters, action plans, discussions, and handbooks.

Probably the easiest contract to spot is a written document signed by both parties in which they agree that the employment will last for a specific amount of time, such as a two-year contract.

However, employers must be careful because contracts can arise in ways employers may not realize. In addition to a written contract, there are other ways to create a contract, including a verbal agreement reached during a discussion; an offer letter; a performance review; an action plan; an employee handbook; progressive discipline policies; and other documents given to employees. Chapter 2 explores contracts in more depth, but for the purposes of this discussion, it is important to realize that contracts, either verbal or written, are another exception to employment at-will, and they can limit the employer's ability to terminate an employee at any time for any or no reason.

When an employer and worker sign a valid contract, the Colorado courts will enforce the promises the employer made in the contract. That means that if the contract says that the employment will last for two years, the employer essentially has limited his or her ability to terminate the employment without cause.

Additionally, if the employer and employee have agreed to a specific term of employment, an employer generally cannot terminate the employment without cause during the employment term without facing potential liability for breach of contract.

Promissory Estoppel Exception—"I Relied on You!"

WORDS OF WISDOM: Employers should say what they mean and mean what they say!

Sometimes employers make promises to employees that do not have all of the legal elements of a contract, and yet the court enforces the employers' promises to avoid injustice. Courts often enforce promises where the employer reasonably should have expected the employee to rely on the promise, the employee did in fact reasonably rely on the promise to his or her detriment, and injustice can be avoided only by enforcement of the promise.

WORDS OF WISDOM: The Colorado Supreme Court has explained that promissory estoppel comes from the basic concept that one who makes promises should be required to keep them—even if there isn't a contract.[8]

For example, in one case called *Pickell v. Arizona Components Co.*,[9] a Colorado employer recruited an employee to leave her job based on assurances that the company would give her better future prospects, paid vacations, a year-end bonus, and full insurance benefits. Ms. Pickell relied on these promises, quit her job, and moved to join the Colorado employer. After only two months, the Colorado employer terminated Ms. Pickell's employment for financial reasons, and she brought a lawsuit.

WORDS OF WISDOM: A valid promissory estoppel claim can cost an employer whatever the court determines justice requires!

The court awarded Ms. Pickell a full year's salary. Ultimately, after many court battles, the Colorado Supreme Court held that a promise of employment for a "reasonable time" is enough to overcome the presumption of employment at-will. The court's decision cost the company Ms. Pickell's salary for a year, as well as lots of legal fees, time, and energy. Colorado employers can avoid these kinds of problems by refraining from making promises they cannot keep and having a well-thought out plan for all hiring decisions. (Chapter 3 discusses practical steps to take during the pre-hire process.)

How to Avoid Employment At-Will Pitfalls

WORDS OF WISDOM: "You're at-will, so I can fire you any time I want!" Translation: "You are hereby cordially invited to sue the company, possibly for a lot of money, if one of the employment at-will exceptions applies!"

Along with the general at-will employment rule and its many exceptions, there are also potential pitfalls. The first pitfall to avoid is making a firing decision based solely on the at-will employment rule. Numerous employers have invited lawsuits by neglecting to consider the exceptions to the at-will employment rule and proclaiming to the fired employee, "Colorado is an at-will employment state, so I can fire you any time!"

As stated earlier, that is not necessarily the case. It is true that an employer can terminate a worker's employment if none of the exceptions applies. However, there are so many exceptions that it is rare for an employer to avoid liability absent some significant wrong-doing by the employee.

A similar pitfall to avoid is making a hasty firing decision, without first analyzing the exceptions to employment at-will. In the heat of the moment, it is easy to make a quick decision and hope to solve the issue of a problem employee by firing the worker. Even when it seems like a slam-dunk employment at-will situation (and probably *especially* when it seems that way), the employer usually should stop and take some time to analyze the situation to avoid potential problems.

A third employment at-will pitfall to avoid is making a firing decision without determining if the employee is covered by an "unintended contract." Employers who plan on relying on the at-will employment rule may be surprised to realize that they are bound by statements made in company documents. Rather than being at-will, the employee actually may have a contract with the company. (Contracts and unintended contracts are discussed more fully in Chapter 2.)

Are the Independent Contractors Really Employees?

WORDS OF WISDOM: Usually the degree of control determines whether a worker is an employee or an independent contractor.

One of the first things to consider when hiring someone to perform a job is whether to hire an employee or an independent contractor. What's the difference between these types of workers? A general rule is that anyone who performs services for an employer is an employee if the employer can control *what* will be done and *how* it will be done. On the other hand, with an independent contractor, an employer has the right to control or direct only the *result* of the work done and *not* the means and methods of accomplishing the result. The degree of control the company exercises over the worker is usually central to the determination of the type of employment, although as discussed later, there is usually no clear cut way to ascertain employment type so each situation should be analyzed on a case-by-case or job-by-job basis.

Advantages and Disadvantages of Independent Contractors versus Employees

According to the U.S. Bureau of Labor Statistics, more than 10 million independent contractors are in the workforce, and at least 60 percent of all businesses use independent contractors to perform a wide variety of work—from accounting and legal services, to computer and technological positions. In tight economies, many employers utilize the services of independent contractors to cut the costs of benefits, taxes, and work tools. Independent contractors can provide for short-term needs, and some employers like the flexibility often provided by independent contractors.

On the other hand, employers may find that independent contractors cannot provide the kind of continuity and loyalty good employees can provide. Additionally, employees often have a stake in the business that independent contractors do not. By definition, the employer has more control over employees than independent contractors, and can direct employee training and supervision to achieve results consistent with the employer's objectives. Also, by hiring employees, employers do not face the same types of problems that can arise with the misclassification of independent contractors who later are determined to be employees.

Determining Classification as Employee or Independent Contractor

It is important to make the determination of employment classification early for several reasons, including resolving tax liability; computing the number of employees for the purposes of many federal, workers' compensation, and unemployment laws; understanding liability for the acts of workers; insurance issues; and other legal duties owed to each other. For example, an employer generally must withhold income taxes, withhold and pay social security and Medicare taxes, and pay unemployment tax on wages paid to an employee. In contrast, a company does not generally have to withhold or pay any taxes on payments to independent contractors and usually has less liability regarding the conduct of the independent contractor.

Unfortunately, some employers have learned that although they may have thought they were working with independent contractors, the federal Internal Revenue Service (IRS) believed that the companies had actually hired employees, "disguised" (or misclassified) as independent contractors. Importantly, the title attached to the job is *not* determinative of job status. Nor is a written contract stating the worker is independent contractor enough to make the worker an independent contractor. Because misclassification of workers has cost some employers millions of dollars, it is useful to learn from their mistakes and minimize the risks of potential liability. Therefore, it is vital to go though the necessary steps to determine whether the worker actually fits the legal definition of independent contractor.

WORDS OF WISDOM: The definition of "employee" may vary, depending on the statute and/or the agency involved. The discussion in this chapter focuses on the IRS definition of "employee" to distinguish between employees and independent contractors.

One of the ways to determine the classification of a worker is by looking at the three broad categories of evidence the IRS uses (which are also often used by courts):

1. Behavioral control;
2. Financial control; and
3. Relationship of the parties.

These categories are referred to as the "control test." According to the IRS, it is important to remember that all of the facts of the situation must be examined to conclude whether the control test is satisfied. No single category in the control test will determine the classification of the employee.

Behavioral Control

The first question an employer should ask in looking at whether the company has behavioral control over a worker is whether the employer has the right to direct and control how the worker does the work. Even if the employer does not actually direct or control how the work is done (for example, if a particular worker needs little supervision), if the employer has the *right* to control the way the worker works, it is more likely that the worker is an employee. Important factors to consider in looking at the right of control are:

1. Instructions; and
2. Training.

A worker may be an employee if the employer gives the worker detailed instructions regarding how the work is to be done, including: when, how, or where to do the work; what tools or equipment to use; what assistants to help with the work; and where to purchase the materials and services. Similarly, if an employer trains the worker to perform tasks in a certain way, then the worker may be an employee. On the other hand, an independent contractor generally provides his or her own tools, equipment, and materials, can hire employees or subcontractors as needed, and usually provides his or her own training.

An example provided by the IRS is a helpful illustration of the different types of behavioral control.[10] Let's look at Joe, the carpenter. He works for a construction company. The company requires him to begin work at 7:00 a.m. each day. The company provides all the tools and materials he needs on the job site. The company gives

Joe a W-2 that shows his wages, tax withheld, and Social Security tax. He is an employee of the company.

Joe also does carpentry work on the side. He has his own tools and buys the materials for these side jobs. As long as Joe meets his customers' deadlines, he can work on the side jobs any time he wishes. Joe receives 1099 Forms for his carpentry jobs that show the income that he has earned, and he must keep records of all of his income (whether he received a Form 1099 or not). Joe has to pay his own self-employment tax. He is a self-employed independent contractor for his side jobs.

Financial Control

After looking at the behavioral control category, the next step is to examine whether the employer has financial control, or the right to direct and control the economic aspects of the work. In determining financial control the IRS considers several factors of evidence, including: significant investment, expenses, and opportunity for profit or loss. No precise dollar amount is used to measure financial control over the worker. If the worker must own or rent costly equipment to do the work, has high, on-going expenses that the company does not reimburse, and has significant freedom to make decisions impacting his or her profit or loss, the worker may be a independent contractor. While an employee may make similar decisions impacting profit or loss, the decisions usually do not affect an employee's salary the way they would an independent contractor.

Relationship of the Parties

In addition to looking at the categories of behavioral and financial control, another aspect to be considered in determining whether the worker is an employee or independent contractor is the way the worker and the company view their relationship.

Sometimes employee benefits can provide evidence regarding the relationship of the parties. For example, the provisions of benefits, such as paid vacation, sick days, health insurance, or a pension may signal employee status. However, some employees do not receive benefits, so while benefits may be an important sign, they are not solely conclusive.

WORDS OF WISDOM: Simply calling a worker an independent contractor in a written contract does not create an independent contractor relationship.

Written contracts can also be helpful to ascertain the relationship of the parties. However, a designation of independent contractor alone is not enough to create a contractor relationship, especially if the other factors, such as behavioral or financial control are present. The actual facts in each situation are more important than the words in a contract, but all other things being equal, a contract may be a deciding factor in making the status determination.

For more information on how to determine whether an individual is an employee or an independent contractor, see www.irs.gov and refer to IRS Publication 15-A—*Employer's Supplemental Tax Guide*,[11] or Topic 762 *Independent Contractor vs. Employee.*[12]

In order to have the IRS determine whether a worker is an employee or an independent contractor, employers can file Form SS-8, *Determination of Employee Work Status for Purposes of Federal Employment Taxes and Income Tax Withholding*, with the IRS.[13]

Problems with Misclassification of Workers—"We Owe How Much?!"

As previously discussed, one of the problems with classifying workers as independent contractors is the cost of back taxes and penalties if the IRS later determines they were actually employees. Another potential problem is the expense of benefits to workers the IRS classifies as employees. Companies can learn from the mistake made by Microsoft Corporation, which had misclassified a work group of freelance proofreaders, software testers, production editors, formatters, and indexers as independent contractors.[14]

The major problem for Microsoft was that the company failed to treat the independent contractors as independent contractors. Although the workgroup individuals were hired to work on specific projects, Microsoft did not treat the workers as people who owned their own independent businesses. Rather, Microsoft treated them like employees—having them work on teams along with regular employees, performing the same functions during the same hours, and reporting to the same supervisors. Microsoft also provided them with workspace, keys to the building, supplies, and office equipment.

Additionally, Microsoft told the individuals in the work group that as independent contractors, they were ineligible for the benefits (e.g., paid vacation, sick leave, holiday pay, short-term disability insurance, group life and health insurance, and participation in 401(k) and stock purchase plans) available to regular, permanent Microsoft employees. The individuals had all signed "Microsoft Corporation Independent Contractor Copyright Assignment and Non-Disclosure Agreements" in which the workers agreed that as independent contractors they were responsible for their own federal and state taxes, withholding taxes, social security, insurance, and other benefits.

Later, the IRS conducted an employment tax audit examining whether Microsoft's classification of the work group individuals as independent contractors was proper. The IRS concluded that Microsoft either exercised, or retained the right to exercise, direction over the services performed by these workers, and that the individuals should have been classified as employees. Microsoft was then required to make payment for overdue employment taxes.

In response to this audit, Microsoft restructured the work group. Microsoft hired several of the former independent contractors as employees and terminated others. Some of the members of the work group sought coverage under various Microsoft benefit plans for benefits during the time that they had been classified as independent contractors rather than employees.

Microsoft said that under the individual agreements, the work group individuals were ineligible for the benefits and denied the workers' request. The workers filed suit in federal court challenging the denial of benefits.[15] The work group individuals ultimately recovered benefits under the company's stock purchase plan because of the stock purchase plan's ambiguity regarding coverage, at significant cost to the company (in addition to the past taxes the company owed as a result of the misclassification of employees as independent contractors).

WORDS OF WISDOM: In addition to properly classifying workers, companies should review benefit plans to make sure that the plans clearly define which workers are entitled to benefits.

The Microsoft case is an example of how things can go wrong when employees are misclassified, resulting in tax liabilities and penalties, as well as the potential cost of benefits ultimately being supplied to misclassified workers. It also is a reminder that merely having an agreement saying that a worker is an independent contractor is not enough.

Section 530 Relief Requirements—"Oh, What a Relief It Is!"

Now, let's say it's audit time for the company. Don't panic. Even if the IRS selects a company for an employment tax audit to determine whether the employer correctly classified and treated workers as independent contractors or employees, if the company meets the Section 530 relief requirements provided by the IRS, it will not owe employment taxes for the workers (even if the company incorrectly classified the workers).[16]

On the other hand, if an employer does *not* meet these relief requirements, the IRS will need to determine whether the workers are independent contractors or employees, and whether the employer owes employment taxes for those workers.

According to the IRS, a business will receive Section 530 relief if the employer meets *all* three of the following requirements:

1. Reasonable basis;
2. Substantive consistency; and
3. Reporting consistency.

Reasonable Basis

To establish that a business had a reasonable basis for not treating workers as employees, the employer can show that:

- The employer reasonably relied on a court case about federal taxes or a ruling issued to the employer by the IRS; or
- The business was audited by the IRS at a time when the employer treated similar workers as independent contractors and the IRS did not reclassify those workers as employees; or
- The employer treated the workers as independent contractors because the employer knew that was how a significant segment of the employer's industry treated similar workers; or
- The employer relied on some other reasonable basis. For example, the employer relied on the advice of a business lawyer or accountant who knew the facts about the employer's business.

If the employer did not have a reasonable basis for treating the workers as independent contractors, then employer does not meet the relief requirements, and the company could be liable for the Social Security tax, federal income tax, and federal unemployment insurance for those workers for up to three years. The employer could also have to pay penalties and interest to the IRS, as well as any taxes and penalties that could be levied by state agencies.

Substantive Consistency

In order to receive Section 530 relief, in addition to a reasonable basis for treating workers as independent contractors, an employer must also meet the requirement of substantive consistency. Substantive consistency requires that the employer must have treated the workers, and any similar workers, as independent contractors. However, if the employer treated similar workers as employees, Section 530 relief is not available.

Reporting Consistency

Finally, to receive Section 530 relief, an employer *must* have filed a Form 1099-MISC for each worker, unless the worker earned less than $600. Section 530 relief is not available for any year an employer did not file the required Form 1099-MISC.

If the employer filed the required Form 1099-MISC for some workers, but not for others, relief is not available for the workers for whom the employer did not file Form 1099-MISC.

Section 530 Results

If an IRS audit finds that an employer's workers are not independent contractors, but instead are employees, if the employer meets the Section 530 relief requirements—reasonable basis, substantive consistency, and reporting consistency—the employer will *not* have to pay employment taxes on the workers. The workers, however, will need to pay their share of the FICA tax on the wages received, but they may be entitled to a refund of any self-employment tax paid.

Practical Guidelines for Preserving Independent Contractor Status

Despite all of the potential pitfalls in classifying independent contractors, there are a few basic steps a company can take to preserve the independent contractor status of their independent contractors. The first, and most basic step, is to treat independent contractors like independent contractors. Remember, independent contractors exercise control over how they accomplish the job, they use their own tools and equipment, they provide their own training and instruction, and sometimes they provide their own employees. In short, they are *independent*, and they should be treated as such.

Other safeguards include asking the right questions before working with independent contractors, gathering documentary evidence from independent contractors, preparing a strong contract with independent contractors, and reviewing other documents.

Questions to Ask Independent Contractors

To make sure that an independent contractor's status will hold up, there are a number of questions an employer can ask before contracting, including:
- Business address and phone number of the independent contractor;
- Tax ID number of the independent contractor's business;
- Structure of the independent contractor's business (i.e. corporation, limited liability company, sole proprietorship, etc);
- List of insurances carried by the independent contractor;
- Professional and/or business licenses held by the independent contractor;
- Number of people employed by the independent contractor;
- Description of business equipment owned by the independent contractor;
- Business cards and/or stationary for the independent contractor;
- How the independent contractor handles billing; and
- References for the independent contractor.

Although these factors will not be determinative, they will help to establish that the worker is an independent contractor and not an employee. Remember, it is important to have a completed Independent Contractor Application for each independent contractor. (See Chapter 3 for a discussion of useful provisions to include in an independent contractor's contract.)

WORDS OF WISDOM: Remember, because the employer is treating the independent contractor differently from employees, the employer should not have an independent contractor complete one of the usual Employment Applications!

Helpful Documentation from Independent Contractors

Employers should also make copies of additional documents for the independent contractor's file in the event of an audit, including some or all of the following:

- The employer's independent contractor contract;
- A copy of the independent contractor's articles of organization or incorporation (if an LLC or incorporated);
- Copies of the independent contractor's certificates of insurance;
- A copy of the independent contractor's invoice form; and
- A copy of IRS Form 1099 issued by other companies.

There may be other documents that would help establish that the independent contractor is running an independent business. The more documentation an employer has in their files, the more protection the employer gives the company from misclassifying the worker—as long as the company continues to treat the worker as an independent contractor.

Comparison Summary: Differences between Employees and Independent Contractors

Factors	Employee	Independent Contractor "IC"
Behavioral Control	Company has the right to direct and control how work is done. Instructions and training are provided by company.	IC has control over how the work done. IC usually provides own training and instructions generally not needed.
Financial Control	Company has right to direct and control financial aspects of work.	IC has significant investment, expenses, and opportunity for profit or loss.
Relationship of Parties	Benefits may be paid, but not required for employee status.	IC generally does not have benefits. Written contract may be evidence of independent contractor status, but not determinative.

Factors	Employee	Independent Contractor "IC"
Tax Consequences and Workers' Compensation	Company pays Social Security, Medicare. Company must withhold for federal/state taxes. Company must issue IRS Form W-2. Company must carry workers' compensation insurance.	Company does not pay Social Security or Medicare and does not withhold taxes for the IC. Company must issue IRS Form 1099 if the company paid IC more than $600 in year. Company does not carry workers' compensation for the IC.
Unemployment	Company must contribute to unemployment insurance fund and pay unemployment tax.	No unemployment fund or tax paid by company.
Benefits	Not required, but company often provides vacation, leave, holidays, health insurance, etc.	No benefits. IC usually carries own benefits.
Government Regulations	Company must follow regulations and laws protecting employees, such as overtime laws.	No overtime, but some laws may still apply, such as discrimination laws.
Liability for Injury	If employee is hurt on the job, workers' compensation may be triggered, and negligence irrelevant.	If the IC is hurt, workers' compensation is not triggered, and negligence must be proven.
Liability for Worker's Conduct	Company generally liable for employees' negligence in course and scope of employment.	Company generally not liable for IC negligence, but may be liable if IC is acting as company's agent.
Ending Relationship	May be at-will.	May be subject to "cause" provisions in the contract.

Liability and Worker Authority

Types of Worker Authority

To understand why "you are who you hire," and what that phrase means, it is helpful to look at the laws of agency and authority, when and how an employer can be held liable for employees' acts, and some ways employers can minimize potential liability for the acts of employees.

Employers have legal duties to their workers, to the state, and to the people and companies who work with their businesses. When an employer hires a worker, the employer is creating a legal relationship with that person and giving that person authority to act on the behalf of the employer. For that reason, employers should have a basic understanding of two types of authority that come from the law of agency:

1. Actual authority; and
2. Apparent authority.

Actual Authority

Actual authority is the authority specifically conveyed by the employer to the employee, and it encompasses *express authority* and *implied authority*. Express authority is the power to perform the particular job for which the employee was hired. For example, a company may give a human resources manager the express authority to hire employees as part of the manager's job description (or written list of duties). However, a job description cannot possibly list every single thing the human resources manager needs to accomplish, so the express authority to hire employees comes with the implied authority to do other things to accomplish the task of hiring the employees. For example, if the job description specifically lists hiring as a function of the human resources manager (express authority) then the *implied authority* of the human resources manager is the authority to take the reasonable steps necessary to hire employees—such as locating applicants, conducting interviews, and completing the necessary paperwork. Both express and implied types of authority are part of the actual authority given by the employer.

Apparent Authority

Apparent authority, on the other hand, may or may not be given intentionally by the employer. Apparent authority is the authority that an employee represents himself or herself as having, and includes the authority a reasonable person would reasonably assume the employee to have based upon the employee's position. Thus, apparent authority is the authority that an employee gets because of his or her rank in the company.

For example, by simply having the title of human resources manager (HR manager), it could appear to third parties as though a HR manager has the authority to sign an employment contract or agree to employ someone for a particular amount of time, even though the HR manager does not have the actual authority to do so. If it is reasonable for third parties to believe that the HR manager has the power to sign an employment contract then the HR manager could, by virtue of apparent authority, bind the company with a contract, even without the actual authority to make contracts.

Ways to Minimize Liability for an Employee's Actions

Because employers "are who they hire," great care must be taken to make sure that both employers and employees understand the scope of a worker's employment authority. Because employees' actions can be interpreted as actions of the company, it is important to be clear about employees' job responsibilities and powers to act on the company's behalf.

WORDS OF WISDOM: An employer is liable for the negligent acts or omissions of his or her employees which are committed within the scope of the worker's employment—this is called *"respondeat superior."*

The scope of an employee's responsibility also is important, because it is possible that employers can be held liable for the wrongs of their employees. In legal terms, this is called *respondeat superior* or vicarious liability. Under the doctrine of *respondeat superior*, an employer is liable for the negligent acts or omissions of his or her employees which are committed within the scope of the employee's employment. Whether the employee's acts are within the scope of the employee's employment depends on the facts and circumstances of each case.

Establishing the scope of an employee's responsibilities can be accomplished through a written job description that spells out the employee's job duties. (Job descriptions are discussed more fully in Chapter 3.) Determining employment scope can also be accomplished through proper disclaimers if necessary. For example, to avoid a situation where the HR manager binds the company to an employment agreement by telling a worker that the worker will be employed for a specific amount of time, the company may want to have a disclaimer in the employee handbook or an acknowledgment form listing the *only* people with the authority to create an employment agreement (i.e. president of the company, vice president of human resources etc.). Of course, a disclaimer alone will not protect the company if the employer allows people to act inconsistently with it or if the employer does not give employees adequate notice of the disclaimer.

FOOTNOTES

[1] Pregnancy Discrimination Act. 42 U.S.C. § 2000e(k) (amended Title VII to include pregnancy, childbirth, and related conditions as categories protected against discrimination).

[2] Title VII, Civil Rights Act of 1964, 42 U.S.C. §§ 2000e-2(a) *et seq.*

[3] Legal Off-Duty Activities—Colorado Anti-Discrimination Act. C.R.S. § 24-34-502.5(1) (the law, with limited exceptions, prevents employers from firing a worker involved in legal activities while off-duty and off-premises, unless the conduct relates to job requirements, or to avoid a conflict of interest).

[4] Marital Status—Colorado Anti-Discrimination Act. C.R.S. § 24-34-402(1)(h)(I) (the law, with limited exceptions, prohibits employers with 25 or more employees from terminating an employee because of marriage to another employee of the employer; however the statute has exceptions for cases where one spouse would supervise another, where money is involved, or where one spouse would have access to the employer's confidential information).

[5] *Lathrop v. Entenmann's, Inc.*, 770 P.2d 1367 (Colo. App. 1989) (employers who fire workers because they filed a workers' compensation claim can be held liable for wrongful termination in violation of public policy).

[6] Public Policy Based on Ethical Codes. *Rocky Mountain Hospital & Medical Service v. Mariani,* 916 P.2d 519, 525 (Colo. 1996) (public policy discharge claim can be based on public policy set out in ethical codes, such as the State Board of Accountancy rules of Professional Conduct; where an employee is fired for refusing to misrepresent facts in violation of her rules of conduct, she may have a claim for wrongful discharge).

[7] Damages for Public Policy Tort Claims. C.R.S. § 13-21-102.5(3)(c) (for claims accruing after January 1, 1998, non-economic damages can be as high as $350,000, and over $700,000 in aggravated cases).

[8] *Kiely v. St. Germain,* 670 P.2d 764, 768-70 (Colo. 1983) (promissory estoppel comes from the basic concept that one who makes promises should be required to keep them, even if there isn't a contract; the Court enforced an oral promise to hire the plaintiff).

[9] *Pickell v. Arizona Components Co.,* 931 P.2d 1184 (Colo. 1997) (a promise of employment for a "reasonable time" is sufficient to overcome the at-will presumption).

[10] IRS, Employees vs. Independent Contractors, http://www.irs.gov/businesses/small/article/0,,id=99921,00.html

[11] IRS, Publication 15-A, Employer's Supplemental Tax Guide, http://www.irs.gov/formspubs/page/0,,id=10831,00.html

[12] IRS, Topic 762 Independent Contractor vs. Employee, www.irs.gov/taxtopics/page/0,,id=16284,00.html

[13] IRS, Forms and Publications, Form SS-8, Determination of Employee Work Status for Purposes of Federal Employment Taxes and Income Tax Withholdings, http://www.irs.gov/formspubs/lists/0,,id=97817,00.html

[14] *Vizcaino v. Microsoft,* 173 F.3d 713 (9th Cir. 1999).

[15] *Id.*

[16] IRS Publication 1976, Section 530 Relief Requirements, www.irs.gov/business/small/article/0,,id=99921,00.html

CHAPTER 2:
Contracts, "Unintended Contracts," and Handbooks

Contract Basics

A basic understanding of how employers can contract with workers and what employers tell workers by way of a company handbook and other documents is helpful in promoting a healthy work environment and minimizing the risks of lawsuits.

Entire volumes of books have been dedicated to explaining the complexities of legal contracts, and it is by no means a simple topic. It is vital for employers to be aware of the different types of contracts, and the pros and cons of the various forms. Many people are under the mistaken impression that unless the agreement is in writing, it is not a contract. However, as discussed throughout this chapter, contracts can be written or verbal and can last for an indefinite period or for a specific amount of time.

In its simplest terms, a contract is a legally enforceable agreement. When an employer hires an employee, a contract is created—even if it is not written down! Usually in an employment contract the employer agrees to pay the employee (in money or in some other way) in exchange for the employee's services. Depending on the agreement of the parties, the contract can last for less than an hour or until the employee retires (or the employment can be terminable at-will, as discussed in Chapter 1).

Elements of a Contract: Offer, Acceptance, and Consideration

Generally, to have a legally enforceable contract there must be an *offer*, *acceptance*, and *consideration*. In plain English, an *offer* is a promise to do or not to do something. The promise must show that the person making the offer, the offeror, is willing to enter into a bargain. The bargain must be clear enough so that the person to whom the offer is made is justified in understanding that the offeror is inviting an acceptance to conclude the bargain.

An *acceptance* is agreeing to the terms of the offer. The *offer* and *acceptance* create an agreement when both parties demonstrate a "meeting of the minds," or the parties both agree on the same bargain or exchange.

But an agreement alone is not enough to establish a legally binding contract. There also must be *consideration*. Consideration is sometimes is called the "benefit of the bargain," or the thing of value that the parties exchange. The consideration includes the benefit gained by one party and the corresponding responsibility of the other party.

One example of a contract could be a coupon from a department store. Using the coupon example to explain the legal elements required for a valid contract, the *offer* is the department store's promise to give the customer something of value; the *acceptance* is the customer presenting the coupon to the department store; and the *consideration* is the benefit of the customer's receipt of a discounted product and the corresponding responsibility of the department store to provide the product at a discount.

WORDS OF WISDOM: In addition to offer, acceptance, and consideration, legally binding contracts must be for a legal purpose, generally between consenting adults with legal capacity (minors can enter into contracts, but the contracts are voidable by the minor—meaning the minor generally can get out of them).

Notice that in the coupon example there was not a written contract in the traditional sense of the word—where both parties sign a document promising to do (or not do) certain things. Instead, the coupon example is a contract created by an offer (the coupon) and acceptance by performance (the shopper's presentation of the coupon to the store).

The coupon example illustrates the point that there are many, many ways to create contracts, and people sometimes enter into contracts without actually calling them contracts. The following is a discussion of a real case in which the court decided a coupon was a contract, demonstrating how seriously the courts can take contracts (and discrimination).

The Dillard Example: The Case of the Million Dollar Perfume Coupon

In a case called *Hampton v. Dillard Dep't Stores, Inc.,*[1] the court enforced a coupon as a contract. The jury found that the coupon was a contract between Ms. Hampton and Dillard and that Dillard had interfered with Ms. Hampton's redemption of a perfume coupon. The jury found Dillard liable for $1,156,000.

What Went Wrong?

In the *Hampton* case, the jury found that Dillard had entered into a contract with Ms. Hampton by making Ms. Hampton an *offer* with a Dillard coupon. Ms. Hampton *accepted* the offer by purchasing clothing and presenting the coupon. The *consideration* was Dillard's promise to give perfume in exchange for her shopping at Dillard. When Ms. Hampton went to redeem her coupon, however, a security guard who had been tracking Ms. Hampton's movements detained her and falsely accused her of stealing. The security guard made the accusation in front of Ms. Hampton's family members, including young children. After reviewing the evidence, the jury found that the security guard had discriminated against Ms. Hampton because of her race.

The Lesson for Employers

What made the *Hampton* coupon case a million dollar case? That could probably be the subject of great debate. However, the reason the *Hampton* case is especially relevant to employers is because it involved a federal law that many former employees have used in employment discrimination cases. The law is commonly referred to as "Section 1981,"[2] and it can be a powerful tool in addressing discrimination in the workplace. Section 1981 is related to contract law because it prohibits racial discrimination in the making, performance, modification, and termination of contracts, and the enjoyment of all benefits, privileges, terms, and conditions of the contractual relationship—including employment relationships. Section 1981 is more powerful than many federal discrimination laws because, unlike other laws which cap the amount of monetary damages a company will pay, there are *no caps* on the monetary damages a jury can award in a Section 1981 case.

The Bottom Line in the Dillard Case

Even though there were no financial damages as a result of Dillard's interference with Ms. Hampton's attempted redemption of the perfume coupon, the jury found that Ms. Hampton had suffered emotional distress as a result of the race discrimination and awarded her $56,000. The jury did not believe the security guard's denials of race discrimination and found that the discrimination was willful or malicious. To deter others from acting the same way, and as a punishment, the jury also awarded Ms. Hampton $1.1 million dollars in punitive damages.

Why Colorado Employers Should Take Special Note

While not every Section 1981 case ends like the *Hampton* case, it certainly should provide employers with a reason to take notice. Colorado employers should especially take note of this case because the appeals court that upheld the jury's verdict is the Tenth Circuit Court of Appeals, which has jurisdiction over federal cases in Colorado.

Employment Contracts

As stated earlier, contracts arise in many different ways and can take different forms. A basic understanding of some of the ways contracts arise can help prevent problems down the line and can help to keep employers out of "unintended" contracts. Unintended contracts are important to know because, as mentioned earlier, people enter into contracts all the time, sometimes without appreciating the fact that they have made a legally enforceable promise. Contracts can arise as either express contracts or as implied contracts.

How Contracts Can Arise

Express/Clear-Cut Contracts

Some contracts are express contracts, meaning that the people who are making the agreement use explicit or clear-cut words to create the contract, either in writing or just by talking. For example, an employer and employee can create an "at-will" employment agreement in writing by signing an employment contract that may include other terms (such as amount of pay and duties), or even by writing one paragraph on a piece of paper. Alternatively, an employer and employee can create a spoken or verbal "at-will" contract relationship during a conversation, such as when the

HR manager makes a clear-cut job offer without an ending date to an employee who accepts the job.

Implied Contracts

In contrast, other contracts are implied contracts, basically meaning that the people who are making the agreement use conduct, or writings along with conduct to create the contract. An example of an implied contract would be when a customer goes into a restaurant and orders a $5.95 hamburger from a server and the server brings the hamburger to the table. Instead of using words to create an agreement, the server simply performs. The customer has a contract to pay for the meal, even though the customer did not sign an agreement when he or she placed the order. When the restaurant performed its part of the bargain by having the server provide the food, the contract was formed.

In the employment context, some employers have learned that they entered into implied contracts with their employees by putting statements in their employee handbooks, which the employees reasonably understood as offers. The employees accepted the offers by working for the employer. An example of an employer entering into an implied contract would be if an employer made statements in the employee handbooks such as "before terminating an employee we will provide first a verbal warning, then a written warning, then probation." Colorado courts have interpreted those statements as binding implied contracts, meaning that if the employer decides for some reason that the employer needs to terminate an employee immediately, then the employer is breaching its contract with the employee if the employer does not follow the promised procedures.[3] There are ways to avoid this kind of a situation, which are discussed in more detail in the handbook section of this chapter.

Understanding how contracts can arise by express words or implied conduct is important to avoid accidentally entering into unintended contracts. However it is also valuable to look at the forms contracts can take and some of the advantages and disadvantages of each. A good understanding of the options will help in the development and strengthening of a legally healthy company and work environment as different situations arise.

Verbal/Spoken Contracts

Let's say a job applicant comes to the office for an interview. During the interview, the employer discusses the duties the job would require and the amount the position will pay. After the interview, the employer is impressed enough with the person to offer her the job on the spot: "We'd love for you to be a part of our team, and I'm happy to offer you the job at the pay we discussed."

The job applicant, overjoyed, immediately says, "Yes! I'd love to start! I accept your offer!" Although no one has signed any paper, the employer has just entered into a contract with a new employee. Because the employer has not discussed the amount of time the employee will be employed, it is presumed to be at-will employment. This is a straightforward example of a verbal at-will employment agreement.

WORDS OF WISDOM: Formal words such as "offer" and "I accept" do not need to be used to create a verbal contract. A verbal contract can be created as long as the parties tell each other in a way that they both understand the bargain, either by words or by what they do.

Now, let's change the facts a little bit. Say the employer liked the job applicant enough to offer her a position for a two-year contract. Even more overjoyed, she accepts in a split second. She works for two weeks, and the employer decides that the job applicant has terrible handwriting. Can the employer terminate the contract and fire the employee without breaching the verbal two-year contract?

This is a trick question, because the second "contract" the employer entered is barred by a law called the "statute of frauds."[4] The statute of frauds requires that any contract that cannot be performed within one year *must be in writing*, or it is barred. Because the two-year verbal agreement exceeds a year, it is not enforceable.

WORDS OF WISDOM: The statute of frauds is a law that voids verbal contracts that cannot be performed within one year.

Unlike the two-year contract, however, the at-will contract created in the first example does not have to be in writing, because it is *possible* that it will be completed within one year. Although the employment could go longer than one year, it is still a valid verbal contract because it is *possible* that the employment could be completed within one year.

Verbal contracts, while easy to create, can be difficult to enforce. When the parties to a contract do not write down their intentions, they can be tough to prove. In an at-will state, like Colorado, theoretically this could work to the benefit of employers, because the employee has the burden to prove that the employment was not at-will.

However, verbal contracts can invite lawsuits where there is a dispute as to the terms of the agreement, and that usually works to no one's benefit. At a minimum, to avoid problems with alleged verbal contracts, employers should at least have an "at-will" provision signed by the employee, whether in a written employment agreement or in an acknowledgment form signed at the time of hiring.

Written Contracts: Agreements, Offer Letters, and Other Documents

Employers can minimize the difficulties presented by verbal agreements by putting their employment contracts in writing. When the word "contract" is used, people generally think of a piece of paper (or several pieces of paper stapled together) that is signed by both parties with the title "Employment Contract" at the top. However, as discussed, this is not the only form a contract can take. In Colorado, offer letters, employee handbooks, and other documents, such as disciplinary documents, work plans, and pay plans can create contracts. Because so many types of documents can create contracts, it is vital for employers to review, or have their legal counsel review, all documents employers give to employees to make sure that the employers are not creating "unintended" contracts.

WORDS OF WISDOM: Some employers use the term "permanent employees" to distinguish certain employees from "temporary employees." Unless an employer intends to employ someone permanently, the employer should replace the term "permanent employee" with "regular employee" in the employer's written documents and in the statements made by recruiters, HR executives, managers, and supervisors.

Written agreements can be beneficial to both parties to clarify the terms of their employment relationship. However, a potential danger can arise if legal counsel is not consulted, or if old written contracts are cut and pasted together for new positions. The potential danger is the danger of unintended consequences. Just because a provision should be used in one contract does not mean that it should be pasted into another, unless the drafter has a clear understanding of the legal meaning of the document and the provision.

WORDS OF WISDOM: A court may enforce a contract for permanent employment or employment through retirement if there has been special consideration or an express stipulation as to the length of employment.[5]

An employment agreement can be as simple as an acknowledgement of at-will employment, or it can be extremely detailed, depending on the needs of the company, the employee, and the job. Because written employment agreements can limit an employer's flexibility and can impose obligations on an employer that are not required by law, employers should *use caution* when entering into written agreements.

If an employer plans to use a contract that has been previously prepared, it would be wise to consult legal counsel beforehand and let the lawyer know that the employer would like a review for the purposes of using the contract again. The laws may have changed, the employer's goals may be different, and patch jobs can lead to trouble in contracts.

WORDS OF WISDOM: If the employer drafts the employment contract, chances are that if the contract is ambiguous or unclear in some respect, and there is a dispute that goes to court, the court will strictly interpret the contract provisions against the employer.

Checklist of Common Provisions: Written Employment Contracts

The following is a checklist of some of the provisions employers may encounter in written employment agreements:

- **Parties Provision** — This includes the names, addresses, and phone numbers of the parties to the agreement.
- **Specific Duration or At-Will Provision** — This lists the time frame of the employment, or confirms the at-will agreement.
- **Employee's Duties/Functions/Services Provision** — This is a description of the services and duties to be provided to the company by the employee; it may be a broad statement reserving the right to add more duties as needed.
- **Confidentiality/Trade Secrets Provision** — This provision gives the company protection for its confidential information.
- **Non-Compete Provisions** — These provisions protect the company from unfair competition (these provisions must comply with the state statute[6] or they are void—see Appendix 1).
- **Liquidated Damages Provision** — If damages for a breach of the agreement cannot be determined, an amount is set forth in advance to compensate for the breach. The amount cannot be simply a punitive amount or it will be invalidated.
- **Non-Solicitation Provision** — This provision protects the company from unfair solicitation of its employees in certain circumstances.
- **Anti-discrimination and Harassment Provision** — The employee acknowledges that he or she must comply with the anti-discrimination and harassment policies of the company as a term and condition of employment.
- **Access to Personnel Files Provision** — This provision describes the company's policy on availability of the personnel file. Since Colorado law does not require private employers to make personnel files available to employees, it is a matter of the company's discretion.

- **Employer's Duties Provision** — This provision lists the employer's obligations.
- **Pay and Benefits Provision** — This includes the amount and timing of the compensation to the employee.
- **Severance Provisions** — These provide additional payments to the employee on termination of employment under certain circumstances (it is not required by law).
- **Alternative Dispute Resolution Provision** — This provides a procedure for resolving disputes without going to court.
- **Termination of Agreement Provision** — This provides a procedure for terminating the employment by the employee and the employer. Some contracts have "cause" provisions, meaning that the employment can only be terminated by the employer for certain reasons. Be careful here, as determining what "cause" is can be tricky if not properly analyzed before the contract is created.
- **Attorney Fees Provision** — This provides attorney fees to the prevailing party if there is a dispute (normally attorney fees are not recoverable in Colorado for breach of a contract unless there is a written agreement for attorney fees in the contract).
- **Choice of Law/Jurisdiction Provision** — This provides that the law of a particular state applies (sometimes the state where the worker lives, works, and provides services will apply even if there is a choice of law provision in the contract, so before including this provision employers with employees in more than one state should understand how the provision might impact the contract).
- **Saving Clause Provision** — This provides that if any provision of the contract is found to be void or unenforceable, the parties intend for the rest of the provisions to remain intact.
- **Modifications Provision** — This provides that the agreement may only be modified in writing by the parties (it usually designates the company official or title authorized to modify the agreement); this can provide some protection against being contractually bound by a later verbal statement by company management.
- **No Other Agreements Provision** — This is a recitation that no other verbal statements before or after the signing of the contract are intended to be part of the contract unless they are specifically written into the contract.
- **Signature block and date**

Some of these provisions may not be useful in every contract, and there may be other provisions that should be included, depending on the circumstances. Some employment agreements can be quite complex, and should not be attempted without a strong knowledge of contract and employment law. Contracts are one of those areas where prevention is the best medicine. It is much more economical to get legal advice in the creation of a contract than to end up in court defending a contract that was not adequately planned at the outset.

WORDS OF WISDOM: When an employer enters into a written employment contract with an employee, both the employer and the employee are promising "good faith and fair dealing." If a company acts in bad faith, and a dispute goes to court, the company may have to pay more damages to the employee than if the company had acted in good faith.

Checklist of Common Provisions: Written Independent Contractor Contracts

The following is a checklist of common provisions in independent contractor contracts:

- **Independent Contractor's Responsibilities Provision** — This provision sets forth the duties and responsibilities of the independent contractor.
- **How Payment is to be Determined Provision** — Some possibilities for this provision include hourly, flat rate, project steps, etc.
- **Provision Allowing Contractor to Hire Assistants** — This provision helps to protect and clarify the independent contractor status as discussed in Chapter 1.
- **Insurance/Workers' Compensation Provision** — This requires the independent contractor to provide insurance and workers' compensation insurance if he or she has employees.
- **Equipment and Supplies Provision** — This clarifies that the independent contractor will provide his or her own work tools and will help clarify and protect the independent contractor status.
- **Contractor's Right to Control How Work Is Performed Provision** — As discussed in Chapter 1, the right of control is a hallmark of the independent contractor's status. If the independent contractor has little or no control over how the work is performed, a court or the IRS might find employee status rather than an independent contractor status. A control provision may be good evidence of independent contractor status, but if employers do not take care to follow the contract provision closely, they will not be helped by the contract.
- **Responsibility for Business Expenses Provision** — This provision states that the independent contractor retains the responsibility for business expenses.
- **No Benefits Provided by Company Provision** — When companies provide benefits to independent contractors, the independent contractors may be deemed to be employees, unless the other factors of independent contractor status are present.

- **Other Clients Provision** — When independent contractors retain the right to have other clients, it is a factor that helps maintain the independent contractor status.
- **Confidentiality and/or Trade Secrets Provisions** — This provision protects the company's confidential and trade secrets.

Other provisions that may be used in an independent contractor contract include a termination provision, an attorney fees provision, a modification provision, and saving clauses.

Remember, when an employer hires an employee or has an agreement with an independent contractor, the employer is entering into a contract, whether written or not. In fact, in some cases, even where there was no written contract in the traditional sense, Colorado courts have found that employers entered into contracts with their employees by issuing an employee handbook.[7] That can be quite a shock to employers who didn't think they had a contract with the employees. This shock can be avoided, and handbooks can be useful, so it is important to review some of the handbook basics.

Employee Handbooks

Another thing companies can do to lay the foundation for a legally healthy work environment is to think about an employee handbook. Many companies have employee handbooks, but they are often out-of-date. If it has been more than a year since your company's employee handbook was updated it is vital to read this section and seriously consider having the employee handbook reviewed by legal counsel. If your company does not have a handbook, it is a good idea to read the following section and consider whether a handbook would be useful. The following section addresses advantages and disadvantages of handbooks, common provisions in handbooks, and potential pitfalls often found in handbooks (and ways to avoid them).

Advantages and Disadvantages of Employee Handbooks

Employee handbooks can help employers lay the foundation for a legally healthy work environment by communicating important information to employees about a company's culture and values, legal information, and practical answers to day-to-day questions employees may have. If employers take the lead in setting a worker-friendly environment by considering the needs of the employees while setting standards for the company, productivity could skyrocket. An employee handbook can be a great opportunity for employers to communicate the needs and expectations of the company to the people who can help the company achieve its goals. Also, the United States Supreme Court has stated that employers have protections from liability when they take these kinds of steps to inform their employees about the company's anti-discrimination and harassment policies.[8]

WORDS OF WISDOM: Be sure all of the employees can understand the employee handbook! Translate it into other languages, and make accommodations for impaired workers (e.g. Braille, large print, audio tapes).

Let employees know in advance what is expected of them. Most employees want to succeed in their jobs, and an employee handbook can help them meet (and exceed) expectations. Employee handbooks also help facilitate consistency and fairness by setting forth guidelines for the equal treatment of employees, including hiring, promotions, pay, and benefits. Handbooks also guide managers and supervisors in handling situations as they arise and promote fairness and equal treatment.

Can an employee handbook really do all of that? Yes and no. It cannot do anything if it is not drafted properly, and it will be no help if no one reads it. These factors are within an employer's control. If there is an existing employee handbook, pull it out and read it. Yes, really read it—cover to cover.

While reviewing the employee handbook consider if it is user-friendly? Is it possible to scan the table of contents or index and find information quickly? Does the handbook make sense? Does it project the appropriate image of the company? If not, it should be updated so that it will be a real tool for the company and employees, rather than thrown in a file somewhere to be pulled out only for lawsuits.

Checklist of Possible Employee Handbook Sections

While employee handbooks can be as diverse as the companies and people who run them, many of them have similar elements.

- A welcome statement, which introduces the company and sets the tone for the handbook and the employment;
- A note that the handbook will answer many employee questions, but of course, cannot cover every situation;
- A description of the "at-will" nature of the employment, in the absence of a written contract to the contrary, and a statement confirming that the handbook and its provisions are NOT a contract and may be modified at any time by the company (this should be stated in big, bold letters);
- A history of the company;
- Hours, pay, and benefits;
- Company expectations;
- Anti-discrimination and harassment policies;

- Complaint procedures and anti-retaliation policies;
- Drug and alcohol policies;
- Attendance and discipline policies;
- Safety policies;
- Work-place violence policies;
- Leave policies (note that if the company has more than 50 employees, and if there is a handbook, the handbook *must* include specific information required by the Family and Medical Leave Act);
- E-mail, voice mail, and Internet use policies; and
- An acknowledgment for employees to sign.

Potential Employee Handbook Pitfalls

While employee handbooks can be extremely helpful tools, the following is a top ten list of mistakes that can lead to trouble:

1. Creating an unintended contract. Colorado courts have bound employers to the statements made in their employee handbooks as contractual promises when the statements can be considered an offer that the employee has accepted by continued employment.

    > **WORDS OF WISDOM:** Employers can protect themselves from unintended handbook contracts by clearly and conspicuously disclaiming the intent to enter into a contract and using language that gives employers flexibility in decisions such as discipline and discharge.

2. Over promising. Sometimes employers have high aspirations and make statements in their handbooks guaranteeing a wonderful work environment and promising a great future to its employees.

    > **WORDS OF WISDOM:** Employers should strive for, but not guarantee, a wonderful work environment. Employers should not make promises that they would not want a court to enforce.

3. Using out of date handbooks. Think the old handbook is a good idea? If the handbook is more than a year old, it may be missing significant protections for the company. The laws have changed, and the handbook should reflect those changes.

> **WORDS OF WISDOM:** Employee handbooks gathering dust on the shelf are as enforceable as brand-new handbooks. Consider the case of the 15-year old handbook... The federal appeals court in our jurisdiction recently upheld a jury decision based on provisions contained in a 15-year-old company handbook.[9] In that case, the employer dismissed several of its supervisory employees in a reduction in force without considering seniority, although its handbook said that seniority would be considered in lay offs. The jury awarded more than $2 million in damages to the employees. Be sure that if there is an employee handbook, it is updated and says what the company wants it to say.

4. Implying guarantees of benefits. Some handbooks discuss benefits available to employees. Unfortunately, sometimes the economy changes or employers need to make changes to their benefits for various reasons. Make sure not to imply a guarantee of benefits.

> **WORDS OF WISDOM:** Tell employees clearly that the benefit plans may change and that the plan documents themselves are controlling over any statements in the employee handbook.

5. Creating mandatory progressive discipline. Some employers find it useful to use progressive, or step, discipline by telling employees that they will receive a verbal warning, written warning, or probation before termination. However, employers should not tell employees that progressive discipline will be used unless the employer is committed to always following these procedures. While these procedures can be effective in giving employees notice of the problems and an opportunity to correct them, if the handbook does not contain a contractual disclaimer and flexible language, it is possible that the company could face a wrongful termination lawsuit in the event that a step is skipped.

> **WORDS OF WISDOM:** If there are progressive discipline procedures in the handbook, be sure to state that they are not mandatory, that they "may" be used (as opposed to "shall" or "will"), and that the employer reserves the right to take any disciplinary step, up to and including termination, even if the other steps have not been taken.

6. Having an "open door" policy when the door is really closed.

> **WORDS OF WISDOM:** Open door policies can be excellent, if they are actually followed. If the door is really closed, not only do these policies backfire, but the failure to follow them creates horrible morale problems and could be used against the company.

7. Promising continued employment. Some aspirational statements in handbooks can be interpreted as promises. It's not a good idea to promise employees that "they will have continued employment as long as ___" (fill in the blank—they do a good job; the company makes money; the economy is good).

> **WORDS OF WISDOM:** Employers should not promise things that are not within their control.

8. Forgetting your audience(s). After an employee handbook is written, there are at least three potential audiences: (1) the employees; (2) the company's lawyer; and (3) if things go wrong, a jury or judge.

> **WORDS OF WISDOM:** Be sure the handbook would be appealing to an employee, a jury, and a judge. An employment lawyer may be able to ensure that the handbook is appealing.

9. Failing to consult the employee handbook when questions come up. Sometimes situations arise and employers can forget what a great resource their handbook can be.

> **WORDS OF WISDOM:** If properly written, an employee handbook can answer many of the questions that arise in tricky situations, such as discipline, leave, and pay. Refer to it, and use it as a guide and helpful tool.

10. Neglecting the employee handbook. Any handbook that is more than one year old should be reviewed by legal counsel.

> **WORDS OF WISDOM:** Employers should think of their handbook as a living document. As a company changes, so will the needs and the questions that arise. For example, if the company is growing, new laws will apply to the company as more employees are added. Also,

many of the protections available to employers can be established by including them in employee handbooks, such as acknowledgements, disclaimers, and policies relating to federal laws.

FOOTNOTES

[1] *Hampton v. Dillard Department Stores, Inc.*, 274 F.3d 1091, 1115 (10th Cir. 2001) *(cert. den.)* 122 S.Ct. 1071 (2002).

[2] 42 U.S.C. § 1981.

[3] *Continental Airlines v. Keenan,* 731 P.2d 708 (Colo. 1987) (an employee manual can constitute an implied contract with an at-will employee; an at-will employee can bring a wrongful discharge claim to enforce termination procedures in an employee manual).

[4] Statute of Frauds. C.R.S. § 38-10-112(a) (renders unwritten contracts unenforceable where they cannot be performed within one year).

[5] Permanent employment. *Schur v. Storage Tech. Corp.,* 878 P.2d 51 (Colo. App. 1994) (a contract for permanent employment is enforceable when: 1) there has been special consideration; or 2) an express stipulation as to the length of employment.

[6] C.R.S. § 8-2-113.

[7] Employee Handbooks. *DeRubis v. Broadmoor Hotel, Inc.,* 772 P.2d 681 (Colo. App. 1989) (at-will employee may bring wrongful discharge claim based on employment manual's grievance procedure, classification for probationary and regular employees, and/or specification of causes for termination); *See also Tuttle v. ANR Freight Systems, Inc,* 797 P.2d 825 (Colo. App. 1990) (non-discrimination provisions in manual may be implied contracts).

[8] *Burlington Industries v. Ellerth,* 118 S.Ct. 2257 (1998); *Faragher c. City of Boca Raton,* 118 S.Ct. 2275 (1988).

[9] *McIlravy v. Kerr-McGee Coal Corp.,* (10th Cir. 2000).

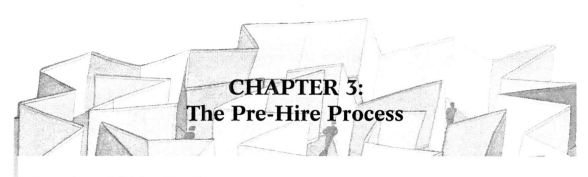

CHAPTER 3:
The Pre-Hire Process

Overview of Hiring Employees

There are many steps an employer can take to strengthen and promote a legally healthy work environment, even before the first worker starts. For employers who already have workers, there are always things to learn to enhance and improve relationships with employees, and in turn, the company's morale and profitability.

Before hiring workers, it is good to have at least a working knowledge of some of the federal and state laws that apply to employers, and the agencies with whom employers can come into contact. In addition, it is helpful to review pre-hire steps, background checks, and interviewing. The brief introductory list of federal and state laws is intended to serve as a quick reference checklist to help guide employers. These laws are discussed in greater detail in other chapters, and there is a more comprehensive list in Appendix 1.

Federal Laws Protecting Employers and Employees

Title VII of the Civil Rights Act of 1964 (Title VII) — Prohibits discrimination and harassment based on race, sex, color, national origin, religion; prohibits retaliation (15 or more employees);[1]

Americans With Disabilities Act (ADA) — Prohibits discrimination and harassment based on disability and requires reasonable accommodation of the employee if it can be accomplished without undue burden (15 or more employees);[2]

Age Discrimination in Employment Act (ADEA) — Prohibits discrimination and harassment based on age; protects individuals 40 and older (20 or more employees);[3]

Equal Pay Act (EPA) — Prohibits discrimination in pay based on gender (1 or more employees);[4]

Fair Labor Standards Act (FLSA) — Sets minimum wage, governs overtime and child labor (1 or more employees);[5]

Pregnancy Discrimination Act (PDA) — Prohibits discrimination on the basis of pregnancy and related conditions (15 or more employees);[6]

Family and Medical Leave Act (FMLA) — Requires unpaid leave for birth or adoption of a child or to care for a serious medical condition (50 or more employees);[7]

Immigration Reform and Control Act (IRCA) — Requires documentation of legal work status and prohibits discrimination on the basis of national origin (1 or more employees);[8]

National Labor Relations Act (NLRA) — Protects employees' rights to act in concert; unions (1 or more employees);[9]

Employee Retirement and Income Security Act (ERISA) — Governs administered benefit plans;[10]

Consolidated Omnibus Budget Reconciliation Act (COBRA) — Requires insurance continuation (20 or more employees);[11] and

Worker Retraining Notification Act (WARN) — Sets forth rules of mass layoffs (100 or more employees).[12]

State Laws Protecting Employers and Employees

Colorado Anti-Discrimination Act (CADA) — Prohibits discrimination and harassment on the basis of race, creed, religion, national origin, color, and marital status (1 or more employees);[13]

Lawful Off-Duty Activities Act — Restricts an employer's ability to terminate employees because of the employees' lawful, off-premises activities during non-working hours (1 or more employees);[14]

Non-Compete Statute — Makes non-compete agreements void unless: in connection with sale of business; for protection of trade secrets; for recovery of training expense; executive and management personnel and their professional staff (1 or more employees);[15]

Colorado Minimum Wage Order — Regulates wages, hours and working conditions for certain employers and employees (similar to FLSA; whichever law gives greater protection will apply) (1 or more employees);[16]

Reference Immunity Statute — Provides protections for employers from civil liability for disclosing information about current or former employees to prospective employers (provides qualified immunity) (1 or more employees);[17]

Various Leave Statutes — Provides leave for various reasons, including jury duty, military leave, voting, and more (see Appendix 1);

Statutory Fraud Statute — Provides penalties for fraudulently inducing relocation of out of state workers;[18] and

Colorado Wage Claim Act — Provides procedures for paying employees in a timely manner (including on separation of employment) and sets forth penalties for violations.[19]

Agencies Employers Should Know

Federal Agencies

United States Equal Employment Opportunity Commission (EEOC) — Federal agency that administers and enforces several federal laws including those that guarantee workers' rights to freedom from employment discrimination, including Title VII, ADA, ADEA, and the Pregnancy Discrimination Act;

United States Department of Labor — Federal agency that administers a variety of federal labor laws including those that guarantee workers' rights to safe and healthful working conditions; a minimum hourly wage and overtime pay; freedom from employment discrimination; unemployment insurance; and other income support;

Bureau of Citizenship and Immigration Services (BCIS) — Bureau within the Department of Homeland Security (DHS) (formerly Immigration Naturalization Service (INS)) — handles administration of immigration and naturalization, including work authorizations and enforcing anti-discrimination provisions and federal immigration laws;

Internal Revenue Service (IRS) — Administers federal taxes; requires tax filings;

Occupational Safety and Health Administration (OSHA) — Administers safety laws designed to protect workers and promote safe working environments;

Social Security Administration (SSA) — Administers social security and requires filings by employers; and

National Labor Relations Board (NLRB) — Federal agency that administers the National Labor Relations Act, conducts secret-ballot elections to determine whether employees want union representation, and investigates and remedies unfair labor practices by employers and unions.

State Agencies

Colorado Civil Rights Division/Colorado Civil Rights Commission — Agency that enforces the Colorado Anti-Discrimination Act; similar to the federal EEOC;

Colorado Department of Labor and Employment — Administers unemployment insurance, workers' compensation, wage and hour enforcement;

Colorado Department of Revenue — Administers tax withholdings and other required filings; and

Colorado State Directory of New Hires (SDNH) — Administers new hire reporting.

While there are many other agencies, departments, and offices that employers may encounter these are a few that may be of assistance. Most of these agencies have excellent websites that provide a great deal of information.

Familiarity with these agencies and the federal and state laws they enforce will help employers make the most of their legal protections, while promoting the positive benefits intended by the employment laws. Because these laws evolve over time, it is important for employers to continue to educate themselves and their employees on an ongoing basis.

Pre-Hire Steps

Once employers have reviewed the federal and state laws and agencies, there are other pre-hire steps they can take to lay a good foundation for a legally healthy work workplace, including: (1) developing clear expectations of what employers want from their workers by carefully defining employee jobs; (2) finding great applicants by gathering information that employers need for the job; (3) conducting meaningful interviews; and (4) selecting the most qualified person for the job.

Defining Jobs

Some employers are so eager to get someone on board that they skip two important steps in getting ready for their employees—doing a job analysis and preparing a written job description.

Job Analysis—What Are the Employer's Needs?

Basically, a job analysis is determining what an employer wants their employee to do. If an employer is creating a new position, the employer will want to list the major things they want the employee to do (and at the same time, the employer can determine those things they do not want the worker to do). If an employer is filling a position that has been vacated, it's a good opportunity to evaluate any additional things that the employee did or did not do that the employer would like to include in the position.

By taking some time to think about the position in detail, employers are taking a huge step in the right direction, not only in making sure they get coverage for the work they want to assign, but also in making sure that they can get the right person with the right qualifications, skills, and abilities.

Whenever employers make employment decisions based on the *requirements* of the job and the *abilities* of the person, they are minimizing the chances of running afoul of the discrimination laws (which are discussed in detail in later chapters).

Job Description—The Roadmap for Success

A written job description is a list of activities an employer wants their employee to perform, sometimes ranked in order of importance. It is the roadmap for success for both an employer and the employees. It can help during applicant interviews, selecting employees, orienting employees to the company, evaluating their work, setting pay, and providing legal protections. If a job description is carefully tailored to the specific job functions, it will help an employer make well-informed choices, and it will help employees know just what is expected of them from the outset. Job descriptions can also help down the line when an employer wants to give their employees feedback using performance evaluations (see Chapter 15 for more information on evaluating employees).

WORDS OF WISDOM: Use gender neutral terms in creating job titles, to avoid the misimpression of discrimination based on gender. Here are some examples: "fireman"="firefighter"; "mailman"= "postal carrier"; "policeman"="police officer"; "chairman"="chair"; "waiter"="server" or "wait staff"; "salesman"= sales associate." Gender neutral terms are not about being "PC" (or politically correct), they are about being more accurate with language and avoiding misunderstandings and potential claims of discrimination.

At a minimum, job descriptions should include the following:

- Date of creation of the description, along with any dates of modifications;
- Job title;
- Type of job (i.e. salaried, hourly, full/part time);
- Job summary;
- List of duties and responsibilities (make sure the duties are the essential functions of the job);
- Required skills;
- Educational requirements, if any; and
- A catch-all phrase, allowing the employer to add more tasks as required by the job.

WORDS OF WISDOM: Factors to consider in determining if a function is essential include: (1) whether the reason the position exists is to perform that function; (2) the number of other employees available to perform the function; and (3) the degree of expertise or skill required to perform the function. (A written job description including the "essential functions" can be important in defending against a claim of disability discrimination—discussed in detail in Chapter 5).

Finding Great Applicants

Once an employer has determined their job needs, the employer can make compensation decisions (see Chapter 13), and begin advertising for the position and accepting applications. Advertising can be as simple as putting an ad in the paper or on-line, or as detailed as a nation-wide search. Employers should plan their budget so that they can advertise in a broad range of places, including publications by and for minorities in the community. Check the EEOC website at www.eeoc.gov or the EEOC Manual at http://www.eeoc.gov/policy/compliance.html for specific guidelines.

Since employers want the best-qualified people, the advertisements should be tailored to the functions of the job and include the necessary skills, knowledge, educational background, and abilities needed; this is another good reason to have a written job description.

WORDS OF WISDOM: Keep the applications, resumes, and other application information of all applicants for at least a year to satisfy the requirements of Title VII[20] and the ADA.[21]

Gathering Meaningful Information

Employers have many resources for getting background information on applicants, including: the applicant (resumes, applications, interviews); former employers and personal references (reference checks); and background checks (checking credit reports, driving records, and conviction records). However, federal laws protect employee privacy by limiting the amount of information a potential employer can legally obtain and use in making employment decisions.[22]

There are many good reasons to gather information about a potential employee. An employer can find out whether a person is the best person for the job and avoid legal claims by other employees that the employer should not have hired the person because of his or her dangerous background. Reasonable preventive measures include screening supervisory job applicants to see if they have a record of engaging in harassment. If so, it may be necessary to reject a candidate on that basis or take additional steps to monitor the individual's actions and prevent harassment.

Always be sure to request only job-related information, whether in the application, from other sources of information, or the interview. There are many reasons to keep requests job-related, including getting the very best candidates. Also, if non job-related information is requested, it can be presumed that it is being used for a negative purpose, such as unlawful discrimination.

WORDS OF WISDOM: According to the EEOC, requesting pre-employment information which discloses or tends to disclose an applicant's race will be interpreted by the EEOC as suggesting that race will be unlawfully used as a basis for hiring.[23] In other words, asking for this information is presumed to be used as a basis for making selection decisions. Therefore, if members of minority groups are excluded from employment, the request for such pre-employment information would likely constitute evidence of discrimination. However, employers may legitimately need information about their employees' or applicants' race for affirmative action purposes or to track applicant flow. One way to obtain racial information and simultaneously guard against discriminatory selection is for employers to use "tear-off sheets" for the identification of an applicant's race. After the applicant completes the application and the tear-off portion, the employer separates the tear-off sheet from the application and does not use the tear-off sheet in the selection process.

Accepting Applications

Use an application that asks for relevant qualifications and experience related to the job, and ask the applicant to list contact information for references. Let the potential employee know that the employer cannot offer a position until the employer has completed a satisfactory reference check. Ask the applicant if he or she will sign a release that the employer can send to the references, in the event that the references will require one before speaking with a potential employer. Although Colorado law provides a qualified immunity for employers who give out reference information,[24] many employers are leery about saying too much without a written release. Employers can have the applicant sign the release when he or she turns in the application.

Conducting Meaningful Interviews

Interviews are an early opportunity to create the positive atmosphere that will inspire a candidate to give his or her best (and to help an employer determine whether a candidate has the skills and abilities to do the job). While interviewing can be an art, there are some simple steps to keep in mind:

- Prepare for the interview by reviewing the job description, the candidate's application and/or resume, any relevant documents related to the job, and the checklist of questions *not* to ask;
- Prepare a list of questions and areas that need to be covered; and
- Review the company's handbook in order to be knowledgeable about the policies and guidelines and to be able to answer any questions the applicant may have.

There are some questions employers should *not* ask, even if they are simply making polite conversation. Because the anti-discrimination laws apply to the hiring process too, employers should stay away from any question that concerns race, religion, disability, age, ethnic background, gender, marital status, or national origin. Limit all questions to those that relate to the job and the applicant's ability to perform the functions of the job.

What Questions Can Employers Ask?

As a general rule, employers can ask any questions related to the job, as long as they do not ask personal questions that could be used to make discriminatory hiring or pay decisions. Here are some examples of questions that are permissible:

- Where have you been employed?
- What is your education? (If required by the job description.)

- Can you perform the essential functions of the job? (Here's another place a job description is handy.)
- Are you 18 or older? (Determine if the applicant is of legal age for the job.)
- Are you legally authorized to work in the United States? (Ask *all* applicants—do not single out people that may be assumed to be foreign.)
- Do you have references we can contact?

What Should Employers Not Ask?

Even if an employer has the best of intentions and would never use the information to make a discriminatory employment decisions, questions about certain irrelevant information can interpreted as discriminatory. Unless there is a legitimate business reason an employer needs certain personal information to make the hiring decision, which is very rare, questions that can get employers into trouble include those that seek information about age, race, national origin, color, religion, disability, marital status, and other personal information. Here are some examples of questions that are *not* permissible:

- How old are you?
- When did you graduate from high school?
- When were you born?
- Are you married?
- Are you engaged?
- Are you planning to get married?
- Do you have children?
- Are you planning to get pregnant?
- Do you have any disabilities?
- Where is your spouse from?
- What is that accent?
- Where are you from?
- Were you born here?
- What is your ethnic heritage?
- What church do you go to?
- Questions about an applicant's impairment or how he or she became disabled (e.g. Why do you use a wheelchair?);
- Questions about past workers' compensation history; and
- What medications, if any, are being taken and medical history.

Because the purpose of anti-discrimination laws is to treat people equally in the workplace, the limits on personal questions make sense. While it may seem difficult to know the boundaries, in general keep these two words in mind: *job related*.

Checking References

- Plan the questions to ask the references. Call or write the references and ask about job related issues, such as employment dates, job titles, rates of pay, tasks performed, work habits, ability to work with others, and whether the applicant is eligible for re-hire;
- Stay away from asking references any questions that could be interpreted as discriminatory; and
- Document reference checks, even unsuccessful tries. List the dates, who gave the information, who conducted the check, information obtained, whether the reference check was by phone or letter. Keep the reference check in a file, along with the application (even for unsuccessful candidates, since the EEOC requires employers to keep them for a year).[25]

Checking Credit Reports

Credit reports may be checked only for a very good business reason, such as where the person hired will be handling large sums of money or exercising financial discretion. The federal Fair Credit Reporting Act limits the use of consumer credit reports as a part of background checks on applicants,[26] and requires that employers notify the applicant in writing in advance of the credit check.[27]

WORDS OF WISDOM: In Colorado, an applicant must consent to a credit check in writing before it is conducted.[28]

If an employer denies employment based on information in the credit report, the employer must: (1) inform the job applicant that the credit report investigation is the basis for the job denial, even if it wasn't the only reason; and (2) provide a copy of the credit report, and a summary of the applicant's credit rights.[29] Credit reporting agencies must provide a copy of this notice with each credit report, so an employer can use this notice to fulfill their responsibility to notify the employee.

WORDS OF WISDOM: An employer may not discriminate against applicants because the applicant has declared bankruptcy, been insolvent, or not paid a dischargeable debt. The federal Bankruptcy Act forbids such discrimination.[30]

Checking Driving Records

If the job requires the employee to drive a vehicle for company business, an employer should check the applicant's driving record for traffic violations, driving related offenses, or more importantly, if the license is suspended or revoked. Employers can obtain driving record information from the Department of Revenue—Motor Vehicle Business Group by providing the applicant's full name, date of birth, address, license number, and a nominal fee. Employers can go into a driver's license office and obtain a copy of the record, or, they can send a written request to the following address: Department of Revenue, Motor Vehicle Business Group, Driver Control Section, Denver, CO 80261-0016. For additional information, visit the Driver Control Section's website at http://www.mv.state.co.us/FAQdc.htm.

Checking Criminal Records

Employers should protect themselves from potential liability for the acts of the people they hire by doing criminal checks on applicants who will drive a company vehicle, have access to master keys (such as for apartment complexes), have a great deal of contact with the public, patients, or children, have access to drugs, carry a weapon, or be bonded. Colorado employers may *not* require an applicant to disclose any information contained in sealed arrest or criminal records.[31]

WORDS OF WISDOM: Checking conviction records generally is permitted, but checking arrest records can get employers into trouble. Arrest records do not show whether someone actually was convicted, so they can be misleading. Also, checking arrest records can lead to liability for the company under anti-discrimination laws.[32]

Colorado has laws pertaining to criminal background checks for employment for non-public schools, education boards, public school districts, nurse's aides, child care centers, nursing care facilities, and emergency medical technicians. Special rules apply to the employment of persons convicted of offenses involving moral turpitude.

To conduct a criminal background check in Colorado, employers can contact the Colorado Bureau of Investigation (CBI), either by visiting the CBI website at http://cbi.state.co.us/ or by sending a written request to 690 Kipling Street, Denver, CO 80215. Criminal history data is based on fingerprint submissions from law enforcement agencies within the State of Colorado. The CBI is not allowed to disclose information from other state or federal databases. Sealed records are not released to the public.

Criminal history reports can be accessed immediately by using the CBI's web-based system and charging to a credit card $5.50 per result viewed. If an employer is paying with anything other than a credit card, submit a written form to the CBI for a manual search ($10.00). The search can take up to three business days to complete, after which the results will be mailed. Forms can be printed off of the website. For more information on the CBI, visit https://www.cbirecordscheck.com/Question/faq.asp.

> **WORDS OF WISDOM:** Put all credit checks and criminal checks in a file separate from the personnel file, because by law credit checks and criminal checks must remain confidential.[33] A separate file will prevent supervisors, or other people without a reason to know the information, from seeing the credit checks and criminal checks when they review personnel files. If anyone removes reference reports from a personnel file, the individual should leave a note in the file as to where the reference reports have been moved.

Job Related Testing

As with background checks, the words *job related* are critical in determining whether to test applicants and employees. Some tests cannot legally be given until after a conditional job offer has been made, including medical examinations. In any event, testing *must* be job related and necessary.

> **WORDS OF WISDOM:** After making a job offer, employers may ask any disability-related questions and conduct medical examinations as long as an employer does this for everybody in the same job category and does not single out someone perceived to be disabled.

Testing falls into many categories, including:
- Achievement tests (special skill or knowledge, e.g. typing, computer);
- Aptitude tests (capabilities and potential, e.g. math aptitude, general intelligence);
- Honesty tests (these are not recommended because of questionable reliability and potential discrimination problems);
- Lie detector tests (while the federal Employee Polygraph Protection Act generally prohibits employers from requiring applicants to take a lie detector test and from asking applicants about previous lie detector tests,[34] the law provides a narrow list of exceptions, including businesses that provide armored car serv-

ices, alarm or guard services or those that manufacture, distribute or dispense pharmaceuticals);[35]

- Physical ability — strength, endurance, overall fitness (these must be job related);
- Personality tests (these are not recommended because they may be considered an invasion of privacy); and
- Drug tests — although Colorado employers may require drug tests under certain circumstances (contact legal counsel for specific advice), they may not ask employees what prescription drugs they are taking.

WORDS OF WISDOM: Pre-offer physical ability tests may violate the ADA if they are considered to be medical exams (however, employers can make a conditional job offer). Also, other tests may violate the ADA, unless the employer makes accommodations as necessary for people with disabilities. See Chapter 5 for more details.

Selecting the Most Qualified Person for the Job

Once an employer has gathered the information from all applicants and references, including the application, resume, interview, and background checks, and has considered the position and abilities and skills of the applicants, the employer will be able to make hiring decisions knowing that they have taken steps toward creating a legally healthy relationship with their new employee. Employers will be ready to move past the pre-hire steps to beginning the employment relationship and getting on with the business of the company.

FOOTNOTES

[1] 42 U.S.C. §§ 2000e to 2000e-17.
[2] 42 U.S.C. §§ 1210 to 12117.
[3] 29 U.S.C. §§ 621 to 634.
[4] 29 U.S.C. § 206(d).
[5] 29 U.S.C. §§ 201 to 219.
[6] 42 U.S.C. § 2000e(k).
[7] 29 U.S.C. §§ 2601 to 2654.
[8] 8 U.S.C. § 1324a.
[9] 29 U.S.C. §§ 151 to 169.
[10] 29 U.S.C. §§ 1001 to 1461.
[11] 29 U.S.C. §§ 1161 to 1168.
[12] 29 U.S.C. §§ 2101 to 2109.
[13] C.R.S. §§ 24-34-401 *et seq.*
[14] C.R.S. § 24-34-402.

[15]   C.R.S. § 8-2-113(2).

[16]   Order No. 22.

[17]   C.R.S. § 8-2-114.

[18]   C.R.S. § 8-2-104; C.R.S. § 8-2-107.

[19]   C.R.S. §§ 8-4-101 to 127.

[20]   EEO-1, Legal Basis for Requirements, www.eeoc.gov/eeo1survey/legalbasis.html; *See also,* Section 709(c), Title VII, Civil Rights Act of 1967.

[21]   42 U.S.C. §§ 1210 to 12117.

[22]   *See e.g.* Fair Credit Reporting Act, 15 U.S.C. § 1681 *et seq.* (protects employees' financial information); *see also,* Americans with Disabilities Act, 42 U.S.C. § 12112(d) (protects certain medical information).

[23]   EEOC, Facts About Race/Color Discrimination, www.eeoc.gov/facts/fs-race.html

[24]   C.R.S. § 8-2-114.

[25]   EEOC, Information for Small Employers, www.eeoc.gov/small/recordsandreports.html

[26]   15 U.S.C. § 1681b(b).

[27]   15 U.S.C. § 1681b(b)(2).

[28]   15 U.S.C. §§ 1681 *et seq.*

[29]   *Id.*

[30]   11 U.S.C. § 525(a) – (b).

[31]   *See,* C.R.S. § 24-72-308.

[32]   *Id.*

[33]   *See generally,* Fair Credit Reporting Act.

[34]   29 U.S.C. § 2002.

[35]   29 U.S.C. § 2006(e) – (f).

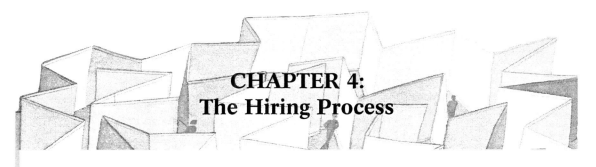

CHAPTER 4:
The Hiring Process

Making the Offer

One of the most exciting parts of employing people is making the job offer, whether verbally (i.e., in person or on the phone) or in writing. When employers extend a job offer to a new employee, they should include the following information:
- Position offered;
- Location and hours;
- Salary;
- Benefits, if any;
- Starting date;
- Required paperwork;

- A date by which the applicant must respond; and
- At-will employment language, unless the employment is for a specific amount of time.

WORDS OF WISDOM: If an employer decides not to offer a position to an applicant, it is respectful to let the applicant know as soon as possible. It's a good policy to send a simple letter telling the applicant that the position has been filled and wishing him or her luck. Keep a copy of the letter in the company's files with the applications (remember the EEOC requires employers to keep application records for a year).[1] If the applicant later decides to bring a failure to hire claim, the employer will have some documentation that may be helpful.

After the Offer is Accepted: Three Important Forms

After the applicant has accepted the job offer, important documents must be completed, including Form W-4 (for taxes and payroll withholding), Form I-9, and the Colorado New Hire Report.

Form W-4—Tax Withholding

Form W-4 is an Employee's Withholding Allowance Certificate IRS form that determines how much federal withholding tax will be deducted from an employee's paycheck. Employers should ask all employees to submit a signed Form W-4 when the employee starts work. The signed Form W-4 should be effective the first pay period. If the employee does not submit a Form W-4, the employer should withhold as if the employee were single, claiming no allowances.

An employee may submit a new Form W-4 at any time. The employer should base the employee's income tax withholding on the most recently submitted Form W-4, unless the IRS has notified the employer to withhold based on a different number of allowances, or unless the Form W-4 is invalid. If an employee submits a new Form W-4, the employer should start withholding based on the new Form W-4 no later than the start of the first payroll period ending on or after the 30th day from the day the new Form W-4 is submitted.

Form I-9—Employment Eligibility Verification

The purpose of employment verification is to ensure that employers only hire citizens and workers who are authorized to work in the United States. The Immigration Reform and Control Act (IRCA)[2] made U.S. employers responsible for verifying the employment eligibility and identity of all employees hired to work in the United States after November 6, 1986. To implement the IRCA, employers are required to complete Employment Eligibility Verification forms (Form I-9) for all employees, including U.S. citizens. Recently, the Immigration and Naturalization Service (INS) was replaced by the Bureau of Citizenship and Immigration Services (BCIS). The BCIS is a bureau within the Department of Homeland Security (DHS). Employers can find more information regarding the BCIS by visiting the BCIS website at http://www.bcis.gov/graphics/aboutus/index.htm. There is a special section for employers at http://www.bcis.gov/graphics/services/employerinfo/index.htm.

While citizens and nationals of the U.S. are automatically eligible for employment, they too must present proof of employment eligibility and identity and complete an Employment Eligibility Verification form (Form I-9). Citizens of the U.S. include persons born in Puerto Rico, Guam, the U.S. Virgin Islands, and the Northern Mariana Islands. Nationals of the U.S. include persons born in American Samoa, including Swains Island.

Employers need to complete Form I-9 only for people actually hired. For purposes of the Form I-9 rules, a person is "hired" when he or she begins to work for an employer for wages or other compensation. If an employee fails to produce one or more required documents, or a receipt for one or more replacement documents (in the case of lost, stolen, or destroyed documents), within three business days of the date employment begins, the employment may be terminated.

WORDS OF WISDOM: If an employee has presented a receipt for a replacement document, he or she must produce the actual document within 90 days of the date employment begins.

If an employer properly completes a Form I-9 and the BCIS discovers that the employee is not actually authorized to work, the employer cannot be charged with a verification violation; however, the employer cannot knowingly continue to employ this individual. The employer will have a good-faith defense against the imposition of penalties unless the government can prove the employer had *actual knowledge* of the unauthorized status of the employee.

According to the BCIS, an employer must examine the document(s) presented by the employee and, if the document(s) reasonably appear on their face to be genuine and related to the person presenting the document(s), the employer must accept them. To do otherwise could be an unfair immigration-related employment practice. However, if a document does not reasonably appear on its face to be genuine and related to the person presenting it, the employer must not accept it. For assistance, employers may contact the Denver District Office of the Bureau of Immigration and

Customs Enforcement (BICE) at 4370 Paris Street, Denver, CO 80239, or visit the BICE web site at http://www.bcis.gov/graphics/fieldoffices/denver/aboutus. htm#anchor1618781.

Every U.S. employer must have a Form I-9 in their files for each new employee, unless the employee was hired before November 7, 1986, and has been continuously employed by the same employer. Also, a Form I-9 need not be completed for individuals who fulfill *all* of the following:

- Providing domestic services in a private household that are sporadic, irregular, or intermittent; and
- Providing services for the employer as an independent contractor (i.e. carrying on an independent business; contracting to do a piece of work according to the independent contractor's own means and methods, subject to control only as to the results of the work, the employer does *not* set the work hours, the employer does *not* provide the necessary tools to do the job; or whom the employer does not have the authority to hire and fire); and
- Providing services for the employer, under a contract, subcontract, or exchange entered into after November 6, 1986. (In such cases, the contractor is the employer of the individual for I-9 purposes; for example, a temporary employment agency.)

The current versions of the Form I-9 and the OBL's *Handbook for Employers* are dated November 21, 1991. Both documents are undergoing revisions to reflect changes in U.S. immigration law since the documents were issued, but the publication dates have not been established. At the time of the publication of this book, the proposed changes and the Form I-9 published in February 1998 were not currently in effect. However, interim changes made on September 30, 1997 are currently in effect.

Unlike tax forms, Form I-9 records are not filed with the U.S. government. The requirement is for employers to maintain I-9 records in their own files for three years after the date of hire or one year after the date the employee's employment is terminated, whichever is later.[3] This requirement means that Form I-9 records need to be retained for all current employees, as well as terminated employees whose records remain within the retention period. Form I-9 records may be stored at the worksite to which they relate, or at company headquarters, or at another location. However, the storage choice must make it possible for the documents to be transmitted to the worksite within three days of an official request for production of the documents for inspection.[4]

WORDS OF WISDOM: U.S. immigration law does not require or forbid storage of a private employer's Form I-9 records in employee personnel files. As a practical matter, however, particularly if a large number of employees are employed by a company, it may be difficult to extract records from individual personnel files in time to meet a three day deadline for production of Form I-9 records for official inspection. Therefore, it may be more practical to keep Form I-9 records in a separate file at the worksite.

The IRCA protects certain individuals from unfair immigration-related employment practices, including refusal to employ based on a future expiration date of a current employment authorization document.[5] The U.S. government entity charged with enforcing the laws protecting against unfair immigration-related employment practices is the Office of Special Counsel for Unfair Employment-Related Discrimination Practices, which is part of the Civil Division of the U.S. Department of Justice.

Employee's Responsibility

A new employee must complete Section 1 of a Form I-9 no later than close of business on his or her first day of work. The employee's signature holds the employee responsible for the accuracy of the information provided. The employer is responsible for ensuring that the employee completes Section 1 in full. No documentation is required to substantiate the Section 1 information provided by the employee.

Employer's Responsibility

The employer is responsible for ensuring completion of the entire Form I-9. No later than close of business on the employee's third day of employment services, the employer must complete Section 2 of Form I-9. To complete Section 2, the employer must review the documentation presented by the employee and record the employee's documentation as required by Form I-9. Proper documentation establishes both that the employee is authorized to work in the U.S. and that the employee who presents the employment authorization document is the person to whom it was issued.

The employer should supply to the employee the official list of acceptable documents for establishing identity and work eligibility. The employer may accept any List A document, establishing both identity and work eligibility, or combination of a List B document (establishing identity) and List C document (establishing work eligibility), that the employee chooses from the list to present (the documentation presented is not required to substantiate information provided in Section 1 of Form I-9). The employer must examine the documents and accept them if the documents reasonably appear to be genuine and related to the employee who presented them.

Requesting more or different documentation than the minimum necessary to meet this requirement may constitute an unfair immigration-related employment practice.

Employers *must* refuse acceptance of the documents if the documentation presented by an employee does not reasonably appear to be genuine or related to the employee who presented them. Employers must then ask for other documentation from the list of acceptable documents that meet the requirements. An employer should not continue to employ an employee who cannot present documentation that meets the requirements.

Are the Documents Genuine?

According to the BCIS, employers are not required to be document experts. In reviewing the genuineness of the documents presented by employees, employers are held to a reasonableness standard. Since most employers do not have access to confirm the information contained in a document, it may happen that an employer will accept a document that is not in fact genuine—or is genuine but does not belong to the person who presented it. Such an employer will not be held responsible if the document reasonably appeared to be genuine or related to the person presenting it. An employer who receives a document that does not appear to be genuine may request assistance from the nearest Immigration field office or may contact the Office of Business Liaison.

Photocopy Concerns

According to the BCIS, there are two separate and unrelated photocopy issues in the employment eligibility verification process. The first issue is whether an employer may accept photocopies of identity or employment eligibility documents to fulfill Form I-9 requirements. Only *original* documents (not necessarily the first document of its kind ever issued to the employee, but an actual document issued by the issuing authority) are satisfactory, with the single exception of a certified photocopy of a birth certificate.

The second issue is whether the employer may or must attach photocopies of the documentation submitted to satisfy Form I-9 requirements to the employee's Form I-9. Attaching photocopies of documentation is permissible, but not required. However, where the practice of photocopying documentation is undertaken by an employer, it must be consistently applied to every employee, without regard to citizenship or national origin.

"Green Cards" are Not Really Green and Other Important Information

The terms *Resident Alien Card, Permanent Resident Card, Alien Registration Receipt Card,* and *Form I-551* all refer to documentation issued to a worker who has been granted permanent residence in the United States. Once granted, the status of permanent residence is permanent. However, the document that an alien carries as proof of this status may expire. The "pink" version of the *Resident Alien Card* and the new *Permanent Resident Cards*, are valid for either two years (for conditional residents) or ten years (for permanent residents). The "white" version of the *Resident Alien Card* does not bear an expiration date.

When these cards expire, the alien cardholders must obtain new cards. An expired card cannot be used to satisfy Form I-9 requirements for new employment. Expiration dates do not affect current employment, since employers are neither required nor permitted to re-verify the employment authorization of aliens who have presented one of these cards to satisfy Form I-9 requirements (this is true for conditional residents as well as permanent residents).

Even if the expiration date is valid, "green cards" must also appear genuine and establish the identity of the cardholder.

Official Inspections of I-9 Files

According to the BCIS, upon request, all Form I-9 records subject to the retention requirement must be made available in their original form or on microfilm or microfiche to an authorized official of the Bureau of Immigration and Customs Enforcement, Department of Labor, and/or the Justice Department's Office of Special Counsel for Unfair Immigration-Related Employment Practices. The official will give employers at least three days advance notice before the inspection. Original documents (as opposed to photocopies) may be requested.

> **WORDS OF WISDOM:** Employers should not fulfill Form I-9 responsibilities by means of documents faxed by a new employee or through identifying numbers appearing on acceptable documents. The employer must review original documents.

For more information regarding official inspections of Form I-9, contact the Office of Business Liaison (OBL). The OBL has informational bulletins regarding the Form I-9 process, plus the *Handbook for Employers*. In addition, the OBL can answer specific questions via e-mail, fax, and phone call.

The Colorado New Hire Report

All Colorado employers are required to send new hire information about every new employee who works or lives in the state of Colorado to the State Directory of New Hires (SDNH).[6] The SDNH receives and processes hiring data, to be used to help the Child Support Enforcement Division of the Colorado Department of

Human Services locate parents, establish paternity, and establish and enforce child support orders. The purpose of new hire reporting is to help individuals stay current with their child support obligations by withholding wages so their children receive support on time.

In Colorado, the information received by the SDNH is also provided to Medicaid, food stamps, Supplemental Security Income, cash assistance, and unemployment compensation programs. The SDNH also supplies the information to the Federal Office of Child Support Enforcement, which passes along the information to other state child support agencies for the same purposes.

Employers are required to report the following information to the SDNH:
- The employee's name, address, and Social Security number; and
- The employer's name, address, and federal identification number (Tax ID).

The SDNH also encourages employers who report electronically or magnetically to report the employee's date of hire, the employee's date of birth, and the employer's payroll address, if different from the employer's address.

Employers must send all new hire reports within 20 days of the employee's first day of work, or by the first payroll period. If an employer reports electronically or magnetically, the employer must report twice a month, not less than 12 nor more than 16 days apart. The SDNH permits reporting by mail, overnight delivery, fax, internet, or magnetic media file layouts.

Creating Personnel Files

Although no specific Colorado or federal law requires employers to keep personnel files, the laws do require employers to maintain certain employee records—including Form W-4, Form I-9, and job applications.[7] Other information about the employee required by law includes:
- Employee's full name;
- Employee's number (many employers use a Social Security number as an employee number, but some employers don't use an employee number at all);
- Employee's home address, including zip code;
- Employee's date of birth;
- Employee's gender;
- Employee's job title; and
- Employee's basic payroll records.

Information that is not required, but would be useful to maintain, includes:
- Employee's performance evaluations;
- Employee's disciplinary records;
- Employee's work history;

- Employee's sick days;
- Employee's vacation days;
- Employee's benefit enrollments;
- Employee's payroll withholding;
- Employee's reference checks; and
- Employee's workers' compensation information.

WORDS OF WISDOM: Because Colorado has no law regarding access to personnel files that applies to private employers, employers may set their own policies regarding an employee's review of his or her own file.

As mentioned in previous chapters, information employers collect about employees should be strictly job-related. Due to privacy concerns and legal restrictions, employers *must* keep all medical, credit, and criminal background records confidential and separate from the rest of the employee's personnel file. Employers also may want to keep the Form I-9 records separate for ease of access in the event of an official review. Limit the personnel file to information that applies only to the employee, such as resumes, performance evaluations, and work history. If required files are kept in separate files, employers can easily produce them to government agencies without providing irrelevant and private personnel information.

Employee Orientation—"Welcome to the Family!"

For many new employees, starting a new job can be an exciting, but stressful time. They may wonder what the company really will be like (now that the recruiting is over), and whether the company will live up to the promises the HR manager made during the hiring process. They wonder what their boss will be like. They wonder how long it will take to get up to speed on their new job. They wonder if their new job will be fun. They wonder if they will make any friends. They wonder if the other employees will like them.

A good orientation is a company's opportunity to get a new employee started off right. To make the most of the opportunity, it is helpful to understand the purposes of orientation, topics employers can present, and things employers can include in the orientation package.

Orientation Purposes

New employee orientation programs reduce employee turnover and help employees reach full productivity faster than they would otherwise. Without a good orientation, employees can find themselves so preoccupied with basic questions that it is difficult for them to integrate into the company and do the job they were hired to do. Orientation can serve at least three purposes for a company: (1) welcoming new employees; (2) conveying important information to new employees; and (3) motivating new employees to do well from their first day.

Welcoming New Employees

Orientation is an opportunity to provide a warm and enthusiastic welcome to new employees. The orientation process can be used to share information on the mission, culture, and goals of a company and the employees' role in advancing them.

Every company has a certain kind of culture, whether it is a formal organizational hierarchy or a more casual environment. The way a new employee is introduced to the company will say a lot about the company's culture and whether the company values their employees as people.

Conveying Important Information

In addition to providing information about the company's culture, orientation can also tell employees what they can expect from the company, including compensation and benefits, employment rights provided by law, and other types of support a company may offer. It also is an opportunity to convey day-to-day operational information and office logistics.

Employers can also help set the tone for an employee's success by telling their employees from day one what the company expects from them. For example, employers should provide specific information about the employees' new job and the part they play in the company. It is an excellent time to acquaint the new employees with the company's philosophies on (and the requirements of) equality in the workplace. A good orientation should include a review of the company handbook as well as training regarding the company's equal employment opportunity and anti-discrimination policies.

Motivating Employees (or Not)

The first day of work can be the beginning of a legally healthy relationship, or it can set the tone for a negative experience. A good orientation program can help employers motivate employees to do well from the beginning. It can help them to understand that not only is their employer interested in helping them to succeed, but that everyone contributes to making the company a quality place to work.

Checklist of Possible Topics for Orientation

Here are some examples of topics employers might want to cover during orientation:

- About the company:
  - Customer service philosophy,
  - Confidentiality,
  - Ethics;
- About the employee's job:
  - Job description,
  - Performance expectations,
  - Immediate supervisor and chain of command,
  - Possibilities for advancement,
  - Training opportunities,
  - Introduction of co-workers and job related interaction;
- General office information:
  - Office equipment location and use,
  - Telephone system, standard greetings, and voicemail system,
  - Computer use and protocol,
  - Location and use of manuals, forms, and supplies,
  - Assignment of keys,
  - Telephone, e-mail, internet use,
  - Time cards/clock,
  - Office organization (i.e., file cabinets, supplies, copier),
  - Office resources (e.g., directories, dictionaries, computer program manuals, staff listings, etc.);
- Conditions of employment:
  - Employment policies and procedures,
  - Probationary periods,
  - Performance evaluations and job descriptions,
  - Privacy rights and personnel files,
  - Grievance and complaint process,
  - Discipline;
- Compensation:
  - Pay periods, pay days, salary schedule,
  - Direct deposit,
  - Salary increases,
  - Other salary provisions;
- Benefits:
  - Medical, dental, vision insurance,

- ○ Disability insurance plans;
- Work schedules:
  - ○ Breaks and lunch,
  - ○ Holidays, vacation, and leaves,
  - ○ Jury duty and subpoenaed witnesses,
  - ○ Overtime hours and compensation,
  - ○ Absence reporting and requests,
  - ○ Family medical leave,
  - ○ Miscellaneous leaves;
- Policies and procedures:
  - ○ Nondiscrimination,
  - ○ Anti-harassment,
  - ○ Individuals with disabilities,
  - ○ Computing and communication technology,
  - ○ Attendance,
  - ○ Zero tolerance of workplace violence,
  - ○ Smoking,
  - ○ Anti-alcohol,
  - ○ Drug-free workplace.

Orientation Package

Here are some documents employers might want to include in an Employee Orientation Package:
- Employee handbook;
- Acknowledgment forms:
  - ○ Receipt of handbook,
  - ○ Anti-discrimination and harassment policies,
  - ○ At-will disclaimer,
  - ○ Receipt and understanding of complaint procedure;
- Employment application (copy);
- Benefits forms;
- I-9 Form;
- W-4 Form;
- Emergency contact form;
- Direct deposit form;
- Wage withholding authorization;
- Certificate of completion;
- Feedback form (How was the orientation? Does the employee have any questions or concerns?).

FOOTNOTES

[1] 2000 CFR, Title 29, Labor, Chapter XIV, Part 1602, Record Keeping and Reporting Requirements Under Title VII and the ADA, http://www.access.gpo.gov/nara/cfr/waisidx_00/29cfr1602_00.html

[2] Bureau of Citizenship Immigration Services, About I-9, Employment Eligibility Verification, http://www.bcis.gov/graphics/howdoi/faqeev.htm

[3] *Id.*

[4] *Id.*

[5] *Id.*

[6] Colorado Department of Human Services, Child Support Enforcement, www.newhire.state.co.us/intro.htm

[7] *See generally,* Colorado Division of Worker's Compensation, http://www.state.co.us/oed/guide/; Bureau of Citizenship and Immigration Services, www.bcis.org; United States Equal Employment Opportunity Commission, www.eeoc.gov

CHAPTER 5:
Equal Employment Opportunity Issues

Overview of Equal Employment Opportunity

Equal employment opportunity can be defined as the treatment of all people in a fair and unbiased manner in all aspects of employment. This includes hiring, training opportunities, promotions, discipline, pay and other compensation, and any other terms and conditions of employment. The federal, state, and local anti-discrimination laws confirm the importance of equal treatment for all people in the workplace. Equal employment opportunity laws prohibit both intentional discrimination (usually based on prejudice and negative stereotypes) and neutral job policies that disproportionately exclude minorities and that are not job related.

Ten Useful Equal Employment Related Definitions

When discussing equal employment opportunity, it is helpful to start with definitions of terms that often arise. The following definitions of equal employment related terms can be found in: *The American Heritage Dictionary of the English Language,* Fourth Edition; Dictionary.com at http://dictionary.reference.com; *Some Facts Psychologists Know About Racism* at http://www.psc.uc.edu/sh/ SH_Racism.htm; and, Wordnet at http://www.cogsci.princeton.edu/~wn/.

1. Discrimination — Unfair treatment of a person or group on the basis of prejudice; treatment or consideration based on class or category rather than individual merit;
2. Prejudice — Irrational suspicion or hatred of a particular group, race, or religion;
3. Stereotype — A person or group considered to conform to an unvarying pattern or manner, lacking any individuality;
4. Ignorance — Being uneducated, unaware, or uninformed;
5. Bigot — One who is strongly partial to one's own group, religion, race, or politics and is intolerant of those who differ. *See also,* Bigotry — The state of mind of a bigot; obstate and unreasoning attachment of one's own belief and opinions, with narrow-minded intolerance of beliefs opposed to them;
6. Race — A classification of human beings into distinguishable groups that are based on innate and immutable physical characteristics, e.g. skin color, hair texture, eye shape. *See also,* Racism — Founded on the belief in one's racial superiority over another, encompassing the beliefs, attitudes, behaviors, and practices that define people based on racial classifications. It involves

a generalized lack of knowledge or experience as it applies to negative beliefs and attitudes, and it uses the inflexible assumption that group differences are biologically determined and therefore inherently unchangeable;

7. Ethnicity — A classification of individuals who share a common ancestry comprised of customs and traditions that are passed on between generations, e.g. religion, dress, and nationality. *See also*, Ethnic group — People of the same race or nationality who share a distinctive culture;

8. Ethnocentrism — Belief in the superiority of one's own ethnic group;

9. Tolerance — The capacity for, or the practice of, recognizing and respecting the beliefs or practices of others;

10. Diverse — Differing one from another; made up of distinct characteristics, qualities, or elements. *See also*, Diversity — The fact or quality of being diverse; difference; variety.

Forms of Employment Discrimination

Unfortunately, discrimination can take many forms. Three legal terms for different kinds of discrimination are:

1. Disparate treatment;
2. Disparate impact; and
3. Retaliation.

Disparate treatment is intentional discrimination against an individual or group of individuals because of protected characteristics. An example of this is refusing to hire a pregnant woman because she is pregnant, which sometimes happens because of stereotypes regarding pregnant women or new mothers.

Unlike disparate treatment, *disparate impact* can be "inadvertent" discrimination, such as a practice or policy that does not specifically apply to one group more than another, but it disadvantages a particular group more than others *without* a business necessity for doing so. Examples of this include unnecessary written tests, height and weight requirements, educational requirements, and subjective practices including interviews.

Retaliation is intentional negative treatment of employees, such as demotion or termination, because they either participated in discrimination complaints or proceedings, or opposed discrimination in the workplace. For a detailed discussion of retaliation, see Chapter 7.

Examples of Discriminatory Employment Practices

Examples of discriminatory employment practices may include decisions based on protected characteristics or categories in the following areas:

• Compensation, assignment, or classification of employees;

- Hiring and firing;
- Transfer, promotion, layoff, or recall;
- Job advertisements;
- Recruitment;
- Testing;
- Use of company facilities;
- Training and apprenticeship programs;
- Fringe benefits;
- Pay, retirement plans, and disability leave; or
- Other terms and conditions of employment.

According to the EEOC, discriminatory practices also include:[1]
- Harassment on the basis of race, color, religion, sex, national origin, disability, or age;
- Retaliation against an individual for filing a charge of discrimination, participating in an investigation, or opposing discriminatory practices;
- Employment decisions based on stereotypes or assumptions about the abilities, traits, or performance of individuals of a certain sex, race, age, religion, or ethnic group, or individuals with disabilities;
- Denying employment opportunities to a person because of marriage to, or association with, an individual of a particular race, religion, national origin, or an individual with a disability; and
- Discrimination because of participation in schools or places of worship associated with a particular racial, ethnic, or religious group.

WORDS OF WISDOM: According to the EEOC, in rare circumstances, employers may discriminate against a particular group, if the employer can show that the requirement is a "bona fide occupational qualification" (BFOQ).[2] A BFOQ is a job requirement allowing an employer to legally discriminate on the basis of sex, age, religion, or national origin. Such requirements are rare. Examples of BFOQs include sex, for a woman working in a women's locker room or modeling dresses. However, sex is not a BFOQ for heavy physical work, because some women are more physically powerful than some men. Race and color should never be used as BFOQs.

Checklist of Protected Classes

Laws protect employees from discrimination based on the following characteristics:

- National origin;
- Race/color;
- Sex;
- Pregnancy;
- Religion;
- Age;
- Disability;
- Citizenship;
- Sexual orientation;
- Marital status;
- Veteran status;
- Military status;
- Union membership;
- Political status; and
- Other individual characteristics that are unrelated to the functions of particular jobs.

WORDS OF WISDOM: Employers may be liable for "compound discrimination," if it can be shown that the employer discriminated based on a combination of the factors listed above. For example, an employer could be responsible for "sex-plus-age discrimination" if the employer terminated a female employee over the age of 40 (because she's an "older woman"), even if the employer treats older male employees and younger female employees favorably. Similarly, an employer could be responsible for "sex-plus-race" discrimination if the employer terminated an African American female employee (because she's a black woman), even if the employer treats black men and white women favorably. Courts are beginning to recognize that combinations of characteristics can expose different groups of people to specific stereotypes (such as the "little old lady" stereotype not faced by younger women) that can interfere with equal employment opportunity in the workplace.

National Origin Discrimination

National origin discrimination means treating someone less favorably because he or she comes from a particular place, because of his or her ethnicity or accent, or because it is believed that he or she has a particular ethnic background. National origin discrimination also means treating someone less favorably at work because of marriage or other association with someone of a particular nationality. To combat national origin discrimination the EEOC states that whether an employee or job applicant's ancestry is Mexican, Ukrainian, Filipino, Arab, American Indian, or any other nationality, he or she is entitled to the same employment opportunities as anyone else.[3]

National Origin Discrimination Examples

Examples of national origin discrimination include:
- Discriminatory employment decisions, such as discriminatory recruitment, hiring, firing, or layoffs;
- Harassment, such as ethnic slurs and other offensive conduct that creates a hostile work environment;
- Language and accent discrimination, such as making decisions based on an employee's foreign accent, unless the accent materially interferes with job performance;
- English-fluency discrimination, such as imposing a fluency requirement where it is not required for the effective performance of the job position; and
- English-only discrimination, such as imposing English-only rules where they are unnecessary for the safe or efficient operation of the employer's business.

WORDS OF WISDOM: The anti-discrimination laws protect non-citizens too![4] However, the remedies may be limited for people without work authorization.

Race/Color Related Discrimination

In addition to protection from national origin discrimination, employment laws protect individuals against employment discrimination on the basis of race and color. Title VII[5] prohibits employment decisions based on stereotypes and assumptions about abilities, traits, or the performance of individuals of racial groups. According to the EEOC, equal employment opportunity cannot be denied because of: (1) marriage to or association with an individual of a different race; (2) membership in or association with ethnic based organizations or groups; or (3) attendance or participation in schools or places of worship generally associated with certain minority groups.[6]

WORDS OF WISDOM: Employment laws protect all people, including non-minority whites, from employment discrimination on the basis of race.

Race/Color Related Discrimination Examples

Examples of race discrimination include:

- Discrimination on the basis of an immutable characteristic associated with race, such as skin color, hair texture, or certain facial features, even though not all members of the race share the same characteristic;
- Discrimination on the basis of a condition which predominantly affects one race unless the practice is job related and consistent with business necessity. The EEOC uses the examples of sickle cell anemia and shaving bumps.[7] Since both sickle cell anemia and shaving bumps predominantly occur in African-Americans, a policy which excludes individuals with sickle cell anemia or a "no-beard" grooming policy must be job related and consistent with business necessity;
- Harassment, such as ethnic slurs, racial "jokes," offensive or derogatory comments, or other verbal or physical conduct based on an individual's race or color if the conduct creates an intimidating, hostile, or offensive working environment, or interferes with the individual's work performance; and
- Segregation and classification of employees, such as segregating minority employees by physically isolating them from other employees or from customer contact, assigning them to predominantly minority establishments or geographic areas, or excluding minorities from certain positions or grouping or categorizing employees or jobs so that certain jobs are generally held by minorities.

WORDS OF WISDOM: The EEOC considers coded applications and resumes that designate an applicant's race, by either an employer or employment agency, evidence of discrimination where minorities are excluded from employment or from certain positions.[8] According to the EEOC one way to obtain racial information and simultaneously guard against discriminatory selection is for employers to use "tear-off sheets" for the identification of an applicant's race.[9] After the applicant completes the application and the tear-off portion, the employer separates the tear-off sheet from the application and does not review the tear-off portion during the selection process.

Sex Discrimination

It is unlawful for employers to discriminate against males or females in the workplace because of their sex.[10] Like national origin and race and color discrimination, decisions based on sexual stereotypes may violate anti-discrimination laws. Like other protected categories, these anti-discrimination protections extend to equal pay and terms and conditions of employment, and they also prohibit sex-based harassment.

WORDS OF WISDOM: Employment laws prohibit same-sex discrimination and harassment, where the conduct is because of the target's sex.

Sex Discrimination Examples

Examples of illegal sex discrimination include:
- Paying a male more than a female for the same job because the female is a woman (e.g., paying the male more because "he has a family to support");
- Stereotyping, such as making employment decisions based on beliefs about different capabilities of men and women (e.g., refusing to promote a female employee who is perceived to be too "macho" or "masculine");
- Disparate impact discrimination, such as using physical strength and ability tests, unless the tests accurately measure the ability to perform functions essential to the job in question; and
- Harassment, such as creating a hostile work environment or by conditioning job decisions on sexual favors.

Pregnancy Discrimination

Laws prohibit employers from making adverse employment decisions because a woman is pregnant. An amendment to Title VII, the Pregnancy Discrimination Act, prohibits discrimination on the basis of pregnancy, childbirth, or related medical conditions.[11]

Pregnancy Discrimination Examples

Women affected by pregnancy or related conditions must be treated in the same manner as applicants or employees with temporary disabilities. Pregnancy discrimination can occur in many ways, including failure to hire a qualified pregnant applicant, treating pregnant employees differently because of pregnancy, and with regard to fringe benefits and insurance.

WORDS OF WISDOM: Employers can pay a high price for pregnancy discrimination. Just ask Wal-Mart. In a recent case, a jury found that Wal-Mart intentionally refused to hire a woman because she was pregnant.[12] According to the lawsuit, the assistant manager told the job applicant to "come back after she had the baby." The EEOC took notice and filed a lawsuit on behalf of the job applicant. After 11 years of repeated trials and appeals, Wal-Mart agreed to pay nearly a quarter of a million dollars and implement comprehensive training concerning the Pregnancy Discrimination Act instead of facing further trial on the issue of punitive damages.

Hiring—"Come Back After You Have the Baby"

As the Wal-Mart case shows, an employer cannot refuse to hire a woman because of her pregnancy-related condition as long as she is able to perform the major functions of the job. Nor can an employer refuse to hire a pregnant woman because of the employer's prejudices against pregnant workers or the prejudices of co-workers, clients, or customers. Dealing with potential pregnancy-related discrimination concerns is another example of a way employers can benefit by having written job descriptions outlining the job functions. Whenever any potential applicant comes in, employers can refer to the job description to make sure that even inadvertent or subconscious biases do not interfere with the company's ability to get the most qualified person for the job, pregnant or not. Remember, pregnancy is only temporary, and a great worker should not be passed up based on negative stereotypes of pregnant women or mothers.

Work Continuation—"You Can't Work, You're Pregnant!"

While it may be tempting to try to "help" a pregnant employee by sending her home to bed before she has asked for leave, an employer must permit the employee to work as long as she is able to perform her job. Also, if the employee is temporarily unable to perform her job because of her pregnancy, she must be treated the same as any other temporarily disabled employee. For example, modified tasks or alternative assignments should be provided, or if other temporarily disabled employees would be accommodated through disability leave or leave without pay, these accomodations should likewise be provided to pregnant employees.

If at some point the pregnant employee must be absent from work because of a pregnancy-related condition, and the employee recovers from that condition, the employer may not require her to stay on leave until the baby's birth. The employee must be allowed to return to work again until she takes her leave. Similarly, an employer cannot have a blanket rule prohibiting employees from returning to work for a specific amount of time after the baby is born (i.e. no rules saying an employee cannot return for six weeks or any other predetermined length of time after childbirth).

Pregnancy and Maternity Leave—"Do You Need Leave?"

Sometimes concerned employers try to use special procedures to determine if a pregnant woman can continue to work. However, as noted above, employers can run into trouble if they treat pregnant women differently from temporarily disabled workers. Employers must use the same procedures they use to determine other employees' abilities to work when determining a pregant woman's ability to work. For example, employers who require employees to give the employer a doctor's statement concerning the employee's inability to work before granting leave or paying sick benefits should require employees affected by pregnancy-related conditions to do the same.

> **WORDS OF WISDOM:** Remember, the FMLA provides 12 weeks of unpaid leave for the birth of a child (for mothers and fathers), and the leave may be taken intermittently.[13] See Chapter 12 for more information regarding leave issues.

Fairness for Health Insurance—"You're Covered!"

While employers generally are not required to provide health insurance for their employees, if the employer does provide health insurance, they must be fair about it. Any health insurance provided by an employer must cover expenses for pregnancy-related conditions on the same basis as costs for other medical conditions.

As to reimbursement for pregnancy-related expenses, whether payment is on a fixed-basis or as a percentage-of-reasonable-and-customary-charge-basis, the payment should be reimbursed exactly as those incurred for other medical conditions. Also, an additional, higher, or larger, deductible cannot be imposed for pregnancy-related expenses. In other words, the amounts payable by the insurance provider can be limited only to the same extent as costs for other conditions.

> **WORDS OF WISDOM:** Employers must provide the same level of health benefits for spouses of male employees as they do for spouses of female employees!

Benefits—A Few Simple Rules

Here are a few simple rules to keep in mind regarding benefits:

- Pregnancy-related benefits cannot be limited to married employees;
- If an employer has an all-female workforce or job classification, and if the employer provides benefits for other medical conditions, the employer must provide benefits for pregnancy-related conditions;
- If an employer provides any benefits to workers on leave, the employer must provide the same benefits for those on leave for pregnancy-related conditions; and
- Employers must treat employees with pregnancy-related disabilities the same as other temporarily disabled employees for accrual and crediting of seniority, vacation calculation, pay increases, and temporary disability benefits.

WORDS OF WISDOM: Under Colorado laws,[14] an employer granting time off to biological parents (women and men) following the birth of a child must, upon request, make the same type of leave available to adoptive parents, in addition to any benefits provided, such as job guarantee or pay. Employers may not penalize employees for exercising these rights.

Reinstatement After Leave—"Welcome Back!"

Employers have a significant investment in their employees. If an employer has trained their employee (hopefully), and has treated their pregnant employee well during the employee's pregnancy (hopefully), then it only makes sense that an employer would welcome their employee back after a temporary absence. In fact, employers *must* hold open a job for a pregnancy-related absence the same length of time the employer holds open jobs for employees on sick or disability leave. If an employer has taken steps to avoid pregnancy discrimination and has learned the lessons Wal-Mart learned the hard way, the employer should be well on the way to avoiding charges of pregnancy discrimination.

Religious Discrimination

Today, more than ever, employers need to be aware of the social and legal issues arising from religious diversity. The workplace is more diverse than ever, in part because of new immigration and changing demographics. The American workplace is shaped not only by traditional Judeo-Christian religions, but also by Muslims, Hindus, Buddhists, Sikhs, and believers of many other faiths. To understand how employers should deal with religious issues, this section explores how religions impact the workplace, employers' legal responsibilities, and tips on creating more inclusive (and effective) workplaces.

Religions at Work

To find out to what extent companies have programs that create a workplace supportive of the religious diversity of their employees (and to see how religion impacts the workplace), the Tanenbaum Center for Interreligious Understanding and the Society for Human Resource Management (SHRM) recently conducted a survey of human resource professionals. Some of the findings of the SHRM are as follows:[15]

- More than one-third (36 percent) of respondents said that there are more religions represented in their workforce than five years ago.
- Less than one-third of respondents' organizations have a written policy on religious diversity. Of those with an official policy, only four percent have one apart from the general diversity statement.
- Christian holidays are the only official religious holidays in 99 percent of workplaces.

In another recent nationwide study surveying 675 employed persons including Buddhists, Hindus, Jews, Christians, Muslims, and Shintoists living in major metropolitan areas within 47 of the 48 contiguous states, *almost half* of those reporting experiences of religious discrimination stated that their performance was adversely affected.[16] This exploratory study also showed:[17]

- When asked about specific behaviors that are discriminatory in nature, 66 percent of all respondents reported that, although it may not have been directed at them, some form of religious bias or discrimination occurred in their workplace, and nearly 45 percent of those reporting discrimination considered changing jobs.
- Buddhist, Hindu, and Muslim respondents *not only experienced religious bias, but expected it.* Buddhists, Hindus and Muslims are the least comfortable and most vulnerable religious groups within the workplace. Of these groups, Muslims are the most vulnerable.
- Seventy percent of the Christians surveyed felt that problems related to religious and racial bias were serious ones in the workplace. This level of concern exceeded that exhibited by the study group. (While Christians made up almost 30 percent of the total survey group, the majority of those surveyed, designated the study group, were Buddhists, Hindus, Muslims, Jews and Shintoists.)
- Two-thirds (67 percent) of all respondents reported being troubled or at least somewhat concerned about religious discrimination in the workplace.

In short, according to the report, this survey indicated that in order to derive the greatest benefit from today's diverse workforce employers need: (1) flexible policies;

(2) attentiveness to and respect for religious and racial diversity; (3) intolerance regarding all forms of bias and prejudice; and (4) proactive stances toward hearing and addressing the concerns of all workers, both native and foreign-born.

The survey stated the same goals advanced by the federal and state laws, Title VII and the Colorado Anti-Discrimination Act. According to the EEOC, religious discrimination is one of the fastest growing types of discrimination charges filed with the agency nationally. In 2002, EEOC charges alleging religious discrimination increased 21 percent over the previous year.[18]

Religion—Title VII and the Colorado Anti-Discrimination Act

Title VII and the Colorado Anti-Discrimination Act recognize the value Americans place on freedom of religion and prohibit employers from discriminating against individuals because of the individual's religion in hiring, firing, and other terms and conditions of employment. Title VII and the Colorado Anti-Discrimination Act also require employers to reasonably accommodate the religious practices of an employee or prospective employee, unless to do so would create an undue hardship upon the employer.

Religion—Hiring and Other Employment Decisions

It is important to hire people based on their qualifications rather than perceptions about their religion, race, or national origin. To avoid discrimination, companies should consider proactive measures for preventing discrimination in hiring and other employment decisions. Employers should communicate with their managers and employees that discrimination based on religion or national origin is not tolerated by the company in any aspect of employment, including hiring. Employers also should adopt objective standards for selecting new employees. See Chapter 3 for more information regarding the pre-hiring process.

Employers cannot schedule examinations or other selection activities in conflict with a current or prospective employee's religious needs; inquire about an applicant's future availability at certain times; or maintain a restrictive dress code. Additionally employers cannot refuse to allow observance of a Sabbath or religious holiday, unless the employer can prove that not doing so would cause an undue hardship to the employer. Employers also cannot make their own judgments about whether a religion is deserving of protection or accommodation, and if employers do so they can expose themselves to significant liability.

For example, a federal jury in Denver found that a Pueblo, Colorado man, Mr. Don Reed, was a victim of religious discrimination after his employer called the man's religious beliefs a "sham."[19] Mr. Reed, who worked for years as an air traffic controller for the Federal Aviation Administration at the Pueblo airport, was fired because he refused to work on Saturdays, after his supervisors denied him permission to take

Saturdays off. Mr. Reed is a member of a "non-denominational" Christian group which marks the Sabbath from sundown Friday to sundown Saturday.

One of Mr. Reed's supervisors called Mr. Reed's beliefs a "religion of convenience" and not a genuine faith, and rejected several compromise work schedules that Mr. Reed had proposed. The FAA fired Mr. Reed after he failed to report to work for six consecutive Saturdays. Mr. Reed then sued the federal government with the assistance of the American Civil Liberties Union and a local law firm.

The federal jury in Denver awarded Mr. Reed a total of $2.25 million, which included back pay and benefits, future pay and benefits, and provisions for emotional pain and suffering, inconvenience, and mental anguish. While Mr. Reed's case was subject to a cap of $300,000 under Title VII, there were attorney fees awarded, not to mention the costs of defending the lawsuit—both in terms of money and in terms of time—lost productivity, and all of the negative impacts inherent in long drawn-out lawsuits. If at all possible, employers should endeavor to avoid this situation by providing reasonable accommodations under Title VII when asked.

Religion—Reasonable Accommodation

As noted above, Title VII and the Colorado Anti-Discrimination Act require employers to reasonably accommodate the religious practices of an employee or prospective employee, unless to do so would create an undue hardship upon the employer.[20] Reasonable accommodations may include the following:

- Flexible scheduling;
- Voluntary substitutions or swaps;
- Voluntary job reassignments;
- Voluntary lateral transfers;
- Leave for religious observances;
- Time and place to pray; and
- Ability to wear religious garb.

According to the SHRM survey, only 25 percent of the respondents' organizations permit holiday swapping, such as working on Ash Wednesday in exchange for taking time off on Yom Kippur.[21] Taking religious needs into account when providing food for employees is the third most requested accommodation (28 percent), yet it is seventh on the list of accommodations offered. Having a written policy regarding religious holiday leave is in the top four requested accommodations (20 percent), while it ranks 11th among those offered by employers.

WORDS OF WISDOM: Mandatory "new age" training programs, designed to improve employee motivation, cooperation, or productivity through meditation, yoga, biofeedback, or other practices may conflict with the non-discriminatory provisions of Title VII. Employers must accommodate any employee who gives notice that these programs are inconsistent with the employee's religious beliefs, whether or not the employer believes there is a religious basis for the employee's objection.

Religion—Undue Hardship

An employer can claim undue hardship when accommodating an employee's religious practices if allowing such practices requires more than ordinary administrative costs. Undue hardship also may be shown if changing a bona fide seniority system to accommodate one employee's religious practices denies another employee the job or shift preference guaranteed by the seniority system.

WORDS OF WISDOM: An employee whose religious practices prohibit payment of union dues to a labor organization cannot be required to pay the dues, but may pay an equal sum to a charitable organization.

In evaluating undue hardship, employers should consider only whether they can accommodate the employee who made the request. If the employer can accommodate the employee, they should do so. Because individual religious practices vary among members of the same religion, employers should not deny the requested accommodation based on speculation that other employees may seek the same accommodation.

If other employees subsequently request the same accommodation and granting it to all of the requesters would cause undue hardship, the employer can make an appropriate adjustment at that time. For example, if accommodating five employees would not cause an undue hardship but accommodating six employees would impose such hardship, the sixth request could be denied.

Age Discrimination

The federal Age Discrimination in Employment Act protects individuals who are 40 years of age or older from employment discrimination based on age.[22]

Age Discrimination Examples

The following are some examples of illegal age discrimination:
- Discriminatory employment advertising, such as including age preferences, age limitations, or age specifications in job notices or advertisements (except for

the "rare circumstances" where age is shown to be a "bona fide occupational qualification" (BFOQ) reasonably necessary to the essence of the business; or,

- Discriminatory employment benefits, such as denying benefits to older employees. An employer may reduce benefits based on age only if the cost of providing the reduced benefits to older workers is the same as the cost of providing benefits to younger workers.

Citizenship Discrimination

Citizenship discrimination occurs when an employer treats some employees (regardless of their national origins, ancestors, etc.) less favorably than other employees because of their citizenship status. For example, citizenship status discrimination occurs when employers grant U.S. citizens blanket preferential treatment over non-citizens.

Disability Discrimination

The Americans with Disabilities Act (ADA) protects qualified individuals with disabilities from employment discrimination.[23] Under the ADA, a person has a disability if the individual has: (1) a physical or mental impairment, that (2) substantially limits a major life activity. The ADA even protects people without disabilities if they have a *record* of a substantially limiting impairment or are *regarded* as having a substantially limiting impairment.

A *substantial impairment* is one that significantly limits or restricts a major life activity such as hearing, seeing, speaking, breathing, performing manual tasks, walking, caring for oneself, learning, or working.

Under the ADA, an individual with a disability also must be qualified to perform the essential functions of the job with or without reasonable accommodation. Employers should carefully examine each job to determine which functions or tasks are essential to the performance of a job, especially before taking an employment action such as recruiting, advertising, hiring, promoting, or firing.

Factors the EEOC considers in determining if a function is essential include:[24]

- Whether the reason the position exists is to perform that function;
- The number of other employees available to perform the function or among whom the performance of the function can be distributed; and
- The degree of expertise or skill required to perform the function.

As discussed in Chapter 3, a written job description prepared before advertising or interviewing for a job will be considered by the EEOC as evidence of the essential functions of a job. Other kinds of evidence that the EEOC will consider include:[25]

- The actual work experience of present or past employees in the job;
- The time spent performing a function;
- The consequences of not requiring that an employee perform a function; and
- The terms of a collective bargaining agreement.

Disability—Reasonable Accommodation

Reasonable accommodation is any change or adjustment to a job or work environment that permits a qualified applicant or employee with a disability to participate in the job application process, to perform the essential functions of a job, or to enjoy the benefits and privileges of employment equal to those enjoyed by employees without disabilities. According to the EEOC, reasonable accommodations may include:[26]

- Acquiring or modifying equipment or devices;
- Job restructuring;
- Part-time or modified work schedules;
- Reassignment to a vacant position;
- Adjusting or modifying examinations, training materials, or policies;
- Providing readers and interpreters; and
- Making the workplace readily accessible to and usable by people with disabilities.

Employers also must make reasonable accommodations to enable individuals with disabilities to participate in the application process and enjoy benefits and privileges of employment equal to those available to other employees. It is a violation of the ADA to fail to provide reasonable accommodation to the known physical or mental limitations of a qualified individual with a disability, unless to do so would impose an undue hardship on the operation of the business.[27]

Disability—Undue Hardship

Employers must provide a reasonable accommodation to qualified individuals with disabilities unless doing so would create an undue hardship. Undue hardship means that an accommodation would be unduly costly, extensive, substantial, or disruptive, or would fundamentally alter the nature or operation of the business. Among the factors to be considered in determining whether an accommodation is an undue hardship are the cost of the accommodation; the employer's size and financial resources; and the nature and structure of the employer's operation.

If a particular accommodation would be an undue hardship, the employer must try to identify another accommodation that will not pose such a hardship. If cost causes the undue hardship, the employer must also consider whether funding for an accommodation is available from an outside source, such as a vocational rehabilitation agency, and if the cost of providing the accommodation can be offset by state or federal tax credits or deductions. Employers must also give the applicant or employee with a disability the opportunity to provide the accommodation or pay for the portion of the accommodation that constitutes an undue hardship.

Disability—Medical Examinations

According to the EEOC, it is unlawful to:[28]

- Ask an applicant whether he or she is disabled, or ask about the nature or severity of a disability; or
- Require the applicant to take a medical examination before making a job offer.

WORDS OF WISDOM: The ADA does not protect illegal drug use.[29] Employers may fire employees or deny illegal drug users employment on the basis of current illegal drug use. The ADA does not prevent employers from testing applicants or employees for current illegal drug use, or from making employment decisions based on verifiable drug test results.

State and Local Discrimination Protections

In addition to the categories discussed above, Colorado state and local laws prohibit discrimination in employment based on sexual orientation, transgender/transsexual status, marital status, veteran status, military status, union membership, and political status. See Appendix 1.

Compensation Discrimination

Federal and state laws prohibit compensation discrimination against the protected categories set forth above, including discrimination based on sex, race, religion, color, national origin, age, and disability.[30] The employment laws prohibiting compensation discrimination include all forms of compensation, including salary, overtime pay, stock options, profit sharing and bonus plans, life insurance, vacation and holiday pay, cleaning or gasoline allowances, hotel accommodations, reimbursement for travel expenses, and benefits.

Compensation Discrimination Examples

Examples of compensation discrimination include:
- Disability discrimination — This includes paying an employee with a disability less than similarly situated employees without satisfactorily accounting for the differential.

- Lingering discriminatory effects of a past discriminatory system — This includes a discriminatory compensation system that has been discontinued but still has lingering discriminatory effects on present salaries. According to the EEOC, if, for example, an employer has a compensation policy or practice that pays Hispanics lower salaries than other employees, the employer must not only adopt a new non-discriminatory compensation policy, it also must: (1) correct any salary differences that began before the adoption of the new policy; and (2) make the victims whole.[31]

- Disparate pay practices — This includes setting compensation predominately held by minorities below the job evaluation study, while setting the pay for jobs predominately held by men or whites consistent with the level suggested by the job evaluation study.

- Disparate impact — This includes maintaining a neutral compensation policy or practice that has an adverse impact on employees in a protected class and cannot be justified as job-related and consistent with business necessity. For example, if an employer provides extra compensation to employees who are the "head of household," i.e., married with dependents and the primary financial contributor to the household, the practice may have an unlawful disparate impact on women.

As discussed in other chapters, employers should ensure that employee compensation is based on nondiscriminatory factors by evaluating compensation plans, practices, and policies. According to the EEOC, employers also should evaluate practices that may indirectly depress the compensation of employees in protected classes.[32] For example, employers should make sure that promotion decisions, performance appraisal systems, and procedures for assigning work are non-discriminatory.

A Word on the Equal Pay Act

The Equal Pay Act (EPA) requires that men and women be given equal pay for equal work in the same establishment.[33] Under the EPA, employers may not pay unequal wages to men and women who perform jobs that require substantially equal skill, effort, and responsibility, and that are performed under similar working conditions within the same establishment. The jobs need not be identical, but they must be substantially equal. It is job content, not job titles, that determines whether jobs are substantially equal.

FOOTNOTES

[1] U.S. EEOC, Federal Laws Prohibiting Job Discrimination, Questions and Answers, http://www.eeoc.gov/facts/qanda.html

[2] 42 U.S.C. § 2000e-2(e)(1). The courts and the EEOC interpret the BFOQ exception very narrowly. *See* 29 C.F.R. § 1604.2(a).

[3] Questions and Answers About the Workplace Rights of Muslims, Arabs, South Asians, and Sikhs Under the Equal Employment Opportunity Laws, Equal Employment Opportunity Commission, http://www.eeoc.gov/facts/backlash-employer.html

[4] Immigration and Nationality Act, 274A, 8 U.S.C. § 1324a.

[5] Employment Discrimination Based on Religion, Ethnicity, or Country of Origin, United States Equal Employment Opportunity Commission, http://www.eeoc.gov/facts/fs-relig_ethnic.html

[6] *Id.*

[7] Facts About Race/Color Discrimination, United States Equal Employment Opportunity Commission, http://www.eeoc.gov/facts/fs-race.html

[8] *Id.*

[9] *Id.*

[10] 42 U.S.C. §§ 2000e *et seq.*

[11] 42 U.S.C. § 2000e(k).

[12] *Wal-Mart to Pay $220,000 for Rejecting Pregnant Applicant in EEOC Settlement,* EEOC Press Release, Dec. 23, 2002, http://www.eeoc.gov/press/12-23-02.html

[13] 29 C.F.R. § 825.205.

[14] C.R.S. § 19-5-211(1.5).

[15] *SHRM®/Tanenbaum Center Survey on Religion in the Workplace,* http://www.tanenbaum.org/programs/diversity/survey2.asp (2001)

[16] *Religious Bias in the Workplace: The Tanenbaum Center's 1999 Survey,* Tanenbaum Center for Interreligious Understanding, http://www.tanenbaum.org/programs/diversity/survey1.asp (1999)

[17] *Id.*

[18] *See,* www.eeoc.gov

[19] *Saturday Sabbath Non-Demoninational Christian Scores Legal Victory for Minority Religions,* C. Leppek, Jewish World Review, Aug. 17, 2001, www.jewishworldreview.com/0801/sabbath.ruling

[20] 42 U.S.C. § 2000e-(j); C.R.S. § 24-34-402(1)(a); Commission Rule 50.1, 3 C.C.R. 708-1.

[21] *SHRM®/Tanenbaum Center Survey on Religion in the Workplace,* http://www.tanenbaum.org/programs/diversity/survey2.asp (2001)

[22] 29 U.S.C. §§ 621 *et seq.*

[23] 42 U.S.C. §§ 12101 *et seq.*

[24] The ADA, Your Responsibilities as An Employer, United States Equal Employment Opportunity Commission, http://www.eeoc.gov/facts/ada17.html

[25] *Id.*

[26] *Id., See also* Small Employers and Reasonable Accommodation, United States Equal Employment Opportunity Commission, http://www.eeoc.gov/facts/accommodation.html

[27] *Id.*

[28] Facts About the Americans With Disabilities Act, United States Equal Employment Opportunity Commission, http://www.eeoc.gov/facts/fs-ada.html; *See also,* The Americans With Disabilities Act: A Primer for Small Business, United States Equal Employment Opportunity Commission, http://www.eeoc.gov/ada/adahandbook.html#dodonts

[29] EEOC, Americans With Disabilities Act: A Primer for Small Business, http://www.eeoc.gov/ada/adahandbook.html#drugalcohol

[30] 42 U.S.C. §§ 2000e *et seq.;* 42 U.S.C. §§ 12101 *et seq.;* 29 U.S.C. §§ 621 *et seq.*

[31] EEOC Compliance Manual, Number 915.003, 12/05/00.

[32] *Id.*

[33] 29 U.S.C. § 206(d).

CHAPTER 6:
The Lowdown on Harassment—
Can't We Even Joke Anymore?

Overview of Harassment

Harassment is no joking matter. The term "harassment" has been abused and misused so much that many people have become desensitized to it and have forgotten the real meaning—and the undeniable effects—of genuine harassment against their fellow human beings.

Imagine if a daily work environment were described by these words (really think about these words): persecution, torment, vexation, anxiety, crisis, depression, discouragement, distress, embarrassment, frustration, misery, oppression, pressure, strain, stress, strife, struggle, affliction, agony, anguish, dejection, deploring, desolation, despair, despondency, distress, heartache, heartbreak, pain, sadness, sorrow, suffering, torture, trial, tribulation, indignity, injury, insult, hell, grief, and suffering. Although these are not legal terms, *Roget's Thesaurus* lists these as synonyms for words describing harassment, and they convey the ugly realities of true harassment.

Now imagine that an employee has to face harassment at work because of things the employee cannot change, things that go to the very essence of who the employee is, like the color of the employee's skin, the employee's ethnic origin, the employee's gender, the employee's disability, or age, or a combination of these parts of what make an individual—an individual.

Envision what would happen if the employees of a business, people employed to carry on important work, were targeted for this kind of treatment on the company's clock. Is it likely that their work performance might suffer? They might even get angry enough to sue the company, especially if they complained to the company and their concerns were ignored with statements like "that's just Joe," or "if you don't like it, you can leave," or even worse, they were retaliated against for making complaints—"fire that troublemaker."

This chapter discusses the difference between "jokes" and harassment, legal definitions of illegal harassment, and examples of illegal harassment.

What is the Difference Between "Funny" Jokes and Harassment?

When talking about employment laws, many people ask, "Can't we even joke anymore?" The answer is "yes, you can joke," even at work. A good sense of humor is important. It can help break tension during a stressful encounter. It can brighten someone's day. It can make someone feel good. The anti-discrimination laws do not prohibit the use of humor in the workplace.

The anti-discrimination laws do, however, prohibit "jokes" that target people for humiliation, denigration, or isolation because of who they are, who their families are, or where they came from. Unfortunately, sometimes it can be easy to cross the line from a joke to harassment, or to use a "joke" as an excuse for harassment.

Harassment is a power play, and jokes are an easy way to disguise the intent to hurt someone. For example, one supervisor may repeatedly "joke" with a Latino employee, saying such things as "don't forget your green card," and "you're Mexican, you should know how to steal." The supervisor intends to make sure that the employee "knows his place" in the world. The supervisor may even try to justify his actions by claiming he was "only joking" and that the Latino employee likes it.

In some instances, there may not be an intent to hurt anyone, but the person on the receiving end interprets the "joke" as cruel. For example, one young woman who had debilitating multiple sclerosis and was bound to a wheelchair found nothing funny about her boss's new "pet name" for her and his related jokes. "Here comes the gimp of the crew," he would say as she wheeled herself into staff meetings. She hoped he was just insensitive, but his continuing comments singled her out in a way that was not funny to her at all. What some people find to be humorous, others may experience as insulting, humiliating, or even threatening.

Because employment laws promise equal treatment in the workplace, regardless of certain protected characteristics, harassment must not be tolerated, even for one minute, regardless of who the harasser or the target happen to be. To understand what the laws prohibit, it is helpful to review the legal definitions of illegal harassment.

> **WORDS OF WISDOM:** Harassers can be company owners, managers, upper level directors, direct supervisors, supervisors in other areas, co-workers, agents of the employer, or non-employees.

What is Illegal Harassment?

Harassment violates federal and Colorado laws if it involves discriminatory treatment based on sex (with or without sexual conduct), national origin, race, color, religion, age, disability, or retaliatory reasons. Harassment, a form of discrimination, is conduct or statements that humiliate, intimidate, exclude, or isolate an individual or group and is based on characteristics unrelated to job performance. Harassment also includes unwelcome attention from a person who knows or should know that the behavior is not welcomed. Harassment can range from written or spoken comments to physical assault and may be accompanied by threats or promises regarding working conditions or opportunities.

Harassment can be a single incident, or a series of incidents, such as:
- Touching;
- Stalking;
- Staring;
- Innuendos or slurs;
- Offensive cartoons, posters, or screensavers;
- "Jokes" based on personal or group characteristics;
- Yelling;
- Name-calling;
- Grafitti; or
- Tire slashing or destruction of personal property.

> **WORDS OF WISDOM:** An employer should correct harassment that is clearly unwelcome regardless of whether a complaint is filed. For example, if there is graffiti in the workplace containing racial or sexual slurs, management should not wait for a complaint before erasing the graffiti. In one case an employer waited too long to erase graffiti in the restrooms saying, "Learn English—or go back to Mexico, where you belong!" After the Hispanic employees complained, the company ignored their complaints and the company was faced with a lawsuit.

To constitute harassment, the conduct must: (1) be sufficiently frequent or severe to create a "hostile work environment"; or (2) result in a "tangible employment action," such as hiring, firing, promotion, or demotion.

WORDS OF WISDOM: The EEOC used to classify harassment as either "quid pro quo" or "hostile environment," based on one of the first Supreme Court rulings to interpret Title VII.[1] However, according to the EEOC,[2] given more recent Supreme Court rulings, it now is more useful to distinguish between: (1) harassment that results in a tangible employment action; and (2) harassment that creates a hostile work environment.

These two types of harassment determine whether employers can effectively use the defense of reasonable preventive and corrective measures. See Chapter 9 for more information regarding company liability for harassment.

Hostile Work Environment

A "hostile work environment" exists if unwelcome conduct of an offensive nature has the purpose or effect of unreasonably interfering with a worker's performance or creates an intimidating, hostile, or offensive environment based on protected characteristics, such as race, religion, national origin, color, pregnancy, disability, age, or sex. Although a hostile work environment can only be proven if the conduct is severe or pervasive, one incident may be sufficient to create a hostile work environment if it is severe enough. Usually if there is a dispute as to whether the conduct occurred, it will be something that a jury will have to decide, meaning that an employer typically will not be able to get the case thrown out by the judge before trial.

WORDS OF WISDOM: In a case decided by the federal appeals court in Denver, the court recognized that even if harassment lasted only three weeks, from between two minutes to fifteen minutes a day, the short exposure time could indicate that the abuse was so offensive as to taint the entire work environment.[3]

Tangible Employment Action

A "tangible employment action" means a significant change in employment status. Examples include hiring, firing, promotion, demotion, undesirable reassignment, decisions causing a significant change in benefits, compensation decisions, and work assignments. According to the EEOC, significantly changing an individual's duties in his or her existing job is a tangible employment action regardless of whether the same salary and benefits are retained.[4] Similarly, altering an individual's duties in a way that blocks his or her opportunity for promotion or salary increases also constitutes a tangible employment action. Harassment that culminates in a tangible employment action can expose employers to possible lawsuits.

WORDS OF WISDOM: Employers should beware of altering tangible job benefits! Even a positive change in employment status may subject the employer to liability for harassment. An example would be a supervisor granting a tangible job benefit to an employee based on the employee's submission to unwelcome sexual demands.

Illegal Harassment Examples

As noted above, illegal harassment includes harassment based on sex, national origin, race, color, religion, age, disability, or retaliatory reasons. The following are some examples of harassment cases based on these protected characteristics.

Harassment Based on Sex

Harassment that is targeted at an individual because of his or her sex violates Title VII and Colorado law even if the harassment does not involve sexual comments or conduct.[5] For example, frequent derogatory remarks about women could constitute unlawful harassment even if the remarks are not sexual in nature—such as comments impugning a woman's intelligence or telling a woman that she should be "at home baking cookies" instead of working in the "man's world."

Additionally, unwelcome sexual advances, requests for sexual favors, and other verbal or physical conduct of a sexual nature also constitute sexual harassment when submission to or rejection of this conduct explicitly or implicitly affects an individual's employment, unreasonably interferes with an individual's work performance, or creates an intimidating, hostile, or offensive work environment. Such comments could include unwelcome "jokes," such as asking women to wear bikinis to work, commenting on a man's body parts, or explicitly asking for sex.

WORDS OF WISDOM: The victim in a harassment case does not have to be the person harassed, but could be anyone affected by the offensive conduct. Even if the target of the harassment does not find it unwelcome, if another employee does find the conduct offensive,

---

and a "reasonable" person would find the conduct offensive, the employer may be liable for harassment.

Same-Sex Harassment

Both men and women can be harassers and victims of sexual harassment, and the victim does *not* have to be of the opposite sex. In a historic ruling, the United States Supreme Court in 1998 recognized that "same-sex" harassment violates Title VII, in *Oncale v. Sundowner Offshore Services, Inc.*[6]

In the *Oncale* case, the target of harassment, Joseph Oncale, worked for Sundowner Offshore Services on a Chevron U.S.A. oil platform in the Gulf of Mexico for four months. During that time, Mr. Oncale's supervisors and co-workers forcibly subjected him to sex-related, humiliating actions in the presence of the rest of the crew. They also threatened him with rape. Mr. Oncale, a 21-year-old man who weighed only 130 pounds, complained to supervisory personnel but the supervisory personnel did nothing. In fact, the company's safety compliance clerk told Mr. Oncale that the supervisors picked on Mr. Oncale too, calling Mr. Oncale a name that suggested homosexuality. Mr. Oncale finally quit for fear that if he didn't leave his job, he would be raped.

Seven years later, after two lower courts heard his case, a unanimous Supreme Court held that Title VII, banning on-the-job sexual harassment, applies when the harasser and victim are the same sex. Sundowner Offshore Services, Inc. settled with Mr. Oncale for an undisclosed amount.

Employers should not assume that a report of harassment related to male-to-male or female-to-female conduct can be ignored because it is legal. Employers should take all harassment seriously and should take immediate steps to rectify any reports of harassment.

Harassment Based on National Origin, Color, and Race

While Title VII and the Colorado Anti-Discrimination Act prohibit harassment based on any national origin, race, or color, the EEOC warns that at this time (i.e., following the attacks of September 11, 2001), employers should be particularly sensitive to potential discrimination or harassment against individuals who are—or are perceived to be—Muslim, Arab, Afghani, Middle Eastern or South Asian (Pakistani, Indian, etc.).[7] Title VII and the Colorado Anti-Discrimination Act prohibitions include harassment or any other employment action based on any of the following:

- Affiliation — This means harassing or otherwise discriminating because an individual is affiliated with a particular religious or ethnic group. Examples include harassing an individual because he or she is Arab or practices Islam, or paying an employee less because he or she is Middle Eastern.

- Physical or cultural traits and clothing — This refers to harassing or otherwise discriminating because of physical, cultural, or linguistic characteristics, such as accent or dress associated with a particular religion, ethnicity, or country of origin. Examples include harassing a woman wearing a hijab (a body covering or head scarf worn by some Muslims), or refusing to hire a man with a dark complexion and an accent believed to be Arab.
- Perception — This means harassing or otherwise discriminating because of the perception or belief that a person is a member of a particular racial, national origin, or religious group whether or not that perception is correct. For example, failing to hire a Hispanic person because the hiring official believed that the individual was from Pakistan, or harassing a Sikh man wearing a turban because the harasser thought he was Muslim.
- Association — This refers to harassing or otherwise discriminating because of an individual's association with a person or organization of a particular religion or ethnicity. Examples include harassing an employee whose husband is from Afghanistan, or refusing to promote an employee because the employee attends a mosque.

One example of unlawful harassment based on cultural traits, color, and national origin is the use of an "English-only" policy to harass employees. In a lawsuit involving a Colorado casino, the author of this book represented a group of former casino housekeepers who, according to the complaint filed in federal court, were subjected to a policy that stated: "IT IS COMPANY POLICY THAT ENGLISH ONLY BE SPOKEN IN THE CASINO AT ALL TIMES. DISCIPLINARY ACTION WILL BE TAKEN IF THIS PROBLEM PERSISTS. ALL EMPLOYEES MUST ACKNOWLEDGE THIS BY SIGNING YOUR NAME BELOW."[8] According to the complaint, the policy was only posted in English, although the casino managers knew that they had hired many people who did not speak or read English.

According to the complaint, the English-only policy applied *only* to the housekeeping department, where the majority of the Hispanic employees worked. The complaint alleged that members of casino management used the skills of the bilingual employees to translate for customers, while also telling the employees that they could not speak Spanish to each other. The casino hired employees, knowing that they spoke no English and then forced the employees to work in silence because they only spoke Spanish, according to the allegations of the lawsuit

While employers may restrict the use of language if they have a legitimate business necessity for such a policy, they may not use such policies as a weapon of harassment. In the Colorado casino case, the evidence showed that the company managers yelled at Hispanic housekeeping employees, "English only! English! English! English!" The evidence also showed that there was no legitimate business purpose for the English-only policy, and in fact, managers admitted that the housekeeping employees did not need to know English to perform the jobs for which they had hired the housekeeping employees—cleaning the casino, scrubbing toilets, and cleaning the very offices in which the managers worked.

As a result of the English-only policy, and the harassing way in which the managers implemented it, the complaint alleged that these workers were humiliated in front of other employees and forced to work in isolation. In fact, there was testimony that some of the other employees even taunted and made fun of the non-English speaking employees. According to the housekeepers, they went to work each day, dreading the ridicule, berating, and forced silence that awaited them—afraid to even utter a Spanish word. Pretty ironic for a state that is named after a Spanish word, "Colorado= color red."

Fortunately for these employees, they were able to speak out through legal counsel against these harassing practices. The employees endured five long years of the legal process and ultimately, as the result of a settlement, the group received compensation in the amount of approximately $1.5 million—the largest monetary settlement ever for an "English-only" national origin harassment case. The casino also agreed to implement training and file reports with the EEOC to insure compliance with Title VII. While the casino denies wrongdoing, the casino made a business decision to settle the lawsuit after the depositions of the witnesses were substantially completed in mid-2003.

Hopefully other employers will learn the lessons that the casino learned the hard way. Respect employees. Treat all employees with the dignity and equality that the law demands. Before passing policies that will restrict the use of languages, contact legal counsel. Make sure that all policies are required by business necessity, and that there is no less-restrictive solution. Closely supervise and monitor managers and supervisors, and do not allow them to pass policies without legal guidance. If an employer discovers that a manager or supervisor has passed a policy without legal guidance, the employer should take prompt remedial action.

Another Colorado lawsuit illustrates how a hostile work environment can result in a tangible employment action, and the price a company can pay for it. In late 2002, a Denver car dealership settled a lawsuit for $450,000 after a manager fired three African-American employees on Martin Luther King, Jr.'s birthday.[9] According to the lawsuit, the manager didn't stop with simply firing the employees. The manager also used crude racial slurs and referred to Martin Luther King, Jr.'s birthday while firing the employees. The slurs created a hostile work environment, which immediately culminated in a tangible employment action—loss of the employees' jobs. Because of the settlement, a jury never had the opportunity to make a finding of hostile work environment or tangible employment action. However, the EEOC clearly thought there was a problem and helped to bring the lawsuit.

Employers should not permit employees to be subjected to harassment based on the employees' national origin, color, or race. Employers should protect their employees, and their company, from harassers.

Harassment Based on Religion

Employers must provide a workplace that is free of harassment based on religion (which sometimes goes hand in hand with national origin and ethnicity). As an example, one employer will pay a $1.11 million settlement for a lawsuit that charged the company with repeatedly harassing four Pakistani-American former employees due to the former employees' national origin and Muslim religion.[10] The lawsuit alleged that supervisors and co-workers repeatedly ridiculed the former employees during the former employees daily Muslim prayer obligations and called the former employees derogatory names, such as "camel jockey" and "raghead." The company agreed to make policy changes, conduct training to prevent future discrimination, and implement a policy guaranteeing an employee's right to request an accommodation for religious needs.

Harassment Based on Age

Recently, courts have expanded the categories of illegal harassment to include age harassment. For example, in a case against a hospital, a 55-year old billing clerk complained of continuous harassment by her supervisor and other employees.[11] The billing clerk had worked in the billing department for nearly 27 years, having started there when she was 28.

The billing clerk overheard her supervisor tell other office employees that "old people should be seen and not heard," and the other employees reported that the supervisor had also said that she did not "think women over 55 should be working." While the billing clerk felt "embarrassed" and "humiliated" by her supervisor's remarks, she also reported that other "older ladies" in the billing department were equally "miserable" over statements made about their ages. According to the lawsuit, one co-worker referred to an area of the office where the older employees worked as "the old side, the dumb side, the worthless side."

In the billing clerk case, a federal court of appeals expanded the forms of illegal harassment to include age discrimination. Although the Supreme Court has not yet ruled on this issue, it is possible that courts around the country will follow suit. Employers would be well advised to include age harassment in their policies.

Harassment Based on Disability

Two federal courts of appeal recently have ruled that disability harassment is against the law.[12] In one case, an employee claimed that she had been subjected to harassment and later fired after her supervisor learned the employee was HIV positive.[13] The employee presented evidence that, after she revealed that she was HIV-positive, her supervisor began treating her differently. For example, the supervisor stopped socializing with the employee and attempted to overhear the employee's telephone conversations. The employee also claimed that the company required her to undergo a number of drug tests and placed her on probation before finally terminating her employment. A jury decided that the company had subjected the employee to disability harassment. After the company appealed, the appeals court upheld the jury's decision. The court stated that the ADA is intended to protect employees with disabilities from harassment, just like the sex discrimination laws.

Harassment Against Others

In addition to the protected categories discussed in the beginning of this chapter, Colorado law also prohibits the harassment of military personnel, as well as the harassment of voters and jurors.[14] Additionally, because the laws are always changing, and because the trend in the courts has been to expand harassment protections to additional classes, employers would be wise to adopt general anti-harassment policies, forbidding harassment against anyone in the workplace. Additional categories employers might consider adding are harassment policies regarding employees who are gay, transgendered, transsexual, and bisexual. Many city and county ordinances already prohibit discrimination based on sexual orientation and gender identity, and those ordinances may be interpreted to prohibit harassment specifically.

WORDS OF WISDOM: Harassment is preventable. No person should be forced to endure harassment based on their personal characteristics when they are simply trying to earn a living. Teach employees to focus on job performance and cultivate a legally healthy work environment by "walking the talk" and engendering tolerance towards the many different people who are working so hard to make the company a success. For practical tips on preventing, investigating, and correcting harassment, see Chapter 8.

FOOTNOTES

[1] *See Meritor v. Savings Bank v. Vinson,* 477 U.S. 57 (1986).

[2] EEOC, Enforcement Guidance: Vicarious Liability for Unlawful Harassment by Supervisors, No. 915.002, 6/18/99, http://eeoc.gov/docs/harassment.html

[3] *McCowan v. All Star Maintenance, Inc.,* No. 00-2040 (10th Cir. 2001), available at http://www.kscourts.org/ca10/cases

[4] EEOC, Enforcement Guidance No. 915.002, supra.

[5] *See O'Shea v. Yellow Tech Services, Inc.,* 185 F.3d 1093 (10th Cir. 1999).

[6] 118 S. Ct. 998 (1998).

[7] Questions and Answers About the Workplace Rights of Muslims, Arabs, South Asians, and Sikhs Under the Equal Employment Opportunity Laws, Equal Employment Opportunity Commission, http://www.eeoc.gov/facts/backlash-employer.html

[8] *EEOC et al v. Anchor Coin et al,* Civil Action No. 01-B-0564 (PAC) in United States District Court for the District of Colorado.

[9] Race Motivated Firings and Epithets Cost Colorado Car Dealership $450,000, US EEOC Press Release, Oct. 9, 2002, http://eeoc.gov/press/10-9-02.html

[10] Pakistani-American Workers to Share $1.1 Million in Harassment Settlement with Stockton Steele, EEOC Press Release, 3/19/03, http://eeoc.gov/press/3-19-03.html

[11] *Courts Now Outlaw Age Harassment,* In Brief, Maricopa Community Colleges, Office of General Counsel (Spring 1997), www.dist.maricopa.edu/legal/dp/inbrief/ageharass

[12] *Flowers v. Southern Regional Physician Services,* 99-31354 (3/30/01 5th Cir.); *Fox v. General Motors Corp.,* 00-1589 (4/13/01 4th Cir.).

[13] *Flowers v. Southern Regional Physician Services,* 99-31354 (3/30/01 5th Cir.).

[14] C.R.S. §§ 28-3-601, 602, 609, 506; C.R.S. §§ 31-10-603, 1522; C.R.S. §§ 13-71-134(1), 126.

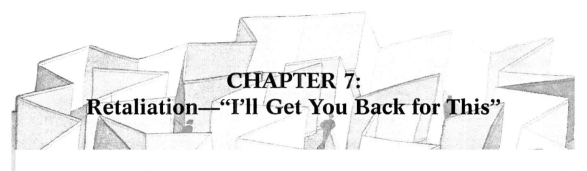

CHAPTER 7:
Retaliation—"I'll Get You Back for This"

Overview of Retaliation

When an employee has made a complaint of discrimination or harassment, tempers can flare. The person (or company) accused of the bad behavior sometimes (rightly or wrongly) feels angry, betrayed, or guilty. It is easy to lash out against the employee who complained. Don't do it. And don't allow other employees to do it.

Employment laws contain strong protections against retaliation for people who either have opposed discriminatory practices or have participated in proceedings relating to allegations of discrimination, harassment, or other types of unequal treatment in the workplace. Nationwide, retaliation charge filings with the EEOC have increased sharply by 33 percent between 1995 and 2002 (from 17,070 to 22,768 filings).[1] Understanding the definition of retaliation, the possible penalties, and strategies to avoid retaliation claims can help employers protect their companies and their employees.

What is Retaliation?

Retaliation against employees can come in many forms. Retaliation can include harassment, firing, negative performance evaluations, and discipline (if it is unwarranted or different from the treatment of other employees). Retaliation can also come in the forms of unwanted transfers, heightened scrutiny, failure to pay wages or bonuses, negative references, or even criminal charges against a former employee.

Title VII specifically protects employees (and former employees) against retaliation for two types of protected conduct: (1) opposing discriminatory conduct; and (2) participating in proceedings relating to discrimination or harassment.[2] Other federal and state laws also specifically forbid retaliation against people who have either asserted their own rights or the rights of others (e.g. the Equal Pay Act, the ADA, the ADEA, the FMLA, and the Colorado Anti-Discrimination Act).

Why Have Anti-Retaliation Laws?

Anti-retaliation laws are designed to protect people from retaliation that would be reasonably likely to deter them from standing up for themselves (or others) by making discrimination complaints. According to the EEOC, voluntary compliance with, and effective enforcement of, anti-discrimination statutes depends in large part on the initiative of individuals to oppose employment practices that they reasonably believe to be unlawful and to file charges of discrimination.[3] If retaliation for speaking out against discrimination were permitted to occur without remedy, it would have a "chilling effect" on the willingness of individuals to say anything against employment discrimination or to participate in the EEOC's process or other employment discrimination proceedings.

Who Can File a Retaliation Claim?

Person Outside of "Protected" Group

Unlike most discrimination or harassment claims, someone alleging retaliation under federal and state laws does not need to be a member of the "protected group" in order to bring a valid claim. For example, an individual claiming retaliation for protesting discrimination against people in the protected age group of 40-years-old or older, need not 40-years-old or older to bring an ADEA claim.[4] Likewise, someone alleging retaliation under Title VII,[5] the Equal Pay Act,[6] or the ADA,[7] need not also allege that he or she was treated differently because of race, religion, sex, national origin, or disability.

Thus, an employee can bring a retaliation claim even if the company did not discriminate against the employee bringing the retaliation claim. The main question is whether the company treated the complaining employee differently (i.e., negatively) because the employee complained on his or her own behalf or for someone else.

WORDS OF WISDOM: Current and former employees may bring a claim of retaliation against a company, whether or not they are in the group originally protected by the law.

Former Employees

A person can claim retaliation by a company even if the retaliation occurred after the employment relationship ended. For example, in a case against Shell Oil Company, a former employee, Mr. Robinson, had worked for Shell Oil for several years.[8] When the company fired Mr. Robinson, he filed a charge of discrimination with the EEOC, claiming that Shell Oil fired him because of his race.

While his charge was pending, Mr. Robinson applied for a job with another company. The company called Shell Oil for a reference. Mr. Robinson alleged that Shell Oil gave him a negative reference in retaliation for his EEOC charge. Mr. Robinson then sued Shell Oil for a violation of the anti-retaliation provision of Title VII. Although two lower courts dismissed his case (because the United States Supreme Court previously had not applied Title VII to former employees), the Supreme Court unanimously reversed their rulings. The Supreme Court ruled that the anti-retaliation provision covers former employees too.

WORDS OF WISDOM: Although a Colorado law provides employers with immunity for giving references,[9] an employer could still face liability for retaliation under Title VII for a negative reference given by an employer regarding a former employee.[10] Under Title VII, the truthfulness of the information in the reference may serve as a defense unless there is proof of pretext (i.e., an excuse to cover up retaliation), such as evidence that the former employer routinely declines to offer information about former employees' job performance and yet violated that policy with regard to an individual who engaged in protected activity.[11]

Employers also should be aware that employment laws protect former employees from retaliation far into the future. If the former employee can prove that an employer gave a negative job reference in retaliation for participation in a discrimination complaint, the protection can last for years. In one case, the where the employer gave a negative reference *three years* after the employment ended, the judge reasoned that because it was the first time the employer had a chance to retaliate, it was up to the jury to decide whether the company had retaliated and how much the company should pay.[12]

Another concern can be if a company settles a discrimination lawsuit with a former employee and then refuses to rehire the employee in the future, the company could face a claim of retaliation. To avoid this problem, many companies try to include a statement in the settlement agreement that the former employee will not reapply with the company for a specified period of time.

WORDS OF WISDOM: Title VII also protects employees from retaliation by a new employer for the employees' protected conduct involving a different employer.[13] For example, an employer cannot refuse to hire someone because the individual previously sued another employer for discrimination.

Close Associates

A person can claim retaliation *even where he or she did not engage in opposition*. The anti-discrimination laws also prohibit retaliation against someone so closely related to or associated with the person who claims discrimination that it would discourage the person claiming discrimination from pursuing those rights.[14] For example, it is unlawful to retaliate against an employee because her daughter, who is also an employee, opposed allegedly unlawful employment practices.

WORDS OF WISDOM: Retaliation against a close relative of an individual who opposed discrimination can be challenged by both the individual who engaged in the protected activity and the relative, where both are employees.

Proving Retaliation

To prove retaliation, an employee (or former employee) must prove three things:
1. Protected conduct (either opposition to discrimination or participation in the complaint process);
2. Adverse action against the complaining party; and
3. A causal connection between the protected activity and the adverse action (the action was taken *because of* the activity).

Protected Conduct—Opposition and Participation

As noted earlier in this chapter, retaliation laws protect both opposition to discrimination and participation in the complaint process.

What Kinds of Opposition are Protected?

Anti-retaliation provisions make it unlawful to discriminate against an individual because the individual has opposed any practice made unlawful under the employment discrimination statutes. This protection applies if an individual either *explicitly* or *implicitly* communicates to his or her employer a reasonable belief that the company has discriminated.

WORDS OF WISDOM: A complaint does not need to include the word "discrimination" to constitute protected opposition. If a reasonable person would interpret statements or conduct as opposition to employment discrimination, even broad or ambiguous complaints of unfair treatment are still protected.

Anti-retaliation laws protect many forms of opposition to discrimination, including threatening to file a charge or formal complaint of discrimination with the EEOC, the Colorado Civil Rights Division (CCRD), a union, or a court.[15] For example, if an employee tells her manager that if the manager fails to raise the employee's salary to that of a male coworker who performs the same job, the employee will file a lawsuit under either the federal Equal Pay Act or the Colorado Anti-Discrimination Act, this statement constitutes "opposition."

Anti-retaliation laws also protect those who actually complain to anyone about alleged discrimination against oneself or others. A complaint or protest about alleged employment discrimination to a manager, union official, co-worker, company EEO official, attorney, newspaper reporter, Congressperson, or anyone else constitutes opposition. Examples of this kind of protected opposition include:

- A call to the president of the employer's parent company to protest religious discrimination by the company;
- A complaint to co-workers about the harassment of a disabled employee by a manager; and
- A complaint to a company foreman about graffiti in the workplace that is derogatory toward women. Note, that although the complaint does not specifically state a belief that the graffiti creates a hostile work environment based on sex, due to the sex-based content of the graffiti the foreman reasonably should interpret the complaint as opposition to sex discrimination. (This is another

example of why training supervisors about discrimination and harassment is vital.)

WORDS OF WISDOM: Opposition may be nonverbal, such as picketing or engaging in a production slow-down.

The following is an example of a general complaint that is *not* protected opposition. An African-American employee requests a wage increase from the company, arguing that he deserves to get paid a higher salary, without stating or suggesting a belief that the company is subjecting him to wage discrimination based on race. Based on these facts alone, there is no basis to conclude that the employer reasonably would have interpreted the employee's complaint as opposition to race discrimination because the challenged unfairness could have been based on *any of several* reasons.

WORDS OF WISDOM: An employee need not be the one who complains in order to be protected from retaliation. A complaint on behalf of someone else, or by an employee's representative, is protected opposition (for both the person who makes the complaint and the person for whom the complaint is made).

Refusal to obey an order because of a reasonable and good faith belief that the order is discriminatory is also protected. For example, a worker at an employment agency refuses to obey her manager's instruction not to refer any African-Americans to a particular client, based on the client's request. The worker's actions are protected opposition.

WORDS OF WISDOM: Refusal to obey an order also constitutes protected opposition if the individual reasonably believes that the order makes discrimination a "term or condition of employment." For example, in one case a court recognized that a correction officer's refusal to cooperate with the defendant's practice of allowing white but not black inmates to shower after work shifts constituted protected opposition.[16] Although the inmates were not "employees," the correction officer could show that his enforcement of the policy made race discrimination a term or condition of his employment (meaning the employer required him to do it to keep his job). Thus, the officer's refusal to obey the order constituted opposition to an unlawful employment practice.

It is important for employers to know that the opposition need only be based on the protester's *reasonable* and *good faith belief* that discrimination has occurred. In other words, anti-retaliation laws protect people against retaliation for opposing *perceived* discrimination, even if the challenged practice later is found to be lawful! Believe it or not, this is to protect informal resolution of problems by encouraging the frank and non-disruptive exchange of ideas between employers and employees.

For example, if a female employee complains to her office manager that her supervisor passed her over for promotion in favor of a male employee for a job for which she was qualified, the female employee has engaged in protected opposition *regardless of whether the promotion decision was in fact discriminatory.* Protected opposition occurs in this example because the employee had a reasonable and good faith belief that discrimination occurred based on her sex. However, if the female employee knew that the job required a CPA license, which she lacked and the male employee had, her complaint would not be protected opposition, because she did not have a reasonable and good faith belief that the supervisor rejected her because of sex discrimination.

Requests for a reasonable accommodation or religious accommodation are also protected. A request for reasonable accommodation of a disability constitutes protected activity under the Americans with Disabilities Act. Although a person making such a request might not literally "oppose" discrimination or "participate" in the administrative or judicial complaint process, he or she is protected against retaliation for making the request.

No Protection for Unreasonable Methods of Opposition

Although anti-retaliation laws provide broad protections against retaliation, they do not protect every complaint of discrimination. The manner of opposition must be *reasonable*. The reasonableness requirement exists because the courts and the EEOC want to balance the right of individuals to oppose employment discrimination (and the public's interest in the enforcement of equal employment opportunity laws) with an employer's need for a stable and productive work environment.

Public criticism of alleged discrimination may be a reasonable form of opposition. Courts have protected an employee's right to inform an employer's customers about the employer's alleged discrimination, as well as the right of employees to engage in peaceful picketing to oppose allegedly discriminatory employment practices.

On the other hand, courts have found that the following activities were *not* protected because they were *not* reasonable:

- Searching and photocopying confidential documents relating to alleged discrimination and showing them to co-workers;

- Making an overwhelming number of complaints based on unsupported allegations and bypassing the chain of command in bringing the complaints; and
- Badgering a subordinate employee into giving a witness statement in support of an EEOC charge of discrimination or attempting to coerce the subordinate employee to change his or her statement.

WORDS OF WISDOM: Anti-retaliation laws do not protect opposition consisting of unlawful activities, such as acts or threats of violence to life or property.

Importantly, the anti-retaliation provisions of employment laws do *not* immunize an employee from appropriate discipline or discharge. This means that if an employee's protests against allegedly discriminatory employment practices interfere with the employee's job performance so much that the employee becomes ineffective in his or her job, the employer may still discipline the employee or terminate the employee's employment.

WORDS OF WISDOM: According to the EEOC, "opposition to perceived discrimination does not serve as a license for the employee to neglect job duties."[17]

What Kinds of Participation are Protected?

Anti-retaliation laws make it unlawful to discriminate against any individual because he or she has made a charge, testified, assisted, or participated in any manner in an investigation, proceeding, hearing, or litigation under the equal employment opportunity laws.

Anti-retaliation laws protect many forms of participation, including the following:

- Challenging employment discrimination under the statutes enforced by the EEOC, in EEOC proceedings, Colorado Civil Rights Division proceedings, or court proceedings; or
- Testifying or otherwise participating in any of the proceedings mentioned above.[18]

WORDS OF WISDOM: Protecting anti-discrimination participation extends even to those who file untimely charges.

It is critical for employers to know that, unlike the anti-retaliation clause relating to opposition, participation is protected *regardless of whether the allegations in the original charge were valid or reasonable*. While the opposition clause applies only to those who protest practices that they reasonably and in good faith believe are unlawful, the participation clause applies to *all* individuals who participate in the statutory complaint process.

Courts consistently have ruled that an employer is liable for retaliating against an individual for filing an EEOC charge, regardless of the validity or reasonableness of the charge. According to the EEOC, to permit an employer to retaliate against a charging party based on the employer's own determination that the charge was unreasonable or otherwise unjustified would "chill" the rights of all individuals protected by the anti-discrimination statutes.[19]

Proving Adverse Action

In addition to proving that there was protected conduct, a person claiming retaliation also must prove that adverse action was taken against him or her. As noted above, there are several types of retaliation, including denial of promotion, refusal to hire, denial of job benefits, demotion, suspension, and termination.

Other types of adverse actions include threats, reprimands, negative evaluations, harassment, or other adverse treatment, such as malicious prosecution, which negatively impact future job prospects. For example, in a case arising in Denver, an employer, a car dealership, initiated a criminal complaint against a former employee alleging check forgery after the employee filed a charge of discrimination with the EEOC.[20]

While the employer denied retaliatory motives, the federal court in Denver found it to be more probable than not that the management of the car dealership caused the initiation of the criminal complaint to retaliate for the discrimination charge. The court found in favor of the former employee. When the case was appealed, the Tenth Circuit Court of Appeals (the appeals court covering federal cases from Colorado and other states) agreed with the lower court and held the employer liable for retaliation.

Although the car dealership tried to argue that retaliatory prosecution is not connected to present or future employment, the Tenth Circuit did not agree. As the court stated:

"While providing a tainted employment reference may have a more direct effect on a former employee's future employment prospects, criminal prosecution will also have an obvious impact. A criminal trial, such as that to which Mr. Reynolds was subjected, is necessarily public and therefore carries a significant risk of humiliation, damage to reputation, and a concomitant harm to future employment prospects."[21]

It is important to note that retaliatory acts designed to interfere with an individual's prospects for employment are unlawful regardless of whether they cause a prospective employer to refrain from hiring the individual. An employer who retaliates cannot escape liability merely because the retaliation falls short of its intended result. However, the fact that the reference did not affect the individual's job prospects may affect the damages awarded.

Although some courts have held that retaliation provisions apply only to retaliation that takes the form of ultimate employment actions, the Tenth Circuit interprets "adverse action" broadly, to include any action having an impact on future employment opportunities."[22]

For example, in a case against the Gates Rubber Company, an employee who had filed charges with the EEOC alleging discrimination based on age, sex, national origin, and retaliation, received negative job evaluations, was placed on probation, and ultimately, was terminated.[23] The employee claimed that her supervisor gave her negative performance evaluations two days after she filed a charge with the EEOC. The employee alleged that the company fired her eight months later based on the negative evaluations.

Although Gates maintained that only the firing, and not the negative evaluations, could constitute "adverse action," the Tenth Circuit disagreed. Because the employee's termination was based on the negative performance evaluations she received after complaining to the EEOC, the court concluded that the employee had shown sufficiently that she suffered an adverse action.

The EEOC also believes that adverse action should be interpreted broadly.[24] The statutory clauses of Title VII prohibit any adverse treatment that is based on a retaliatory motive and is reasonably likely to deter the charging party or others from engaging in protected activity. However, according to the EEOC, petty slights and trivial annoyances are not actionable, as they are not likely to deter protected activity.

More significant retaliatory treatment, however, can be challenged regardless of the level of harm. The degree of harm suffered by the individual goes to the issue of damages, not liability (meaning how much money, if any, should be paid, not whether the company did something wrong).

Proving Causal Connection

Even if an employee or former employee can prove that there was protected activity and adverse employment action, the individual must also prove that there was a *causal relation* between the protected activity and adverse employment action to establish a claim of retaliation. The causal relation can be proved either by direct or circumstantial evidence.

Direct evidence of a retaliatory motive is any written or verbal statement by the company that the company undertook the challenged action because the individual engaged in protected activity. Direct evidence also includes any statement by the company that explicitly demonstrates a bias toward the individual based on the individual's protected activity, along with evidence linking that bias to the adverse action. Such a link could be shown if the decision-maker made the statement at the time of the adverse action. Of course, direct evidence of retaliation is rare.

An example of direct evidence is the hypothetical case of Maria. Maria, a former employee, filed a charge against her previous employer alleging that her supervisor had sexually harassed Maria and forced Maria to resign. Maria then sued the company and reached a settlement. When Maria applied for a new job at a different company, the new company gave her a job offer, subject to a reference check. When the new company called her former supervisor, he said that Maria was a "troublemaker," that she had started a sex harassment lawsuit, and that she was not anyone the new company "would want to get mixed up with." Maria was not hired by the new company and she suspected retaliation by her former employer.

When the EEOC investigated Maria's situation, the investigator discovered notes regarding the phone conversation between the former employer and the potential employer. These notes are direct evidence of retaliation because they prove on their face that the company told the potential employer about her protected activity.

It is rare, however, for someone who retaliates to make notes of it. According to the EEOC, the most common method of proving that retaliation was the reason for an adverse action is through circumstantial evidence.[25]

Proving retaliation through circumstantial evidence usually begins with an initial inference of retaliation. An initial inference of retaliation arises where there is proof that the protected activity and the adverse action were related. Typically, the link is demonstrated by evidence that: (1) the adverse action occurred shortly after the protected activity; and (2) the person who undertook the adverse action was aware of the complainant's protected activity before taking the action.

The employer can rebut the inference by offering legitimate non-retaliatory reasons for the challenged actions, including poor job performance, inadequate qualifications for the position sought, violation of work rules or insubordination, and, with regard to negative job references, truthfulness of the information in the reference.

Even if the employer produces evidence of a legitimate, nondiscriminatory reason for the challenged action, however, the employer will still be liable for a violation if this explanation is a pretext designed to hide the true retaliatory motive. Typically, an employee proves pretext by showing evidence that the company treated the employee differently from similarly situated employees or that the company's explanation for the adverse action is not believable.

The following situation would be an example of pretext. Debra alleges that her company denied her a promotion because the company viewed her as a "troublemaker" after Debra opposed the under-representation of women in management jobs. The company promoted another female employee, Kathy. Although the company argues that Kathy was better qualified for the job because she had a Masters in Business Administration, while Debra only had a college degree, the EEOC investigator finds that this explanation is pretextual. Debra had significantly greater experience working at the company, and experience has always been the most important criterion for selection for management jobs in the company.

Employers Can Pay a High Price for Retaliation

Costs to employers for retaliation can include the expenses of lawsuits, judicial intervention in their businesses, loss of goodwill in the community (and with clients or customers), and the intangible costs of the negative impact on employees.

Under Title VII[26] and the ADA,[27] the EEOC can sue for temporary or preliminary relief before completing the processing of a retaliation charge if the retaliation victim or the EEOC will likely suffer irreparable harm because of the retaliation. The temporary or preliminary relief allows a court to stop retaliation before it occurs or continues. Although courts have ruled that financial hardships are not irreparable, other harms that accompany loss of a job may be irreparable. For example, one case forced retirees to show irreparable harm and the retirees obtained a preliminary injunction where they had lost work and future prospects for work, consequently suffering emotional distress, depression, a contracted social life, and other related harms.[28]

Compensatory and punitive damages also are available for retaliation claims brought under the EPA[29] and the ADEA,[30] as well as under Title VII[31] and the ADA.[32] Recently the EEOC announced the settlement of three retaliation lawsuits against employers, netting a combined total of $570,000 for the employees.[33] These cases all involved allegations of discriminatory discharge of employees for exercising federally protected rights.

One of the lawsuits alleged that a manager fired a female employee in retaliation for the employee exercising her right to complain of what she reasonably believed to be gender discrimination.[34] Specifically, the employee complained that the company provided training and certification to the male employees, but consistently denied her requests for such training and certification because of her sex. The company will pay $100,000 to the female employee. In addition to the payment of monetary relief, the company is required to employ injunctive measures during the next three years, including the distribution and posting of an anti-discrimination policy to all employees, annual training of its managers on Title VII retaliation by experienced employment trainers, and semi-annual reporting to the EEOC regarding the company's compliance process. The EEOC will monitor the company's compliance with all provisions for three years.

In a similar lawsuit, the EEOC charged a company with allowing a company vice president's sexually offensive conduct to go unchecked and subsequently terminating a female employee for complaining about the vice president's sexually offensive conduct.[35] The litigation was resolved with the company agreeing to pay two claimants $220,000 as well as agreeing to implement extensive injunctive relief, including annual training at all of the company's facilities in the state for both management and supervisory employees, posting a laminated notice regarding company policies, and semi-annual monitoring reports.

WORDS OF WISDOM: The compensatory and punitive damages obtained under the EPA and the ADEA are not subject to statutory caps![36]

According to the EEOC, proven retaliation constitutes a practice undertaken "with malice or with reckless indifference to the federally protected rights of an aggrieved individual."[37] This is the standard required for an award of punitive damages. Punitive damages often will be appropriate in retaliation claims brought under any of the statutes enforced by the EEOC.

Tips on How to Avoid Retaliation Claims

How can an employer prevent retaliation against, and preserve relationships with, current employees? Here are six suggestions that are discussed in more detail in Chapter 9:

1. Be proactive. Set clear policies regarding how to treat claims of discrimination.
2. Regularly teach managers, supervisors, and employees about the equal opportunity employment laws and company policies, and make equal treatment a part of the company's culture.
3. If an employer receives a complaint, the employer should take a deep breath and step back from any emotional reaction so as to think clearly about the best steps to take.
4. Treat the complaint confidentially to the extent that the company can investigate it promptly. Refer to the investigation checklists discussed in Chapter 8.
5. Reassure the complaining party that the company will not tolerate any type of retaliation and instruct the complainant to tell the company immediately if retaliation occurs. As to former employees, be sure that an EEOC filing does not affect the nature of any references given.
6. Take steps to monitor the treatment of all employees, make sure that there is a legitimate basis for any actions taken, and document all decisions.

Employers can protect their employees and their company from retaliation. When employers encourage an atmosphere of open discussion and prompt remedial actions, they can prevent problems while they are big enough to see and yet small enough to solve.

FOOTNOTES

[1] EEOC, Charge Statistics FY 1992-2002, http://eeoc.gov/stats/charges.html

[2] 42 U.S.C. § 2000e-3(a).

[3] EEOC Compliance Manual, No. 915.003, 5/20/98, http://eeoc.gov/docs/retal.html

[4] 29 U.S.C. § 623(d).

[5] 42 U.S.C. § 2000e-3.

[6] 29 U.S.C. § 215(a)(3).

[7] 42 U.S.C. § 12203(a).

[8] *Robinson v. Shell Oil Co.,* 519 U.S. 337 (1997).

[9] C.R.S. § 8-2-114.

[10] *Robinson v. Shell Oil Co.,* 519 U.S. 337 (1997).

[11] *Id.*

[12] *Haynes v. Shalala,* 902 F. Supp. 259 (D.D.C. 1995).

[13] EEOC Compliance Manual, No. 915.003, *supra.*

[14] *Id.*

[15] *See Id.*

[16] *Id.*

[17] *Id.*

[18] *Id.*

[19] *Id.*

[20] *Berry v. Stevinson Chevrolet,* 74 F.3d 980, 986 (10th Cir. 1996).

[21] *Id.*

[22] *Id.*

[23] *Toth v. Gates Rubber Co.,* 216 F.3d 1088 (10th Cir. 2000).

[24] EEOC Compliance Manual, No. 915.003, *supra.*

[25] *Id.*

[26] 42 U.S.C. §§ 2000e *et seq.*

[27] 42 U.S.C. § 12101, *et seq.*

[28] *EEOC v. Chrysler Corp.,* 733 F.2d 1183, 1186 (6th Cir.), reh'g denied,738 F.2d 167 (1984); *See also EEOC v. City of Bowling Green,* Kentucky, 607 F. Supp. 524 (D. Ky. 1985) (granting preliminary injunction preventing defendant from mandatorily retiring policy department employee because of his age; although plaintiff could have collected back pay and been reinstated at later time, he would have suffered from inability to keep up with current matters in police department and would have suffered anxiety or emotional problems due to compulsory retirement).

[29] 29 U.S.C. § 206(d).

[30] 29 U.S.C. §§ 621 *et seq.*

[31] 42 U.S.C. §§ 2000e *et seq.*

[32] 42 U.S.C. §§ 12101, *et seq.*

[33] Three Florida Employers to Pay Total of $570,000 for Unlawful Retaliation, in EEOC Settlements, EEOC Press Release, 3/18/03, http://eeoc.gov/press/3-18-03.html

[34] *Id.*

[35] *Id.*

[36] EEOC Compliance Manual, No. 915.003, *supra.*

[37] *Id.*

CHAPTER 8:
Prevent, Investigate, Correct—The Top Three Words in Developing an Anti-discrimination and Harassment-free Workplace

Overview of Developing an Anti-discrimination and Harassment-free Workplace

The law protects employers who take reasonable steps to prevent, investigate, and correct claims of discrimination and harassment. The prevention of discrimination or harassment includes maintaining and implementing anti-discrimination and harassment policies and complaint procedures as well as training managers, supervisors, and employees on those policies and procedures. The investigation of discrimination or harassment includes taking complaints seriously and getting to the bottom of the complaints by asking the right questions of the witnesses and reviewing appropriate documents in a timely fashion. Correcting discrimination or harassment may involve education, reprimands, transfers, or even termination. Employers can use each of these measures not only to eradicate workplace discrimination, but also to take advantage of a legal defense of "reasonable care" to prevent discrimination in the first place and to immediately remedy it if it should occur.

Prevention is Better than the Bitter Pill of Litigation

After four long years of a bitter court battle over an emotionally toxic discrimination case, one human resources manager was heard to say, "If only they (the top managers) would have listened to what I was saying five years ago, we wouldn't have even had this lawsuit. Now they're paying ten times more than the training seminars I recommended—not including the huge fees they paid for their legal defense." In most cases, if employers and employees use reasonable care to prevent harassment, there will be no reason to go to the courthouse.

Two of the easiest steps employers can take to prevent discrimination or harassment are:

1. Creating and implementing anti-discrimination and harassment policies and a complaint procedure (and reviewing the policies and procedure at least once a year with legal counsel to make sure they are adequate under current law); and

2. Training and monitoring managers, supervisors, and employees on the anti-discrimination and harassment policies and complaint procedure (Chapter 10 discusses no-charge and low-cost training options available to employers).

Creating and Implementing Policies

As discussed in Chapter 2, creating anti-discrimination and harassment policies is the easy part (especially if an employer has a good employment attorney who understands the employer and the business). While the creation of the policies and procedure is critical, even more critical is implementing the policies. Having anti-discrimination and harassment polices and ignoring them may be the worst thing an employer could do. (However, not having any policies at all is also a very bad idea!)

WORDS OF WISDOM: Once a company has created anti-discrimination and harassment policies, be sure to distribute them to the employees periodically. Distributing the policies will have at least three benefits to the company: (1) it will be a good reminder to the employees; (2) it will demonstrate that the company is committed to being a good employer and following the law; and (3) it can provide the company with good evidence that the company took reasonable steps to prevent discrimination in the event that something goes wrong.

Once the anti-discrimination and harassment policies are created, employers should disseminate them effectively to the employees. Provide every employee with a copy of the policies and take care to write the policies and complaint procedure in a way that will be understood by all employees in the employer's workforce. Not only should employers (or their lawyers) write the policies in plain language, they also should translate the policies into other languages if necessary to convey the meaning to workforce members who do not read English.

WORDS OF WISDOM: Employers can demonstrate that they have used reasonable care in preventing and correcting harassment by instructing all supervisors to report complaints of harassment to appropriate officials, regardless of whether the supervisors are specifically designated to receive complaints. Reporting complaints to appropriate officials can even be included in the supervisors' written job descriptions (see Chapter 3), in employee handbooks, in employment agreements, and in at-will acknowledgments (see Chapter 2).

Other measures to ensure effective dissemination of the policies and complaint procedure include posting them in central locations and incorporating them into employee handbooks.

Elements of Anti-discrimination and Harassment Policies and a Complaint Procedure

According to the EEOC, anti-discrimination and harassment policies and a complaint procedure should contain, at a minimum, the following elements: (1) prohibited conduct clause, (2) anti-retaliation clause, (3) complaint process, (4) alternate channels to report clause, (5) confidentiality clause, (6) investigation clause, and (7) corrective action clause.[1]

Prohibited Conduct

The prohibited conduct clause should explain clearly what is prohibited. Good policies make it clear that the employer will not tolerate harassment based on sex *(with or without sexual conduct)*, race, color, religion, national origin, age, disability, sexual orientation, or protected activity (i.e., opposition to prohibited discrimination or participation in the statutory complaint process). This prohibition should cover harassment by *anyone* in the workplace—supervisors, co-workers, and non-employees. The prohibited conduct clause is where it is important for employers to take the lead. Company management should convey the seriousness of the prohibition by communicating that upper management fully supports the policies and will take all complaints seriously.

Anti-retaliation

The anti-retaliation clause should include an assurance that employees who make complaints of harassment or provide information related to such complaints will be protected against retaliation. Without such an assurance, anti-discrimination and harassment policies and the complaint procedure will not be effective.

Complaint Process

A *clearly described* complaint process provides *accessible avenues* of complaint. Employers should design their complaint procedure to encourage employees to come forward! The earlier employees report, the faster employers can correct the situation and avoid much bigger problems. A complaint procedure should not be rigid, since that could defeat the goal of preventing and correcting harassment.

Alternative Channels to Report

Because a supervisor may be a harasser, if employees always are required to complain first to their supervisors, the complaint procedure will be considered ineffective. An alternate channel for reporting complaints should be included in the complaint process.

Confidentiality

The confidentiality clause should include an assurance that the employer will protect the confidentiality of harassment complaints *to the extent possible.* Confidentiality may not always be possible and should not be guaranteed, because an employer cannot conduct an effective investigation without revealing certain information to the alleged harasser and potential witnesses. However, employers should share information about the allegation of harassment only with those who need to know about it, and keep all records confidential on the same basis.

> **WORDS OF WISDOM:** If an employee complains of harassment but asks an employer to keep it confidential and take no action, the employer must investigate anyway! Once the company is on notice of the problem, it must investigate or it could be held liable.

Investigation

The investigation clause should provide a complaint process that provides a prompt, thorough, and impartial investigation.

Corrective Action

The corrective action clause should include an assurance that the company will take immediate and appropriate corrective action when the company determines that harassment has occurred.

> **WORDS OF WISDOM:** When an employee complains to management about alleged harassment, the employer is obligated to investigate the allegation regardless of whether the complaint conforms to a particular format or is made in writing!

Training and Monitoring

Training Employees

In addition to creating and implementing anti-discrimination and harassment policies, employers can demonstrate that they use reasonable care to prevent harassment by training and educating their workforce about employee responsibilities under the policies. The training should explain the types of conduct that violate the employer's anti-discrimination and harassment policies, the seriousness of the policies, the responsibilities of supervisors and managers when they learn of alleged harassment, and the prohibition against retaliation.

The training also should explain the complaint procedure to ensure that employees understand it. If an employee ever brings a lawsuit, the employer will have a defense if the employee unreasonably failed to use the complaint procedure. If the employer has provided specific training on the procedure, it would be hard for an employee to argue (with a straight face) that the employee didn't know the complaint procedure.

WORDS OF WISDOM: Employers should include a section in formal evaluations of supervisors and managers to evaluate the way in which the supervisors and managers carry out their responsibilities under the anti-discrimination and harassment policies. (See Chapter 15.)

Monitoring the Workplace

Employers should keep records of all harassment and discrimination complaints and review them when a complaint is made. Reviewing records will help reveal any patterns of harassment or discrimination by the same individuals. Without these records, the employer could be unaware of a pattern of harassment or discrimination by the same individual. Such a pattern would be relevant to credibility assessments and disciplinary measures.

How to Investigate Claims of Harassment and Discrimination

In addition to taking steps to prevent discrimination and harassment, wise employers proactively set up a mechanism for a prompt, thorough, and impartial investigation into alleged harassment and discrimination. As soon as employers learn about a complaint, they should determine if a detailed fact-finding investigation is required and if intermediate measures should be taken before the investigation is completed.

A Detailed Fact-finding Investigation

If the alleged harasser does not deny the accusation, there is no need to interview witnesses, and the employer can immediately determine appropriate corrective action. If a fact-finding investigation is necessary, the investigation should be launched immediately (see steps to take below). The amount of time that it will take to complete the investigation depends on the particular circumstances of the situation.

Taking Intermediate Measures

If the alleged harasser and the alleged target have frequent contact because of their positions, employers should take steps to ensure that the possibility of further harassment does not occur. Employers should consider taking measures such as making scheduling changes to avoid contact between the parties, transferring the alleged harasser, or placing the alleged harasser on non-disciplinary leave with pay pending the conclusion of the investigation. The determination of the best measures, if any, depends on the severity of the accusations and the risk that the parties will come into contact with each other.

WORDS OF WISDOM: Do not kill the messenger! When an employer receives a complaint of discrimination, the employer should not automatically transfer or burden the person who complained, or the employer may risk a retaliation claim (see Chapter 7).

Investigation Goals

The investigation should have at least five goals:
1. To provide a solid, thorough, and factual basis for decisions by the employer;
2. To produce trustworthy and reliable documentation that the employer can use to support management actions;
3. To uncover any misconduct;
4. To identify employees suspected of the misconduct; and
5. To end the conduct and prevent further discriminatory or harassing conduct.

The Investigator

The investigation could lay the groundwork for a quick and easy resolution, or it may be used later to defend against a charge or lawsuit for discrimination or harassment. Employers have several options when choosing an investigator, including:
- Internal HR employees or other employees who know how to conduct discrimination and harassment investigations;
- Professional HR investigation consultants; or
- Legal counsel (who are in-house or specially retained).

There are advantages and disadvantages to each of these options, depending on the circumstances and the gravity of the situation. While HR employees or other internal employees may be a good option, especially from the perspective of immediate cost-containment, there is the risk that internal employees will be perceived as biased, that internal employees may not be objective, or that internal employees will not make good witnesses if the matter goes to trial. Professional HR investigation consultants may provide a measure of objectivity and, if selected carefully, may be extremely capable of conducting the investigation (and serving as witnesses if necessary). However, professional HR investigation consultants may be expensive and cost may be a factor. While attorneys who focus their practices on employment law may be a good option from the legal perspective, there is a risk that an employment attorney could be called as a witness in a lawsuit, meaning that the company could deprive itself of the attorney/client privilege that normally protects communications with legal counsel.

WORDS OF WISDOM: If the employer uses outside attorneys, consultants, or investigators to investigate the discrimination or harassment claim, the investigation may be subject to the notice and reporting requirements set forth under the federal Fair Credit Reporting Act.[2]

In any event, the employer should ensure that the individual who conducts the investigation will objectively gather and consider the relevant facts. Under no circumstances should the alleged harasser have supervisory authority over the individual who conducts the investigation, nor should the alleged harasser have any direct or indirect control over the investigation. Whoever conducts the investigation should be well-trained in the skills required for interviewing witnesses and evaluating credibility, and also should possess the skills, demeanor, and credibility necessary to be a good witness in front of a jury.

WORDS OF WISDOM: If employers want to be represented by their legal counsel in anticipated litigation, it may not be a good idea to turn their legal counsel into a witness by having their legal counsel conduct the investigation. Instead, employers should consult with legal counsel separately or let legal counsel direct others to perform the investigation.

Investigation Tips

Investigations are not always easy, but with planning and care, wise employers can use investigations as tools for understanding what really happened.

Pre-Investigation

- Plan — Before launching an investigation, the investigator should plan the investigation, keeping in mind the goals of the investigation and the best methods for achieving those goals.

- Read — The investigator should review the complaint, read the company's policies and procedures (and follow them), and look at any other relevant documents or files, including personnel files. The investigator should be educated about the legal elements, requirements, and prohibitions of relevant state and federal discrimination and harassment laws and should review relevant state and federal discrimination and harassment laws pre-investigation as necessary.
- Write — The investigator should write a list of witnesses, questions, and documents.
- Expedite — Do not delay. Early investigation can protect the employees, as well as the company. Courts have found that where companies investigate quickly and take prompt, remedial action, they can often avoid liability.

During the Investigation

- Be Discreet — Hold individual interviews in a private place to keep the investigation confidential and avoid undue influence by other witnesses.
- Keep an Open Mind — Some employers believe that discrimination or harassment could not occur in their workplace or by their supervisors or that if discrimination or harassment occurred, they certainly would know about it. Nevertheless, because it is possible for discrimination and harassment to occur, use the investigation as a tool to find out what happened. Remember, most harassment and discrimination does not occur out in the open for everyone to see.
- Interview — Talk with the complainant, the alleged wrongdoer, and any witnesses identified as a result of the interviews or as indicated by the documents.
- Write — Take good notes of the interviews and log all actions taken in the investigation.

WORDS OF WISDOM: Early in the investigation, be sure to identify, locate, and secure documents that might be necessary—including memos, correspondence, time cards, policies, personnel files, e-mails, journals, and logs. Even if such documents are normally shredded or discarded as part of a routine procedure, missing documents could cause problems of proof or even accusations of tampering with evidence!

Questions to Ask Parties and Witnesses

According to the EEOC,[3] the following are examples of questions that may be appropriate to ask the parties and potential witnesses (of course, any actual investigation must be tailored to the particular facts of each situation):

- Ask "who, what, when, where, and how" — *Who* committed the alleged harassment or discrimination? *What* exactly occurred or was said? *When* did it occur and is it still ongoing? *Where* did it occur? *How often* did it occur? *How* did it affect you?
- How did you react? What response did you make when the incident occurred or afterwards?
- How did the alleged harassment or discrimination affect you? Has your job been affected in any way?
- Are there any persons who have relevant information? Was anyone present when the alleged harassment or discrimination occurred? Did you tell anyone about it? Did anyone see you immediately after the incident?
- Did the person who harassed or discriminated against you harass or discriminate against anyone else? Do you know whether anyone else complained about harassment or discrimination by that person? If so, to whom did they complain, and when? What happened?
- Are there any notes, physical evidence, or other documentation regarding the incident?
- Do you know of any other relevant information?
- How would you like to see the situation resolved?

Interviewing the Complainant

Interviewing the complainant can be a good opportunity to avoid a lawsuit—if the interview is handled with care. Chances are good that the complainant is uncomfortable and scared, and it may be that he or she has suffered. Make the person feel comfortable. Investigators can make the complainant comfortable by:

- Thanking the individual for coming forward;
- Emphasizing the company's goal of providing a safe working environment for all employees;
- Restating the company's commitment to its anti-retaliation policies;
- Asking the individual to report immediately any retaliatory activity;
- Telling the complainant that although steps will be taken to preserve confidentiality to the greatest extent possible, it is likely that third party witnesses will need to be interviewed; and
- Confirming that the company will determine what kind of investigation is warranted and will take appropriate measures.

Interviewing the Alleged Harasser or Discriminator

Remember, the alleged harasser or discriminator may or may not have engaged in the conduct accused. Provide only enough information to allow the accused individual to respond to the complaint. Get the accused individual's side of the story, and ask for as much detail as possible. Ask for dates, time, places, activities, and witnesses. Explain that the company has received allegations, but that at this time the company has not yet drawn any conclusions about the truthfulness of the claims. Ask the accused individual to volunteer any information that he or she thinks may be relevant and remind the accused individual that honesty is the best policy.

WORDS OF WISDOM: When talking with the alleged harasser or discriminator, review the company's anti-retaliation policy with the accused individual and emphasize that the accused individual must not retaliate, intimidate, or otherwise harass the complaining employee, or anyone else involved in the investigation. Remind the accused individual that he or she is not permitted to encourage others to retaliate. Stress the confidential nature of the investigation and instruct the accused individual not to talk with others about the matter.

Here are some potential questions the investigator may wish to ask the alleged harasser or discriminator:

- Briefly explain the allegations, ask, "What is your response?"
- If the accused individual claims that the allegations are false, ask why the complainant might lie.
- Are there any persons who have relevant information?
- Are there any notes, physical evidence, or other documentation regarding the incident?
- Do you know of any other relevant information?

Interviewing Third Parties

Be careful to identify witnesses who may have information. When the investigator meets with witnesses, meet with them individually in a private location and explain the purpose of the interview. Go over the company's anti-retaliation policies and stress the requirements of confidentiality. If possible, first try to get as much information from the witness as possible without disclosing who complained or the identity of the accused by asking broad, open-ended questions. Find out whether the witness has any information about each incident or allegation, and ask for the names of any other potential witnesses.

WORDS OF WISDOM: When interviewing a third party witness, the investigator may want to have the witness write a statement, or the investigator

---

may want to document the interview and have the witness review it for accuracy, make any corrections necessary, and sign and date it.

The following are questions the investigator may wish to ask third party witnesses:

- What did you see or hear? When did this occur? Describe the accused individual's behavior toward the complainant and toward others in the workplace.
- What did the complainant tell you? When did the complainant tell you this?
- What did the accused individual tell you? When did the accused individual tell you this?
- Do you know of any other relevant information?
- Are there other persons who have relevant information?

Making Credibility Determinations

If the investigation reveals conflicting versions of relevant events, the investigator will have to weigh each party's credibility, or believability. Credibility assessments can be critical in determining whether the alleged misconduct in fact occurred. According to the EEOC,[4] factors to consider include:

- Inherent Plausibility — Is the testimony believable on its face? Does it make sense?
- Demeanor — Did the person seem to be telling the truth or lying?
- Motive to Falsify — Did the person have a reason to lie?
- Corroboration — Is there witness testimony (such as testimony by eye-witnesses, people who saw the person soon after the alleged incidents, or people who discussed the incidents with the complainant or accused individual at around the time that the incidents occurred) or physical evidence (such as written documentation) that corroborates the party's testimony?
- Past Record — Did the accused individual have a history of similar behavior in the past?

According to the EEOC, no individual factor is conclusive as to believability or credibility.[5] For example, the fact that there are no eye-witnesses to the alleged misconduct does not necessarily defeat the complainant's credibility, since harassment and discrimination often occur behind closed doors. Furthermore, the fact that the accused individual engaged in similar behavior in the past does not necessarily mean that he or she did so again.

Reaching a Determination

Once all of the evidence is in, interviews are finalized, and credibility issues are resolved, the determination should be made as to whether conduct occurred that violated harassment or discrimination laws. The determination could be made by the investigator, a management official, or legal counsel based upon a review of the investigator's report. Sometimes it is difficult for management to reach a determination because of direct contradictions between the parties and a lack of documentary or eye-witness corroboration. In such cases, the employer may need to assess credibility as discussed earlier and make a determination based on the credibility assessment. According to the EEOC, if no determination can be made because the evidence is inconclusive, the employer should still undertake further preventive measures, such as training and monitoring.[6]

How to Remedy Harassment and Discrimination

Remedial measures should do three things:
1. Stop the harassment or discrimination;
2. Correct the effects of harassment or discrimination on the employee; and
3. Ensure that the harassment or discrimination does not recur.

As long as the remedial measures effectively achieve these goals, they do not need to be the measures requested or preferred by the complainant. Remember, when determining remedial measures, that if the harassment or discrimination does not stop, the employer could be found liable. At the same time, if the punishment does not fit the crime, the company may be open to claims by the accused individual, including wrongful discharge and defamation.

Stopping the Harassment or Discrimination

Select disciplinary measures that are proportional to the seriousness of the offense. Do not punish the complainant. If it is necessary to separate the parties, transfer the harasser and not the complainant (unless the complainant prefers otherwise—then be sure to document the complainant's request and have the complainant sign the request). Remedial responses that penalize the complainant are not effective in correcting the harassment or discrimination and could constitute unlawful retaliation.

When determining the appropriate remedial action, make sure to take action consistent with prior similar situations. To determine the appropriate action, consider the following:
- The severity, frequency, and pervasiveness of the conduct;
- Whether any third parties corroborated the claims;
- The response of the accused individual and his or her willingness to accept fault; and
- What corrective action will ensure that the behavior will not continue or be repeated.

Appropriate corrective action can include combinations of the following:

- Verbal warnings (be sure to document verbal warnings in writing);
- Written warnings;
- Counseling;
- Suspension;
- Transfer of the accused individual to a different department or location;
- Demotion;
- Reduction of wages;
- Training or counseling of the harasser or discriminator to ensure that he or she understands why his or her conduct violated the employer's anti-discrimination and harassment policies;
- Monitoring of the harasser or discriminator to ensure that the harassment or discrimination stops; and
- Termination of employment.

WORDS OF WISDOM: Any time an employer determines that corrective action must be taken for discrimination or harassment, it is a good idea to ask legal counsel whether to conduct company-wide training. Sometimes the complaint the employer receives is only the tip of the iceberg.

Correcting the Effects of Harassment or Discrimination

In addition to stopping the harassment or discrimination, use remedial measures to correct the *effects* of the harassment. Design measures to put the complainant in the position he or she would have been in had the misconduct not occurred. According to the EEOC, measures employers can take to correct the effects of harassment or discrimination on a complainant include:[7]

- Restoration of leave taken because of the harassment or discrimination;
- Expungement of negative evaluation(s) from the complainant's personnel file that arose from the harassment or discrimination;
- Reinstatement;
- An apology by the harasser or discriminator; and
- Correction of any other harm caused by the harassment or discrimination (e.g., compensation for losses).

Ensuring that Harassment or Discrimination Do Not Recur

After stopping the harassment or discrimination and correcting its effects, continue to monitor the situation with the complainant every few weeks. Make sure that no harassment or discrimination recurs and that retaliation does not occur. Make notes of the follow-up and put the notes in the investigatory file.

Wise employers will take steps to prevent, investigate, and correct complaints of harassment or discrimination and will continue to educate themselves and their employees on the benefits of a tolerant, harassment-free and discrimination-free workplace.

FOOTNOTES

[1]   EEOC, Enforcement Guidance: Vicarious Liability for Unlawful Harassment by Supervisors, No. 915.002, 6/18/99, http://www.eeoc.gov/docs/harassment.html#qa-2

[2]   15 U.S.C. §§ 1681 to 1681v.

[3]   EEOC Enforcement Guidance, No. 915.002, *supra.*

[4]   *Id.*

[5]   *Id.*

[6]   *Id.*

[7]   *Id.*

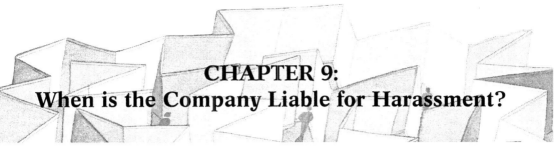

CHAPTER 9:
When is the Company Liable for Harassment?

The Basic Rules Regarding Employer Liability for Harassment

Employers should strive to end harassment and promote equality in the workplace. The United States Supreme Court has explained in two cases that both employees and employers have responsibilities to prevent and stop harassment. In *Burlington Indus., Inc. v. Ellerth* and *Faragher v. City of Boca Raton*,[1] the Supreme Court made it clear that *employers* are responsible for the acts of company supervisors. At the same time, *employees* are responsible to take reasonable steps to avoid or limit the harm from harassment.

This chapter does not discuss proving harassment, which is addressed in Chapter 6. Instead, this chapter explains the employer's responsibility for harassment once it has been determined that harassment has occurred. For the purposes of this chapter, assume that there was, in fact, harassment, and the only question is whether the employer should be found responsible for it.

Harassment by Managers and Supervisors

According to the Supreme Court, an employer is always responsible for harassment by a supervisor that results in a "tangible employment action."[2] Employers are always responsible for harassment by a supervisor that results in a tangible employment action because employers act through their supervisors, as discussed in

Chapter 1. When a supervisor takes a tangible employment action against an employee, because employers act through their supervisors, the supervisor's actions constitute an act of the employer. The legal term for the idea of responsibility for the acts of the supervisors is *vicarious liability* (meaning imposing responsibility for the acts of one person on another person because of their relationship).

WORDS OF WISDOM: A "tangible employment action" means a significant change in employment status. Examples of tangible employment actions include hiring, firing, promotion, demotion, undesirable reassignment, decisions causing a significant change in benefits, compensation decisions, and work assignments. According to the EEOC, significantly changing an individual's duties in his or her existing job is a tangible employment action regardless of whether the same salary and benefits are retained.[3] Similarly, altering an individual's duties in a way that blocks his or her opportunity for promotion or salary increases also constitutes a tangible employment action. Beware of tangible job benefits! Even a positive change in employment status may subject the employer to liability for harassment by a supervisor, for example, where the supervisor grants a tangible job benefit to an employee based on the employee's submission to unwelcome sexual demands.

The Supreme Court has explained that vicarious liability for supervisor harassment is appropriate because the employer has delegated authority to the supervisor, and this authority aids the supervisor in his or her misconduct.[4] An individual who is temporarily authorized to direct another employee's daily work activities qualifies as the employee's "supervisor" during that time period.

WORDS OF WISDOM: In some circumstances, an employer may be subject to vicarious liability for harassment by a supervisor who does not have actual authority over the employee! Such a result is appropriate if the employee reasonably believed that the harasser had such power (i.e., apparent authority—as discussed in Chapter 1). For example, an employer may be subject to vicarious liability for harassment by a supervisor who does not have actual authority where the chains of command are unclear or where the employee reasonably believes that a harasser with broad powers has the ability to significantly influence employment decisions affecting the employee—even if the harasser is actually outside the employee's chain of command.

If the harassment does *not* lead to a tangible employment action (such as where the work environment is hostile but the supervisor did not take disciplinary measures against the target of the harassment), the employer is liable *unless* it proves two things:

1. The employer exercised reasonable care to prevent and promptly correct any harassment; *and*
2. The employee unreasonably failed to complain to management or to avoid harm otherwise.[5]

WORDS OF WISDOM: Regardless of the person's title, an individual qualifies as an employee's "supervisor" if the individual has the authority to recommend tangible employment decisions affecting the employee (even if the individual does not have the final say regarding the employment decisions) or if the individual has the authority to direct the employee's daily work activities.

Harassment by Co-Workers

When harassment is perpetrated by a co-worker (as opposed to a manager or supervisor) an employer is liable for the harassment if the employer *knew or should have known* of the misconduct by the co-worker, unless the employer can show that the employer took immediate and appropriate corrective action.

WORDS OF WISDOM: Employers also may be liable for harassment by non-employees, such as customers, but the EEOC and courts consider the employer's control over the non-employee's misconduct to determine whether to impose liability, and if so, how much liability to impose.[6]

Harassment by the "Alter Ego" of the Employer

An employer is liable for unlawful harassment whenever the harasser is of a sufficiently high rank within a company to fall within the class of individuals who may be treated as the company's proxy. This essentially means that the harasser *is equivalent* to the employer. Under these circumstances, the employer is directly liable for the employer's own actions. It is not a case of *respondeat superior*, where the individual's actions are attributed to the company. It is a case of direct liability, where the individual's actions are the actions of the company itself. Essentially, it is as if the individual *is* the company because of the individual's high rank within the company. Under these circumstances, the employer cannot raise the *Faragher/Ellerth* defense (discussed later in this chapter), even if the harassment did not result in a tangible employment action.

The United States Supreme Court explained that courts can attribute full responsibility automatically to the employer for the actions of the following officials:[7]

- President;
- Owner;
- Partner;
- Corporate officer.

The Law Protects Careful Employers: *Faragher/Ellerth* Defense

As mentioned earlier, if supervisor harassment does *not* lead to a tangible employment action, the employer is liable for the harassment *unless* it proves two things:

1. The employer exercised reasonable care to prevent and promptly correct any harassment; *and*
2. The employee unreasonably failed to complain to management or avoid harm otherwise.[8]

The employer bears the burden of proof on *both* elements. The employer bearing the burden of proof on both elements means, for example, that the employee need *not* prove that he or she complained, or that if the employee did not complain that it was reasonable for him or her not to complain.

Employer's Duty to Exercise Reasonable Care

An employer trying to avoid liability for a company supervisor's harassment must prove that the employer undertook reasonable care to prevent and promptly correct harassment.[9] As discussed in Chapter 8, reasonable care generally requires an employer to establish, disseminate, and enforce anti-harassment policies and a complaint procedure and take other reasonable steps to prevent and correct harassment. Of course, even the best policies and complaint procedure will not alone satisfy the burden of proving reasonable care if the employer failed to implement their process effectively. For example, an employer has not exercised reasonable care in preventing harassment if management ignored previous complaints by other employees about a harasser, even if the employer has adequate policies and complaint procedure and properly responded to an employee's complaint of harassment.

Employee's Responsibility to Avoid or Limit Effects of Harassment

In addition to proving that the employer used reasonable care to prevent and correct harassment, the employer must also prove that the employee unreasonably failed to take advantage of any preventive or corrective opportunities provided by the employer or unreasonably failed to avoid harm.

As noted earlier, if an employer can prove that they used reasonable care and that the employee could have avoided all of the harm but unreasonably failed to do so, the employer should avoid all liability for unlawful harassment. For example, according to the EEOC, if an employee experienced a pattern of harassment that created an unlawful hostile environment, but the employee unreasonably failed to complain to management before the employee suffered emotional harm and the employer exercised reasonable care to prevent and promptly correct the harassment, then the employer will avoid all liability.[10]

Employee's Failure to Complain

A determination as to whether an employee unreasonably failed to complain or otherwise avoid harm depends on the particular circumstances and information available to the employee *at that time*. According to the EEOC, an employee should not necessarily be expected to complain to management immediately after the first or second incident of relatively minor harassment, as workplaces need not become battlegrounds where every minor, unwelcome remark based on race, sex, or another protected category triggers a complaint and investigation.[11] The EEOC instructs that an employee might reasonably ignore a small number of incidents, hoping that the harassment will stop without resort to the complaint process. The employee may directly say to the harasser that the employee wants the misconduct to stop, and then wait to see if that is effective in ending the harassment before complaining to management. However, if the harassment continues, then further delay might be found unreasonable.

According to the EEOC, there might be other reasonable explanations for an employee's delay in complaining or failure to utilize the employer's complaint process, such as:[12]

- Retaliation — An employer cannot establish that an employee unreasonably failed to use the company's complaint procedure if that employee reasonably feared retaliation.
- Obstacles — An employee's failure to use the employer's complaint procedure would be reasonable if that failure was based on unnecessary obstacles to complaints, such as inaccessible points of contact for making complaints or unnecessarily intimidating or burdensome requirements for making complaints.
- Ineffective Complaint Mechanism — An employer cannot avoid liability based on the employee's failure to complain if the employee's failure to complain was based on a reasonable belief that the process was ineffective, such as where the complaint procedure required the employee to complain initially to the harass-

ing supervisor, or where the employee was aware of instances in which co-workers' complaints failed to stop harassment.

WORDS OF WISDOM: The employer has to prove that the employee's belief or perception underlying the employee's failure to complain was unreasonable.

Other Efforts to Avoid Harm

The employee can make efforts to avoid harm, including making a prompt complaint to the EEOC while the harassment is ongoing, filing a union grievance, or reporting harassment to a joint employer. With these and any other efforts to avoid harm, the timing of the complaint could affect liability or damages. If the employee could have avoided some of the harm by complaining earlier, then damages could be reduced.

The ultimate goal is for both employers and employees to take reasonable steps to avoid harassment and its damaging effects. When employers plan to follow the laws by implementing and enforcing clear and effective policies, they can make the most of the protections the laws give to careful employers.

FOOTNOTES

[1] *Faragher v. City of Boca Raton,* 524 U.S. 775 (1998); *Burlington Industries , Inc. v. Ellerth,* 524 U.S. 742 (1998).

[2] *Faragher,* 524 U.S. at 762.

[3] EEOC, Enforcement Guidance: Vicarious Liability for Unlawful Harassment by Supervisors, No. 915.002, 6/18/99, http://eeoc.gov/docs/harassment.html

[4] *Faragher,* 524 U.S. at 762.

[5] *Faragher,* 524 U.S. at 806-807.

[6] *See Lockhard v. Pizza Hut Inc.,* 78 FEP Cases 1026 (10th Cir. 1998)("[a]n employer who condones or tolerates the creation of [a hostile work] environment should be held liable regardless of whether the environment was created by a co-employee or a nonemployee, since the employer ultimately controls the conditions of the work environment").

[7] *Faragher,* 118 S. Ct. at 2284.

[8] *Id.*

[9] *Id.*

[10] EEOC, Enforcement Guidance No. 915.002, *supra.*

[11] *Id.*

[12] *Id.*

CHAPTER 10:
Everything You Wanted to Know About the EEOC But Were Afraid to Ask

Overview of the EEOC

Believe it or not, the Equal Employment Opportunity Commission (EEOC) can be a great resource for employers. While the mere mention of the agency's name can cause trepidation for some employers, and while other employers prepare for battle when they anticipate dealings with the EEOC, the agency provides many tools to help employers prevent, investigate, and correct discrimination problems within companies. Employers striving for legally healthy workplaces can utilize the EEOC's tools, which are easily available to employers, but often are undiscovered until it is too late. This chapter gives an overview of the EEOC, EEOC resources for employers, and opportunities for resolution of charges when things go wrong.

What Does the EEOC Do?

The EEOC is an independent federal agency created by Congress in 1964 to eradicate discrimination in employment.[1] One function of the EEOC is to interpret employment discrimination laws. The EEOC also enforces laws that prohibit employment discrimination on the basis of race, color, sex, national origin, religion, retaliation, age, and disability. Additionally, the EEOC provides many services to employers, including training on federal civil rights laws, prevention activities, investigations, and enforcement of employment laws.

While the EEOC gets a lot of press for the agency's enforcement activities, such as litigation when things go wrong, the enforcement activities are only a small fraction of what the EEOC does. In addition to enforcement activities, the EEOC provides outreach for employers, training resources, technical assistance, alternative dispute resolution, and free written and on-line materials that answer many of the questions that employers face on a day-to-day basis.

The EEOC and Outreach, Education, Technical Assistance, and Training

The EEOC views its outreach, education, and technical assistance efforts as vital components of its mission to eradicate employment discrimination.[2] The agency's outreach program is designed to encourage voluntary compliance with the anti-discrimination laws and assist employers, employees, and stakeholder groups with understanding and preventing discrimination. Employers should take advantage of the EEOC's expertise in the area of employment discrimination.

The EEOC's Services for Outreach and Education

The EEOC offers *no-cost* outreach and educational programs which make EEOC staff available for presentations and participation in meetings with employees, employers, community organizations, and other members of the general public. The EEOC representatives are available, on request and at no cost, to provide information and answer questions about laws enforced by the EEOC and EEOC procedures. The following are some ways for employers to make use of the EEOC's no-cost education services:

- Conference or seminar — The EEOC will send a representative to discuss recent developments in EEOC laws and EEOC policy issues to educate a company's managers and supervisors.
- Cultural festival or job fair — The EEOC will set up a booth and disseminate information to employees and applicants.
- Small business liaisons — EEOC field offices have designated small business liaisons to answer questions and provide assistance to small businesses.

- Interactive workshops — The EEOC sponsors several interactive workshops under the New Freedom Initiative for employers with 15-100 employees with questions about employing individuals with disabilities,.

The EEOC's Fee-Based Training—Technical Assistance Programs (TAPS)

The EEOC also provides fee-based technical assistance programs. EEOC staff and other federal and state officials as well as private attorneys with EEOC expertise may be speakers. The seminars emphasize how to prevent EEOC problems from developing and how to resolve discrimination complaints effectively if complaints do arise. Real-life case studies and examples often are used to show how equal employment requirements apply to specific employment practices. Updates on important legal developments, EEOC policies and procedures, and vital information about the EEOC's latest initiatives and alternative dispute resolution program are discussed. Specialized topics will differ by seminar and may include in-depth sessions on issues such as: sexual and racial harassment; complex ADA issues, including the ADA's relation to other employment laws; and religious and national origin discrimination. Whenever practicable, small group breakouts, question and answer periods, interactive formats, and informal discussions are used in the seminars, which enable participants to receive answers to specific EEOC concerns.

The EEOC's Customer-Based Training

EEOC staff members, from field and headquarters offices, are available on a limited basis to provide specialized training on various employment discrimination topics for all types of employers and employees. The training can take place at work sites or at an organization's meeting or training event. According to the EEOC, the length of training varies based on the company's needs. Some of the most popular topics requested for on-site training include:[3]

- Sexual harassment — Preventing and eliminating sexual harassment and lessening legal liability;
- Racial, national origin, and other forms of illegal harassment — Preventing and eliminating racial, national origin, and other forms of illegal harassment and lessening legal liability;
- Understanding the ABC's of the EEOC; and
- The Americans with Disabilities Act and reasonable accommodation.

The EEOC's Publications and Resources for Employers

EEOC publications—including the texts of the laws enforced by the EEOC, facts about employment discrimination, and enforcement guidances and related documents—are available free of charge, either on the EEOC website at www.eeoc.gov or by mailing the EEOC Publications Request Form to the U.S. Equal Employment Opportunity Commission Publications Information Center, P.O. Box 12549, Cincinnati, Ohio 45212-0549, (800) 669-3362 (voice), (800) 800-3302 (TDD), (513) 791-2954 (FAX).

Some of the information also available on the EEOC's website includes:

- *EEOC Compliance Manual* — One of the best "gold nuggets" for employers is the *EEOC Compliance Manual*, which addresses many of the particular situations employers face. While most of the manual is not available on-line, there are several sections available at http://www.eeoc.gov/policy/compliance.html;
- EEOC Regulations — Regulations specifying implementation of employment statutes can be found at http://www.eeoc.gov/regs/index.html;
- EEOC Enforcement Guidance — Links to information used by EEOC investigators and litigators in handling charges can be found at http://www.eeoc.gov/policy/guidance.html;
- EEOC Information for Small Employers — Links to questions and answers and other resources can be found at http://www.eeoc.gov/small/index.html;
- Laws enforced by the EEOC — Links to statutes enforced by the EEOC can be found at http://www.eeoc.gov/laws.html; and
- Quick Start for Small Employers — Fact sheets and additional information can be found at http://www.eeoc.gov/qs-employers.html.

The EEOC's Enforcement Activities: When Things Go Wrong

The EEOC has the authority to receive, initiate, and investigate charges of discrimination filed against employers who have 15 or more employees. According to the EEOC, the agency's role in an investigation is to fairly and accurately evaluate allegations in light of all the evidence obtained.[4]

Enforcement Procedure

With the agency's headquarters in Washington, D.C., and through the operation of 50 field offices nationwide, the EEOC coordinates all federal equal employment opportunity regulations, practices, and policies. Any individual who believes he or she has been discriminated against regarding his or her employment may file an administrative charge with the EEOC. After investigating the charge, the EEOC determines if there is "reasonable cause" to believe discrimination has occurred against the individual (the charging party). If the EEOC finds reasonable cause to believe that discrimination has occurred, the EEOC attempts to conciliate the charge by reaching a voluntary resolution between the charging party and the company (called the respondent).

If conciliation is not successful, the EEOC may bring suit in federal court. The EEOC may also issue a "right-to-sue notice" to the charging party, allowing the individual to file an individual action in court without the EEOC's involvement.

Charge Handling System

The EEOC receives approximately 80,000 private sector charges annually.[5] When the EEOC processes a charge, the agency classifies the charge in one of three basic categories:

- Category A — The EEOC recognizes quickly that it is likely that discrimination has occurred and gives these charges priority investigative and settlement efforts (according to most recent statistics, approximately 40 percent of all charges fell into this category);[6]
- Category B — The EEOC requires further investigation to determine if a violation has occurred (according to most recent statistics, approximately 57 percent of all charges fell into this category);[7] and
- Category C — The EEOC determines that the charges include non-jurisdictional or unsupported charges and closes these charges immediately (according to most recent statistics, only about 2 percent of all charges fell into this category).[8]

Settlements are encouraged at all stages of the charge handling process.

What Happens When a Charge Has Been Filed Against a Company?

Employers should take a deep breath and stay calm when a charge is filed against their company. Employers should then contact their legal counsel. Employers will be notified that a charge of discrimination has been filed and they will be provided with the name and contact information for the investigator assigned to their case. A charge does *not* constitute a finding that a company engaged in discrimination. The EEOC has a responsibility to investigate and determine whether there is a reasonable cause to believe discrimination occurred.

WORDS OF WISDOM: The EEOC notice will caution an employer that it is unlawful to retaliate against the charging party for filing the charge. There have been many cases where the EEOC or the court found that even though there was no discrimination, the employer retaliated against the employee for filing a charge and the employer had to pay significant damages!

In many cases, the employer may opt to resolve a charge early in the process through mediation or settlement. At the start of an investigation, the EEOC will advise an employer if the charge is eligible for mediation, but employers should feel free to ask their legal counsel about the settlement option. Mediation and settlement are *voluntary resolutions.*

During the investigation, the employer and the charging party will be asked to provide information. The investigator will evaluate the information submitted to determine whether unlawful discrimination has taken place.

Steps Employers May Be Asked to Take

- Submit a statement of position — This is an employer's opportunity to tell the employer's side of the story and the employer should take advantage of it. If the employer hasn't already, this would be a good time to get legal counsel involved. If litigation occurs, the documents the employer submits may be used in litigation.
- Respond to a request for information (RFI) — The RFI may ask an employer to submit copies of personnel policies, the charging party's personnel files, the personnel files of other individuals, and other relevant information.
- Permit an on-site visit — While an employer may view such a visit as being disruptive to company operations, according to the EEOC, the agency's experience has been that such visits greatly expedite the fact-finding process and may help achieve quicker resolutions.[9] In some cases, if requested documents are made available for viewing or photocopying, an on-site visit may be an alternative to a request for information.
- Provide employee contact information for witness interviews — Employers may be present during interviews with management personnel, but an investigator is allowed to conduct interviews of non-management level employees without the employer's presence or permission.
- Present the employer's side of the story — If the charge was not dismissed by the EEOC when it was received, that means there was some basis for proceeding with further investigation. There are many cases where it is unclear whether discrimination may have occurred and an investigation is necessary. Employers are encouraged to present any facts that they believe show the allegations are incorrect or do not amount to a violation of the law. An employer's input and cooperation will assist EEOC in promptly and thoroughly investigating a charge.
- Work with the investigator — The EEOC may be able to help an employer identify the most efficient and least burdensome way to gather relevant evidence. (Again, employers should consult legal counsel to assist them with this process.)

- Submit a prompt response to the EEOC — Employers should submit a prompt response to the EEOC and provide the information requested, even if they believe the charge is frivolous. If there are extenuating circumstances preventing a timely response from an employer, contact the investigator to work out a new due date for receipt of the information.
- Provide complete and accurate information in response to requests from the investigator.
- Keep relevant documents — If an employer is unsure whether a document is needed, ask the company's employment lawyer. By law, employers are required to keep certain documents for a set period of time and employers can get into trouble if the documents are destroyed.

When the Investigation is Completed

Once the investigator has completed the investigation, the EEOC will make a determination on the merits of the charge. If the EEOC determines that there is no reasonable cause to believe that discrimination occurred, the charging party will be issued a letter called a *dismissal and notice of rights* that tells the charging party that he or she has the right to file a lawsuit in federal court within 90 days from the date of receipt of the letter. The employer will also receive a copy of the *dismissal and notice of rights* document.

If the EEOC determines there is reasonable cause to believe discrimination has occurred, both parties will be issued a *letter of determination* stating that there is reason to believe that discrimination occurred and inviting the parties to join the agency in seeking to resolve the charge, through an informal process known as *conciliation*. Where conciliation fails, the EEOC has the authority to enforce violations of employment related statutes by filing a lawsuit in federal court. If the EEOC decides not to litigate, the charging party will receive a *notice of right to sue*. The charging party may file a lawsuit in federal court within 90 days from the date of receipt of the document.

How Can the Charge Be Resolved?

Can the charge be resolved without going to court? Possibly. The EEOC offers employers many opportunities to resolve charges of discrimination without going to court. Successfully resolving the case through a voluntary process may save an employer time, effort, and money. Methods of resolution include mediation, conciliation, and settlement. If the voluntary efforts fail, some cases end up in litigation.

Mediation

The EEOC has greatly expanded the agency's mediation program, which is free, quick, voluntary, and confidential. If the charge filed against an employer is eligible for mediation, the employer will be invited to take part in the mediation process. Mediation avoids lengthy and unnecessary litigation. If mediation is successful, there is no investigation and the charge is closed. If mediation is unsuccessful, the charge is referred for further investigation.

Mediation is a confidential process. The mediators do not tape record or transcribe sessions, and the mediator discards all notes taken during mediation. If mediation is unsuccessful, the EEOC investigators cannot use information learned during the mediation later if litigation is commenced against the employer.

If the parties can reach a settlement agreement during the mediation, the employer need not make any admission of any violation of laws enforced by the EEOC. Settlement agreements secured during mediation are enforceable.

Settlement

The parties can settle charges of discrimination at any time during the investigation. Settling a charge early may save an employer the time and effort associated with investigations. If the parties, including the EEOC, reach a voluntary agreement, the charge will be dismissed. Like mediation, agreements reached through settlement are enforceable and settlement agreements enable the parties to avoid lengthy, costly, and unnecessary litigation.

Conciliation

Federal laws require the EEOC to attempt to resolve findings of discrimination through "informal methods of conference, conciliation, and persuasion."[10] When the EEOC determines, after investigation, that there is "reasonable cause" to believe that discrimination has occurred, the EEOC will notify the parties by letter and will invite the parties to participate in conciliation discussions. During conciliation, the EEOC investigator will work with the employer and the charging party to develop an appropriate remedy for the discrimination. The EEOC encourages employers to take advantage of this final opportunity to resolve the charge prior to the EEOC considering the matter for litigation.

Litigation

The EEOC files lawsuits in a wide variety of professional fields addressing egregious discrimination on behalf of individuals in various occupations. In addition, the EEOC files *amicus curiae* or "friend of the court" briefs in appellate and trial courts in support of EEOC positions, usually in cases involving issues important to the development of the laws the EEOC enforces.

Possible Damages

If a company is found to have discriminated in violation of the EEOC-enforced laws, the remedies that may be assessed against the company include:

- An order from the court to eliminate discriminatory practices;
- Hiring, wage adjustments, promotion, or reinstatement—depending upon the nature of the action taken against the individual; and
- Monetary remedies.

Monatary remedies available under the laws enforced by the EEOC are as follows:

- Lost wages and prejudgment interest (all statutes);
- Liquidated/double damages (for violations of ADEA and EPA);
- Compensatory damages (for violations of Title VII and ADA cases involving intentional discrimination);
- Punitive damages (for violations of Title VII and ADA cases in which the employer acted with reckless disregard of the federally protected rights of the individual); and
- Attorney fees for the charging parties' lawyers.

The sum of the punitive damages and future compensatory damages may not exceed the following amounts, per person:

- $50,000 for employers with 15-100 employees;
- $100,000 for employers with 101-200 employees;
- $200,000 for employers with 201-500 employees; and
- $300,000 for employers with more than 500 employees.[11]

The costs stated above do not include the costs for an employer's legal counsel, administrative expenses and lost productivity, and the personal and emotional tolls litigation can take on employees. These costs are very good reasons to pay attention to prevention, to make the investment in solid legal counsel before problems arise, and to strive for a legally healthy workplace.

FOOTNOTES

[1] EEOC Investigations, What an Employer Should Know, http://www.eeoc.gov/small/investigations.html

[2] EEOC Statutory Authority, http://www.eeoc.gov/statauth.html

[3] EEOC Customer Specific Training, http://www.eeoc.gov/outreach/customerspecific.html

[4] EEOC Investigations, What an Employer Should Know, *supra.*

[5] EEOC Enforcement Activities, http://www.eeoc.gov/enforce.html

[6] *Id.*

[7] *Id.*

[8] *Id.*

[9] EEOC Investigations, What an Employer Should Know, *supra.*

[10] 42 U.S.C. § 2000e-5(b).

[11] EEOC Enforcement Guidance: Compensatory and Punitive Damages Available Under § 102 of the Civil Rights Act of 1991, 7/14/92, www.eeoc.gov/docs/damages.html

CHAPTER 11:
Employment Related Immigration Information—
Our Friends From Abroad

Overview of Employment Immigration Information

Immigration laws are complex, and in a post-September 11th world, the laws and policies can be important for employers who work with our friends from abroad. This chapter highlights the basics of employment immigration as well as providing references for employers who need more detailed information.

Where Did the INS Go? Introducing the Bureau of Citizenship and Immigration Services (BCIS)

On March 1, 2003, service and benefit functions of the U.S. Immigration and Naturalization Service (INS) transitioned into the Department of Homeland Security (DHS) as the Bureau of Citizenship and Immigration Services (BCIS). President Bush nominated Mr. Eduardo Aguirre to lead the BCIS, and the Senate confirmed Mr. Aguirre's appointment on June 19, 2003. The BCIS is responsible for the administration of immigration and naturalization adjudication functions and establishing immigration services, policies, and priorities.[1] The functions of the BCIS include:

- Adjudication of immigrant visa petitions;
- Adjudication of naturalization petitions;
- Adjudication of asylum and refugee applications;
- Adjudications performed at the service centers; and
- All other adjudications performed by the INS.

Fifteen thousand federal employees and contractors working in approximately 250 headquarters and field offices around the world comprise the BCIS.

Office of Business Liason

The Office of Business Liaison (OBL) is a division of the BCIS. The primary function of the OBL is to educate the business community on employment, business, investment, training, and employer education-related immigration issues. The BCIS website contains helpful information about the OBL and its services, including:

- Frequently asked questions about employment eligibility;
- Concurrent filing of Form I-140 (Immigrant Petition for Alien Worker) and Form I-485 (Application to Register Permanent Residence or Adjust Status);
- Filing of Form I-485 (Application to Register Permanent Residence or Adjust Status);
- Premium processing service;
- Temporary workers information, such as how to apply for visas, fees, maximum stay requirements, and other pertinent information;
- H1B Visas for non-immigrant workers who will be employed temporarily in a specialty occupation or as a fashion model of distinguished merit and ability;
- Employment verification pilot programs (SAVE Program); and
- NAFTA professionals (TN Visas), including who qualifies and how to obtain such Visas.

For more information regarding the OLB, see http://www.bcis.gov, and go to the employer's information link.

Sponsoring Immigrants for Lawful Permanent Residency

An immigrant is a foreign national who has been authorized to live and work permanently in the United States. If an employer wants to sponsor someone for lawful permanent residency based on permanent employment in the United States, the employer must go through a multi-step process:[2]

1. Foreign nationals and employers must determine if the foreign national is eligible for lawful permanent residency under one of the BCIS's paths to lawful permanent residency.

2. Most employment categories require that the U.S. employer complete a labor certification request (Form ETA 750) for the applicant, and submit the labor certification request to the Department of Labor's Employment and Training Administration. The Department of Labor must either grant or deny the certification request. Qualified alien physicians who will practice medicine in an area of the United States which has been certified as underserved by the U.S. Department of Health and Human Services are relieved from this requirement.

3. The BCIS must approve an immigrant visa petition, Form I-140 (Petition for Alien Worker), for the person wishing to immigrate to the United States. The employer wishing to bring the applicant to the United States to work permanently files Form I-140. However, if a Department of Labor certification is needed, the application can only be filed *after* the certification is granted. The employer acts as the sponsor (or petitioner) for the applicant (or beneficiary) who wants to live and work on a permanent basis in the United States.

4. The State Department must give the applicant an immigrant visa number, even if the applicant is already in the United States. When the applicant receives an immigrant visa number, it means that an immigrant visa has been assigned to the applicant.

5. If the applicant is already in the United States, the applicant must apply to adjust to permanent resident status after a visa number becomes available. If the applicant is outside the United States when an immigrant visa number becomes available, the applicant will be notified and must complete the process at his or her local U.S. Consulate office.

Five Categories of Eligibility Based on Employment Skills

While there are many categories of eligibility for permanent residency status based on a number of qualifications, there are five categories based on employment skills:

1. EB-1 Priority Workers — Foreign nationals of extraordinary ability in the sciences, arts, education, business, or athletics; outstanding professors or researchers; and managers and executives subject to international transfer to the United States.

2. EB-2 Professionals with Advanced Degrees or Persons with Exceptional Ability — Foreign nationals of exceptional ability in the sciences, arts or business; advanced degree professionals; or qualified alien physicians who will practice medicine in an area of the U.S. which is underserved.

3. EB-3 Skilled or Professional Workers — Foreign national professionals with bachelor's degrees (not qualifying for a higher preference category);

skilled workers (with a minimum of two years training and experience); and unskilled workers.

4. EB-4 Special Immigrants — Foreign national religious workers and employees and former employees of the U.S. Government abroad.
5. EB-5 Immigrant Investors.

If an employer wishes to sponsor (or petition for) a foreign national to work in the United States on a permanent basis, the employer must file Form I-140 (Petition for Alien Worker). Filing requirements differ for each of the five categories. Form I-140 must be filed at the BCIS Service Center that serves the area where the immigrant will work.

The Denver District Office for the BCIS is located at 4730 Paris Street, Denver, Colorado, 80239. It is open to the public from 7:30 a.m. to 2:30 p.m., Monday through Thursday. The Denver District Office for the BCIS is closed to the general public on Fridays, except for individuals attending scheduled naturalization ceremonies, and is closed on Saturdays, Sundays, and federal holidays. The telephone number for employer related immigration matters (Office of Business Liaison) is 1-800-357-2099.

Types of Immigrant and Non-Immigrant Status

Immigrant

An immigrant, also known as a "permanent legal resident" is a foreign national (a citizen of another country) who has been authorized to live and work permanently in the United States. An immigrant holds a "green card" (which is not actually green).

Non-Immigrant

A non-immigrant is a foreign national who comes to the United States temporarily and has no intention of abandoning his or her permanent residence abroad. A non-immigrant is restricted in the work activities he or she can legally perform, and most non-immigrant visa categories do not authorize employment. If work authorization is granted, it is for fixed periods of time, usually for one employer. Common examples of nonimmigrant categories include:

- B-1 — Business visitors (visiting the U.S. on behalf of foreign employers);
- F-1 — Students with work authorization, including practical training;
- H-1B — Temporary workers (including most professionals);
- L-1 — Intra-company transferees; and
- Canadians working under the special immigration provisions of the North American Free Trade Agreement (NAFTA).

Undocumented Individuals

"Undocumented" individuals are people who have entered the country without legal permission. Except in rare circumstances, undocumented individuals are not allowed to work legally. However, those who once entered the country illegally may later become documented and may legally work.

Special Classifications

Some individuals fall into classifications not listed above, including refugees, political asylees, temporary resident aliens, and nationals of certain countries who have been granted temporary protected status, among others. These special classifications have unique requirements and employment rules. For additional information regarding these special classifications, employers can go to the BCIS website at http://www.bcis.gov and/or consult legal counsel.

Laws Employers Should Know About—IRCA and IIRAIRA

Two of the immigration laws employers may encounter are the Immigration Reform and Control Act of 1986 (IRCA)[3] and the Illegal Immigration Reform and Immigrant Responsibility Act of 1996 (IIRAIRA).[4] Basically, these acts require that employers:

- Take affirmative steps to verify that employers are not employing unauthorized workers by completing I-9 Forms and reviewing permissible documentation (see Chapter 4);
- Make sure that employers do not knowingly hire or continue to employ undocumented workers; and
- Prohibit discrimination in hiring and employment based on citizenship and national origin.

WORDS OF WISDOM: An employer who singles out individuals of a particular national origin or individuals who appear to be foreign to provide employment verification may have violated both the IRCA[5] and Title VII.[6]

What to Do Upon Discovery of an Unauthorized Worker

If an employer learns that an employee whose documentation appeared to be in order for Form I-9 purposes is not actually authorized to work, the employer should question the employee and provide another opportunity for review of proper Form

I-9 documentation. If the employee does not provide satisfactory documentation, the employee's employment should be discontinued. If the employer knew or should have known an employee was unauthorized to work, civil and criminal penalties may be imposed upon the employer.[7]

What to Do Upon Discovery of False Documentation

False documentation includes counterfeit documents or documents belonging to someone other than the employee presenting the documents. On occasion, an employee who initially presented false documentation to gain employment later obtains proper work authorization and presents it to the employer. U.S. immigration law does not require the employer to terminate the employee's services, however the internal personnel policies of the employer may apply. If the employer elects to retain the employee, the Form I-9 should be corrected.

WORDS OF WISDOM: IRCA's anti-discrimination provisions apply to employers with a smaller number of employees than the employers covered by EEOC-enforced Title VII laws. IRCA's national origin discrimination provisions apply to employers with between 4 and 14 employees (who would not be covered by Title VII, which generally applies only to employers with 15 or more employees).[8] The IRCA is enforced by the U.S. Department of Justice.

For more information regarding the IRCA's anti-discrimination provisions see http://www.usdoj.gov/crt/osc.

Because employment immigration laws are complex and can be confusing, employers should seek counsel and educate themselves on the laws as necessary.

FOOTNOTES

[1] http://www.bcis.gov/graphics/aboutus/thisisimm/index.htm

[2] *See generally,* Bureau of Citizenship and Immigration Services, http://www.bcis.gov/graphics/howdoi/immstatemp.htm

[3] 274A, 8 U.S.C. § 1324a.

[4] Pub. L. No. 104-208, § 306(d), 110 Stat. 3009 (1996).

[5] Note 3, *supra.*

[6] 42 U.S.C. §§ 2000e *et seq.*

[7] BCIS, About Form I-9, Employment Eligibility Verification, http://www.bcis.gov/graphics/howdoi/faqeev.htm

[8] EEOC, Other Employment Issues, http://www.eeoc.gov/small/otherissues.html#what%20is%20IRCA

CHAPTER 12:
Leave Issues—Give Me a Break

Overview of Leave Issues

During the course of their employment, many employees will need to take leave for varied reasons. Although no Colorado or federal law requires employers to grant paid vacation benefits, there are some circumstances under which employment laws require paid leave (such as brief leaves for jury duty and voting). More often, employment laws provide for unpaid leave (such as medical and military leaves). This chapter is a quick primer on the federal and state laws regarding leave issues, the reasons behind them, and the basic provisions regarding leave issues employers should know.

Federal Law: Family and Medical Leave Act (FMLA)

Purposes of the FMLA

The FMLA allows employees to balance their work and family life by taking reasonable unpaid employment leave for certain family and medical reasons.[1] The FMLA seeks to balance the employers' interests and minimize the potential for employment discrimination on the basis of gender, while promoting equal employment opportunity for men and women.

The FMLA in a Nutshell

The following is a general summary of FMLA provisions:
- Covers only certain employers (covered employers);
- Affects only those employees eligible for the protections of the law (eligible employees);
- Provides entitlement to unpaid leave for certain reasons;
- Requires maintenance of health benefits during leave;
- Mandates job restoration after leave, with a few exceptions;
- Sets requirements for notice and certification of the need for FMLA leave;
- Protects employees who request or take FMLA leave; and
- Includes certain employer recordkeeping requirements.

Covered Employers

Private employers who employ 50 or more employees for at least 20 workweeks in the current or preceding calendar year, including joint employers and successors of covered employers, are covered employers for the purposes of the FMLA. The FMLA also includes some public entities and schools as covered employers.[2]

Eligible Employees

To be eligible for FMLA leave, an employee must work for a covered employer *and*:

- Have worked for that employer for at least 12 months;
- Have worked at least 1,250 hours during the 12 months prior to the start of the FMLA leave; and
- Have worked at a location where at least 50 employees are employed at the location or within 75 miles of the location.[3]

Entitlement to Unpaid Leave

Covered employers must grant eligible employees up to a total of 12 workweeks of unpaid leave during any 12-month period for one or more of the following reasons:

- For the birth and care of the newborn child of the employee;
- For placement with the employee of a son or daughter for adoption or foster care;
- To care for an immediate family member (spouse, child, or parent) with a serious health condition; or
- To take medical leave when the employee is unable to work because of a serious health condition.[4]

Intermittent or Reduced Schedule Leave

The FMLA permits employees to take leave on an intermittent basis or to work a reduced schedule under certain circumstances. Intermittent or reduced schedule leave may be taken when medically necessary to care for a seriously ill family member, or because of the employee's serious health condition. Intermittent or reduced schedule leave may be taken to care for a newborn or newly placed adopted or foster care child only with the employer's approval.[5]

Only the amount of leave actually taken while on intermittent or reduced schedule leave may be charged as FMLA leave. Employees may not be required to take more FMLA leave than necessary to address the circumstances that cause the need for leave.[6] Employers may account for FMLA leave in the shortest period of time that their payroll systems uses, provided it is one hour or less.[7]

Employees who need intermittent or reduced schedule leave for foreseeable medical treatment must work with their employers to schedule the leave so as not to unduly disrupt the employer's operations, subject to the approval of the employee's health care provider.[8] In those cases, the employer may transfer the employee temporarily to an alternative job with equivalent pay and benefits that accommodate recurring periods of leave better than the employee's regular job.[9]

WORDS OF WISDOM: Substitution of Paid Leave—Employers may require the employee to use accrued paid leave, vacation leave, and/or personal leave to cover some or all of the FMLA leave taken— if the requirement to take accrued leave is set forth in advance in employer policies.[10]

Serious Health Condition

"Serious health condition" means an illness, injury, impairment, or physical or mental condition that involves:

- Any period of incapacity or treatment connected with inpatient care (i.e., an overnight stay) in a hospital, hospice, or residential medical care facility; or
- A period of incapacity requiring absence of more than three consecutive calendar days from work, school, or other regular daily activities that also involves continuing treatment by (or under the supervision of) a health care provider; or
- Any period of incapacity due to pregnancy, or for prenatal care; or
- Any period of incapacity (or treatment therefore) due to a chronic serious health condition (e.g., asthma, diabetes, epilepsy, etc.); or
- A period of incapacity that is permanent or long-term due to a condition for which treatment may not be effective (e.g., Alzheimer's, stroke, terminal diseases, etc.); or,
- Any absences to receive multiple treatments (including any period of recovery) by, or on referral by, a health care provider for a condition that likely would result in incapacity of more than three consecutive days if left untreated (e.g., chemotherapy, physical therapy, dialysis, etc.).[11]

WORDS OF WISDOM: Leave to care for a newborn child or for a newly placed adopted or foster child must conclude within 12 months after the birth or placement.[12]

Maintenance of Health Benefits

A covered employer is required to maintain group health insurance coverage, including family coverage, for an employee on FMLA leave on the same terms as if the employee continued to work.[13] Where appropriate, arrangements should be made for employees taking unpaid FMLA leave to pay their share of health insurance premiums. For example, if the group health plan involves co-payments by the employer and the employee, an employee on unpaid FMLA leave must make arrangements to pay the employee's normal portion of the insurance premiums to maintain insurance coverage, as must the employer. Such payments may be made under any arrangement voluntarily agreed to by the employer and employee.[14]

An employer's obligation to maintain health benefits under the FMLA stops if and when an employee informs the employer of the employee's intent not to return to work at the end of the leave period, or if the employee fails to return to work when the FMLA leave entitlement is exhausted.[15] The employer's obligation to maintain health benefits under the FMLA also stops if the employee's premium payment is more than 30 days late and the employer has given the employee written notice at least 15 days in advance advising the employee that coverage will cease if payment is not received.[16]

WORDS OF WISDOM: In some circumstances, the employer may recover premiums the employer paid to maintain health insurance coverage for an employee who fails to return to work from FMLA leave.[17]

Additional Benefits

Other benefits, including cash payments chosen by the employee instead of group health insurance coverage, need not be maintained during periods of unpaid FMLA leave. Certain types of earned benefits, such as seniority or paid leave, need not continue to accrue during periods of unpaid FMLA leave provided that such benefits do not accrue for employees on other types of unpaid leave.[18]

For other benefits, such as elected life insurance coverage, the employer and the employee may make arrangements to continue benefits during periods of unpaid FMLA leave. An employer may elect to continue such benefits to ensure that the employee will be eligible to be restored to the same benefits upon returning to work. At the conclusion of the unpaid FMLA leave, the employer may recover only the employee's share of premiums the employer paid to maintain other "non-health" benefits during unpaid FMLA leave.[19]

Job Restoration

Upon return from FMLA leave, an employee must be restored to his or her original job, or to an "equivalent" job, which means virtually identical to the original job in terms of pay, benefits, and other employment terms and conditions.[20] In addition, an employee's use of FMLA leave cannot result in the loss of any employment benefit that the employee earned or was entitled to before using (but not necessarily during) FMLA leave.[21]

WORDS OF WISDOM: "Key" Employee Exception—Under limited circumstances where restoration to employment will cause "substantial and grievous economic injury" to a company's operations, an employer may refuse to reinstate certain highly-paid, salaried "key" employees. In order to deny job restoration to an employee, the employer must notify the employee in writing of the employee's status as a key employee (as defined by FMLA) and the reasons for denying job restoration, as well as provide the employee a reasonable opportunity to return to work after notifying the employee of his or her status as a "key" employee.[22]

Employee Notice

Eligible employees seeking to use FMLA leave may be required to provide:
- 30-day advance notice of the need to take FMLA leave when the need is foreseeable;[23]
- Notice "as soon as practicable" when the need to take FMLA leave is not foreseeable (as soon as practicable generally means at least verbal notice to the employer within one or two business days of learning of the need to take FMLA leave);[24]
- Sufficient information for the employer to understand that the employee needs leave for FMLA-qualifying reasons;[25] and
- Where the employer was not made aware that an employee was absent for FMLA reasons and the employee wants the leave counted as FMLA leave, timely notice (generally within two business days of returning to work) that the leave was taken for an FMLA-qualifying reason.[26]

WORDS OF WISDOM: The employee need not mention "FMLA" when requesting leave to meet the requirement of putting the employer on notice of FMLA-qualifying leave if the employee gives a qualifying reason why the leave is needed![27]

Employer Notice

Covered employers must take the following steps to provide information to employees about FMLA:

- Post a notice approved by the Secretary of Labor explaining employee rights and responsibilities under FMLA (employers can obtain a poster from the Department of Labor by visiting the DOL website at http://www.dol.gov/esa/regs/compliance/posters/fmla.htm);

- Include information about employee rights and obligations under FMLA in employee handbooks or other written materials, including collective bargaining agreements; or

- If handbooks or other written materials do not exist, provide general written guidance about employee rights and obligations under FMLA whenever an employee requests leave (employers can obtain a poster from the Department of Labor by visiting the DOL website at http://www.dol.gov/esa/regs/compliance/posters/fmla.htm); and

- Provide a written notice designating the leave as FMLA leave and detailing specific expectations and obligations of an employee who is exercising his or her FMLA entitlements. The employer may use the "Employer Response to Employee Request for Family or Medical Leave" Form WH-381, to meet this requirement. Form WH-381 can be obtained by visiting the "forms" link at Department of Labor Website at www.dol.gov. Written employer notice should be provided to the employee within one or two business days after receiving the employee's notice of need for leave.[28]

WORDS OF WISDOM: According to FMLA regulations, where an employer's workforce is comprised of a significant portion of workers who are not literate in English, the employer shall be responsible for providing FMLA notices in a language in which the employees are literate. The Department of Labor Website provides posters in Spanish and may provide translations in other languages. See www.dol.gov. [29]

Certification

An employer may require that the need for leave for a serious health condition of the employee or the employee's immediate family member be supported by medical certification issued by a health care provider. The employer must allow the employee at least 15 calendar days to obtain the medical certification. Moreover, an employer may, at its own expense, require the employee to obtain a second medical certification from a health care provider. The employer may choose the health care provider for the second opinion, except that in most cases the employer may not regularly contract with or otherwise regularly use the services of the health care provider.[30]

If the opinions of the employee's health care provider and the employer's health care provider differ, the employer may require the employee to obtain medical certification from a third health care provider, again at the employer's expense. The third opinion shall be final and binding. The third health care provider must be approved jointly by the employer and the employee.[31] The optional Department of Labor's "Certification of Healthcare Provider" Form WH-380, can be obtained at the DOL website at http://www.dol.gov/esa/whd/fmla/#form. Although the Form WH-380 is optional, it is recommended.

Health Care Provider

Health care providers who may provide medical certification of a serious health condition include:

- Doctors of medicine or osteopathy authorized to practice medicine or surgery (as appropriate) by the state in which the doctor practices;
- Podiatrists, dentists, clinical psychologists, optometrists, and chiropractors (limited to treatment consisting of manual manipulation of the spine to correct a subluxation as demonstrated by X-ray to exist) authorized to practice in the state and performing within the scope of their practice under state law;
- Nurse practitioners, nurse-midwives, and clinical social workers authorized to practice under state law and performing within the scope of their practice as defined under state law;
- Christian Science practitioners listed with the First Church of Christ, Scientist in Boston, Massachusetts;
- Any health care provider recognized by the employer or the employer's group health plan's benefits manager; and
- A health care provider listed above who practices in a country other than the United States and who is authorized to practice under the laws of that country.[32]

Protection of Employees Requesting or Taking FMLA Leave

The FMLA makes it unlawful for any employer to interfere with, restrain, or deny the exercise of any right provided by the FMLA. It is also unlawful for an employer to discharge or discriminate against any individual for opposing any practice, or because of involvement in any proceeding, related to the FMLA. Employers cannot use the taking of FMLA leave as a negative factor in employment actions such as hiring, promotions, or disciplinary actions; nor can FMLA leave be counted under "no fault" attendance policies.[33]

WORDS OF WISDOM: Spouses employed by the same employer may be limited to a combined total of 12 workweeks of family leave for: the birth and care of a child; the placement of a child for adoption or foster care, and to care for the newly placed child; and to care for an employee's parent who has a serious health condition.[34]

What Records Must Employers Keep?

The FMLA provides that covered employers shall make, keep, and preserve records pertaining to their obligations under the FMLA.[35] No particular order or form of records is required. However, employers must keep the records specified by the regulations for no less than three years and make them available for inspection, copying, and transcription by representatives of the Department of Labor upon request.[36]

The FMLA records may be maintained and preserved on microfilm or other basic source document of an automated data processing memory provided that adequate projection or viewing equipment is available, that the reproductions are clear and identifiable by date or pay period, and that extensions or transcriptions of the information can be and are made available upon request. Records kept in computer form must be made available for transcription or copying.[37]

Covered employers who have eligible employees must maintain records that disclose the following:

- Basic payroll and identifying employee data, including name, address, and occupation; rate or basis of pay and terms of compensation; daily and weekly hours worked per pay period; additions to or deductions from wages; and total compensation paid;
- Dates FMLA leave is taken by FMLA eligible employees (e.g., available from time records, requests for leave, etc., if so designated). Leave must be designated in records as FMLA leave; leave so designated may not include leave required under state law or an employer plan which is not also covered by FMLA;
- If FMLA leave is taken by eligible employees in increments of less than one full day, the hours of the leave;
- Copies of employee notices of leave furnished to the employer under FMLA, if in writing, and copies of all general and specific written notices given to

employees as required under FMLA and the regulations. Copies may be maintained in employee personnel files;

- Any documents (including written and electronic records) describing employee benefits or employer policies and practices regarding the taking of paid and unpaid leaves;
- Premium payments of employee benefits; and
- Records of any dispute between the employer and an eligible employee regarding designation of leave as FMLA leave, including any written statement from the employer or employee regarding the reasons for the designation and for the disagreement.[38]

Records and documents relating to medical certifications, re-certifications, or medical histories of employees or employees' family members created for the purposes of the FMLA, shall be maintained as confidential medical records in separate files and records from the usual personnel files, and if the ADA is also applicable, such records shall be maintained in conformance with ADA confidentiality requirements,[39] except that:

- Supervisors and managers may be informed regarding necessary restrictions of the work or duties of an employee and necessary accommodations;
- First aid and safety personnel may be informed (when appropriate) if the employee's physical or medical condition might require emergency treatment; and
- Government officials investigating compliance with FMLA (or other pertinent law) shall be provided relevant information upon request.[40]

Colorado Law Regarding Employment Leave

Maternity and Paternity Leave for Adoptions

Colorado does not have a state version of the FMLA, but Colorado does provide that an employer who permits employees paternity or maternity time off for biological parents following the birth of a child shall make such time off available for individuals adopting a child, if the employee requests time off. If the employer has established a policy providing time off for biological parents, that period of time shall be the minimum period of leave available for adoptive parents.[41]

Requests for additional leave due to the adoption of an ill child or a child with a disability shall be considered on the same basis as comparable cases of such complications accompanying the birth of such a child to an employee or employee's spouse. Any other benefits provided by the employer, such as job guarantee or pay, shall be available to both adoptive and biological parents on an equal basis. An employer shall not penalize an employee for exercising the rights provided by this law.[42]

WORDS OF WISDOM: The state law requiring leave for adoptive parents on the same basis as natural parents does not apply to an adoption by the spouse of a custodial parent.[43]

Jury Duty

Colorado state law requires employers to grant employees leave for grand jury or trial jury duty.[44] For the first three days of jury duty, employers are required to pay regular wages, but not to exceed fifty dollars per day unless by mutual agreement between the employee and employer. Regular employment includes part-time, temporary, and casual employment if the employment hours may be determined by a schedule, custom, or practice established during the three-month period proceeding the juror's term of service.[45]

The jury duty law also prohibits employers from depriving an employed juror of employment or any benefits as a result of jury duty. In addition, the jury duty law also prohibits harassment, threats, and coercion of an employee because of jury duty. Employers may not make any demands of any employed juror that will substantially interfere with the effective performance of juror service.[46]

WORDS OF WISDOM: The employed juror may sue his or her employer in court for damages and/or an order from the court for a violation of the jury duty law and may seek triple damages and reasonable attorney fees for willful misconduct by the employer. Criminal provisions also apply in the event of the willful harassment of a juror.[47]

Voting

Colorado law also protects employees' rights to vote. The Colorado voting law specifically provides that any registered voter entitled to vote in any municipal election held within the state is entitled to two hours of leave between the time of opening and time of closing the polls. Employers may not discharge a voter for leaving to vote, nor can the employer deduct any wages or salary, even for hourly workers. However, employed voters must apply for leave to vote prior to the election day. While the employer may specify the hours during which the employee may take leave to vote, if the employee requests leave at the beginning or end of the work shift the employer must comply with the request.[48]

WORDS OF WISDOM: The Colorado voting law does not require leave for employees who are scheduled to be off work for three or more hours between the time of opening and the time of closing of the polls.[49]

The Colorado voting law also provides that it is unlawful for any employer (or the agent of an employer) to refuse any employees the privilege of taking time off to vote as provided by the law, or to influence the vote of any employee.[50]

WORDS OF WISDOM: Within 90 days before any election, employers may not exhibit any handbill, notice, or placard containing any threat, notice, or information that work will cease, wages will be reduced, or any other threat in the event of the election of any particular candidate or issue. The Colorado voting law also forbids putting pay in an envelope with any political statements on it. Criminal penalties apply to violations of these provisions.[51]

Military Leave

Both federal and state laws require employers to give leave to employees who serve in the military. The federal law is called the Uniformed Services Employment and Reemployment Rights Act (USERRA).[52] The state law is called the Military and Veterans Act. The purposes of USERRA and the Military and Veterans Act are:

- To encourage non-career service in the uniformed services by eliminating or minimizing the disadvantages to civilian careers and employment which can result from such service;
- To minimize disruption to the lives of persons performing service in the uniformed services as well as to their employers, their fellow employees, and their communities, by providing for the prompt reemployment of such persons upon their completion of such service; and
- To prohibit discrimination against individuals because of their service in the uniformed services.

Federal Law: Uniformed Services Employment and Reemployment Rights Act (USERRA)

The following is a brief summary of some of the provisions of the federal laws governing military leave. Because there are many more provisions, as well as numerous court interpretations, employers should consult legal counsel with particular questions before taking specific actions. The following section addresses basic provisions, such as which individuals are covered and general rights to reemployment and benefits.

Who is Covered?

The USERRA applies to an "employee," meaning any person employed by an employer, including citizens, nationals, and permanent resident workers. For purposes of the USERRA, "employer" is defined as any person, institution, organization, or other entity that pays salary or wages for work performed or that has control over employment opportunities.[53]

Notice Requirements

Ordinarily, the employee is required to provide advance notice of the need to take a leave of absence. This requirement is waived if it would be unreasonable or impossible to provide such notice, or if advance notice is prevented by military necessity.[54]

Rights to Reemployment and Benefits

A person who is reemployed under the federal law is entitled to the seniority and other rights and benefits determined by seniority that the person had on the date of the commencement of service in the uniformed services, plus the additional seniority and rights and benefits that such person would have attained if the person had remained continuously employed.[55]

The USERRA does not require the employer to provide any benefits to which the employee would not otherwise be entitled if the employee had not taken the leave.[56] Also, if the employee would be required to pay the cost of benefits while not on leave, the employee may be required to pay the employee cost while on military leave if other employees on leaves of absence are required to do so.[57] Because there are additional special provisions regarding benefits and benefit plans in the USERRA, employers should consult legal counsel with specific concerns.

Leave Treated as Furlough or Leave of Absence

A person who is absent from a position of employment by reason of service in the uniformed services shall be deemed to be on furlough or leave of absence while performing such service. This individual is entitled to such other rights and benefits *not determined by seniority* as the employer provides to other employees having similar seniority, status, and pay who are on furlough or leave of absence under a contract, agreement, policy, practice, or plan in effect at the beginning of the military leave or while the individual is out on military leave.[58]

Notice of Intent Not to Return

A person who is absent from a position of employment by reason of service in the uniformed services, and who knowingly provides written notice of intent not to return to a position of employment after service in the uniformed services, is not entitled to the rights and benefits described in the preceding paragraphs.[59]

Limits on Ability to Terminate Employee

Employers may not terminate an employee who is reemployed after a military leave of absence, except for cause, within one year after the date of such reemployment, if the person's period of service before the reemployment was more than 180 days. If the person's period of service before the reemployment was more than 30 days but less than 181 days, the employer may not terminate an employee within 180 days after the date of reemployment.[60]

Employee's Substitution of Paid Leave for Military Leave

Any person whose employment with an employer is interrupted by a period of service in the uniformed services shall be able to use paid vacation, annual leave, or similar leave time before the beginning of the military service if he or she so requests. However, employers may not require use of the paid leave.[61]

Leave for Funeral Honors Duty

An employer shall grant an employee who is a member of a reserve component an authorized leave of absence from a position of employment to allow that employee to perform funeral honors duty as authorized by the USERRA.[62]

Length of Reemployment Protection Rights

Generally, the USERRA grants employees certain rights to be reemployed so long as the cumulative period of military service does not exceed five years. To be eligible for reemployment, the employee must either report for reemployment or submit an application for reemployment within a specified period after concluding service in the uniformed services.[63] Exceptions from the five-year limitation are made for periods of war or other national emergency.[64]

Colorado Military and Veterans Act

Private Employees—Annual Military Leave

Colorado law requires employers to provide up to 15 days a year of unpaid leave for military training for non-temporary employees who are duly qualified members of the Colorado National Guard or the reserve forces of the United States. Employees who provide evidence of the satisfactory completion of such training, and who are still qualified to perform the duties of their positions are entitled to be restored to their previous or similar employment positions in the same status, pay, and seniority.[65]

Such absence for military training will in no way affect the employee's right to receive normal vacation, sick leave, bonus, advancement, and other advantages of his or her employment normally to be anticipated in his or her particular position.[66]

Penalties and Remedies

Criminal penalties and civil remedies apply to violations of the Colorado Military and Veterans Act.[67]

Anti-discrimination Provisions

Under Colorado law, no person shall discriminate against any officer or enlisted person of the military forces of the state because of the officer or enlisted person's membership in the military.[68] In addition, no employer, officer, or agent of any corporation, company, or firm or other person shall take the following actions:

- Refuse to hire any person for, or discharge any person from, employment because of the person's status as an officer or enlisted person of the military forces of the state;
- Hinder or prevent the person from performing any military service he or she may be called upon to perform by proper authority; or
- Dissuade any person from enlistment in the National Guard by threat or injury to such person with respect to the person's employment, trade, or business.[69]

Penalties and Remedies of Anti-discrimination Provision

Any person violating any of the provisions of the anti-discrimination section of the Colorado Military and Veterans Act is guilty of a misdemeanor and, upon conviction, shall be punished by a fine of not more than five thousand dollars. In addition, the aggrieved person may bring an action at law for damages for such noncompliance or apply to the district court for such equitable relief as is just and proper under the circumstances.[70]

WORDS OF WISDOM: Employers can do more than the law requires! While employment laws regarding leaves for medical reasons, to vote, for jury duty, and for military service provide the minimum requirements for employee leaves, employers always can elect to provide more generous leave policies, as long as the employers treat similarly situated employees consistently.

FOOTNOTES

1. 29 U.S.C. § 2601.
2. 29 U.S.C. § 2611(4).
3. 29 U.S.C. § 2611(2).
4. 29 U.S.C. § 2612(a)(1).
5. 29 U.S.C. § 2612(b)(1).
6. *Id.*
7. 29 C.F.R. § 825.203(d).
8. 29 U.S.C. § 2612(e)(2)(A).
9. 29 U.S.C. § 2612(b)(2).
10. 29 U.S.C. § 2612(d)(2); 29 C.F.R. § 825.207; 29 C.F.R. § 825.301(b)(1)(iii).
11. 29 U.S.C. § 2611(11); 29 C.F.R. § 825.114.
12. 29 U.S.C. § 2612(a)(2).
13. 29 U.S.C. § 2614(c)(1).
14. 29 C.F.R. § 825.210.
15. 29 C.F.R. § 825.209(f).
16. 29 C.F.R. § 825.212(a)(1).
17. 29 U.S.C. § 2614(c)(2).
18. 29 C.F.R. § 825.209(h).
19. 29 C.F.R. § 825.213(b).
20. 29 U.S.C. § 2614(a)(1); 29 C.F.R. § 825.215(a).
21. 29 U.S.C. § 2614(a)(2).
22. 29 U.S.C. § 2614(b); 29 C.F.R. § 825.217.
23. 29 U.S.C. § 2612(e)(1); 29 C.F.R. § 825.302(a).
24. 29 U.S.C. § 2612(e)(1); 29 C.F.R. § 825.302(a) – (b).
25. 29 C.F.R. § 825.302(c).
26. 29 C.F.R. § 825.208.
27. 29 C.F.R. § 825.302(c).
28. 29 U.S.C. § 2619; 29 C.F.R. § 825.300; 29 C.F.R. § 825.301.
29. 29 C.F.R. § 825.300(c).
30. 29 U.S.C. § 2613(a) – (c); 29 C.F.R. § 825.305; 29 C.F.R. § 825.307(a) – (b).
31. 29 U.S.C. § 2613(d); 29 C.F.R. § 825.307(c).
32. 29 U.S.C. § 2611(6); 29 C.F.R. § 825.818.
33. 29 U.S.C. § 2615; 29 C.F.R. § 825.220.
34. 29 U.S.C. § 2612(f).
35. 29 U.S.C. § 2616(b).
36. 29 C.F.R. § 825.500(b).
37. *Id.*

[38] 29 C.F.R. §825.500(c).

[39] 29 C.F.R. § 825.500(g).

[40] *Id.*

[41] C.R.S. § 19-5-211(1.5).

[42] *Id.*

[43] *Id.*

[44] C.R.S. § 13-71-134.

[45] C.R.S. § 13-71-126.

[46] C.R.S. § 13-71-134.

[47] *Id.*

[48] C.R.S. § 1-7-102(1).

[49] C.R.S. § 1-7-102(2).

[50] C.R.S. § 31-10-1522(1)(a), (b).

[51] C.R.S. § 31-10-1522(1)(c), (1)(d), (2).

[52] 38 U.S.C. §§ 4301 to 4333.

[53] 38 U.S.C. § 4303(3), (4).

[54] 38 U.S.C. § 4312(a)(1), (b).

[55] 38 U.S.C. § 4316(a).

[56] 38 U.S.C. § 4316(b)(3).

[57] 38 U.S.C. § 4316(b)(4).

[58] 38 U.S.C. § 4316(b)(1).

[59] 38 U.S.C. § 4316(b)(2).

[60] 38 U.S.C. § 4316(c).

[61] 38 U.S.C. § 4316(d).

[62] 38 U.S.C. § 4316(e)(1).

[63] 38 U.S.C. § 4312(a).

[64] 38 U.S.C. § 4312(c).

[65] C.R.S. § 28-3-609.

[66] C.R.S. § 28-3-610.

[67] C.R.S. § 28-3-611.

[68] C.R.S. § 28-3-506(1).

[69] *Id.*

[70] C.R.S. § 28-3-506(2).

CHAPTER 13:
A Wage and Hour Primer—Everybody Loves Payday!

Overview of Wages

Everybody loves payday, right? Some employers who are working their way through the federal and state laws may not like it so much. This chapter provides an overview of the federal and state wage and hour laws in hopes of making it easier for employers to navigate the maze of regulations and laws in this area.

Fair Labor Standards Act (FLSA) and Colorado Minimum Wage Order Number 22

The Fair Labor Standards Act (FLSA) is the federal law that establishes minimum wage, overtime pay, recordkeeping, and child labor standards affecting full-time and part-time workers.[1] Colorado Minimum Wage Order Number 22 has several provisions similar to the FLSA.[2] The following discussion about the FLSA and Colorado Minimum Wage Order Number 22 addresses who is covered by the FLSA, the employment relationship, minimum wage, overtime, common exemptions, recordkeeping and posting requirements, as well as an overview of what the FLSA does *not* require.

Covered Employers

Although the FLSA states that it covers businesses with an annual gross volume of business or sales of $500,000 or more,[3] it also covers employers who are engaged in "interstate commerce."[4] This means that the FLSA applies to virtually all businesses because the courts have interpreted "interstate commerce" extremely broadly. For example, interstate commerce has been interpreted to include employers who regularly use the mail, telephones, or telegraph for interstate communication; or employers who keep records of interstate transactions; or employers who handle, ship, or receive goods moving in interstate commerce.

Employment Relationship

Chapter 1 discussed some of the differences between employees and independent contractors for the purposes of tax consequences. For the purposes of the FLSA, it is also important to distinguish between employees and independent contractors; however, the tests under the FLSA used to make that determination are different from the tests used by the IRS. Under the FLSA, an employee is one who, as a matter of economic reality, follows the usual path of an employee and is dependent on the business which he or she serves.[5]

WORDS OF WISDOM: Unlike the IRS test discussed in Chapter 1, for purposes of the FLSA certain factors don't matter in determining whether there is an employment relationship, including where work is performed, the absence of a formal employment agreement, or the time or mode of pay.

For the purposes of the FLSA, relevant factors in distinguishing an independent contractor from an employee include:[6]
- The extent to which the services rendered are an integral part of the business;
- The permanency of the relationship;
- The amount of the alleged contractor's investment in facilities and equipment;
- The nature and degree of control by the business;
- The alleged contractor's opportunities for profit and loss;
- The amount of initiative, judgment, or foresight in open market competition with others required for the success of the claimed independent contractor; and
- The degree of independent business organization and operation.

> **WORDS OF WISDOM:** Domestic service workers such as day workers, housekeepers, chauffeurs, cooks, or full-time babysitters are covered by the FLSA if their cash wages from one employer are at least $1,000 in a calendar year (or the amount designated pursuant to an adjustment provision in the Internal Revenue Code), or they work a total of more than 8 hours a week for one or more employers.[7]

Minimum Wage

FLSA-covered nonexempt workers are entitled to a minimum wage of not less than $5.15 an hour.[8] The law provides minimum wage exceptions under limited circumstances to full-time students, youths under the age of 20 in their first 90 days of employment, tipped employees, some disabled workers, and student-learners.[9]

> **WORDS OF WISDOM:** The FLSA prohibits deductions from wages for such items as cash or merchandise shortages, employer-required uniforms, and tools of the trade, if the deductions reduce the wages of employees below the minimum wage or reduce the amount of overtime pay due under the FLSA.[10]

Overtime Pay

Overtime pay at a rate of not less than one and one-half times their regular rate of pay is required after 40 hours of work in a workweek for FLSA-covered nonexempt workers.[11] Some exceptions to the 40 hours per week standard apply under special circumstances to police officers and fire fighters employed by public agencies and to employees of hospitals and nursing homes.[12]

WORDS OF WISDOM: Overtime violations can be costly. Precision Cleaning Services, a Colorado-based janitorial service that contracts with retailers including Wal-Mart, Kmart, Target, Home Depot, Rite-Aid, and other stores in 10 states nationwide, will pay $409,954.72 in back overtime wages to 621 employees following a FLSA investigation conducted by the U. S. Department of Labor's (DOL) Wage and Hour Division in 2002.[13] According to the DOL, an investigation of Precision Cleaning Services revealed that janitorial workers were being paid straight time for all hours worked beyond 40 per week and that certain salaried supervisors were also entitled to overtime compensation. No additional penalties were assessed in the Precision Cleaning Services case because the company had no prior history of violations under the FLSA.

FLSA Exemption Issues

What does it mean to be exempt from the FLSA? Employers do not need to pay "exempt" employees overtime or minimum wages, depending on the exemption.[14] Employers should be aware of the common exemptions to the FLSA.

"White Collar Exemptions"— Executive, Administrative, Professional, and Outside Sales

So called "white collar" employees are exempt from the minimum wage and overtime requirements of the FLSA,[15] provided these employees meet certain tests regarding job duties and responsibilities and are compensated "on a salary basis" at not less than stated amounts. Subject to certain exceptions set forth in the regulations, in order to be considered "salaried," employees must receive their full salary for any workweek in which they perform any work without regard to the number of days or hours worked. This rule applies to each employee that has a salary requirement (outside sales employees, and certain licensed or certified doctors, lawyers, and teachers have no salary requirement).[16] The special exemption requirements that apply to each category of "white collar" employees are summarized on the following pages.

Executive Exemption

The executive exemption is applicable to employees who meet the following requirements:

- Have management as their primary duty;
- Direct the work of two or more full-time employees;
- Have the authority to hire and fire or make recommendations regarding decisions affecting the employment status of others;
- Regularly exercise a high degree of independent judgment in their work;
- Receive a salary which meets the requirements of the exemption; and
- Do not devote more than 20 percent of their time to non-management functions (40 percent in retail and service establishments).[17]

Administrative Exemption

The administrative exemption applies to employees who meet the following requirements:

- Perform office or non-manual work which is directly related to the management policies or general business operations of their employer or their employer's customers, or perform such functions in the administration of an educational establishment;
- Regularly exercise discretion and judgment in their work;
- Assist a proprietor or executive or administrator, perform specialized or technical work, or execute special assignments;
- Receive a salary which meets the requirements of the exemption; and
- Do not devote more than 20 percent of their time to work other than that described above (40 percent in retail and service establishments).[18]

Professional Exemption

The professional exemption is applicable to employees who perform work requiring advanced knowledge and education, work in an artistic field which is original and creative, work as a teacher, or work as a computer system analyst, programmer, software engineer, or similarly skilled worker in the computer software field, and who:

- Regularly exercise discretion and judgment;
- Perform work which is intellectual and varied in character, the accomplishment of which cannot be standardized as to time;
- Receive a salary which meets the requirements of the exemption (except doctors, lawyers, teachers and certain computer occupations); and
- Do not devote more than 20 percent of their time to work other than that described above.[19]

Outside Sales Exemption

The outside sales exemption is applicable to employees who engage in making sales or obtaining orders away from their employer's place of business and who do not devote more than 20 percent of the hours worked by non-exempt employees of the employer to work other than the making of such sales.[20]

WORDS OF WISDOM: The DOL proposes to update and revise the regulations relating to the "white collar" exemptions, including executive, administrative, professional, outside sales, and computer employees. Currently, to be considered exempt, employees must meet certain minimum tests related to their primary job duties and be paid on a salary basis at not less than specified minimum amounts. These basic tests have been essentially unchanged since the 1950s. As of September of 2003, the United States Senate had voted to block the proposed changes to the exemptions, and the U.S. House rejected a similar bill in July.[21] However the Department of Labor intends to press the issue forward.[22]

Common Trouble Spots for Employers Applying the White Collar Exemption

According to the DOL, some common mistakes employers make in applying the white collar exemption are as follows:[23]

- Employers without a formal sick leave policy docking salaried, exempt employees for time missed from work because of sickness;
- Employees not receiving full salary payments each week;
- Employees performing routine production type duties that seem related to general business operations but which have no bearing on setting management policies;
- Employees who hold degrees performing jobs which are not professional in nature or to which the degree they hold is not applicable;
- Employers confusing acquired job skills with the exercise of independent judgment and discretion; and
- Employees placed on salary and classified as exempt without regard to duties or percentage of time spent in exempt duties.

Computer Specialists Exemption

Certain computer professionals paid at least $27.63 per hour (a salary of at least $170.00 per week) are exempt from the overtime provisions of the FLSA.[24]

Commissioned Sales Employees Exemption

Commissioned sales employees of retail or service establishments are exempt from overtime if:

1. More than half of the employee's earnings come from commissions; and
2. The employee averages at least one and one-half times the minimum wage for each hour worked.[25]

WORDS OF WISDOM: Employers should double check exemptions often, as they frequently change. Legal counsel can help review exemptions, or employers can contact the DOL. See www.dol.gov.

Additional Exempt Workers

Other workers exempt from the minimum wage and overtime pay provisions of the FLSA include: workers on small farms, newspaper delivery workers, some switchboard operators, and employees of seasonal amusement or recreational businesses.[26] The following chart of additional FLSA exemptions is provided as a general reference.[27]

Employee Type	Exempt from Overtime	Exempt from Minimum Wage	Exempt from Child Labor
Agricultural Buyers	X		
Aircraft Sales	X		
Airline Employees	X		
Amusement/Recreational Employees	X		
Babysitters (if less than 8 hours a week and less than $1,000/yr from a single employer)	X	X	
Boat Sales	X		
Companions for Elderly Individuals	X	X	
Domestic Employees / Live-in	X		
Farm Sales	X		
Federal Criminal Investigators	X	X	
Firefighters/less than 5 employees in public fire departments	X		
Fishing	X	X	
Forestry Employees/less than 9 employees	X		
Fruit and Vegetable Harvest Transporters	X		
Livestock Auction Employees	X		
Local Delivery Drivers	X		
Newspaper Deliverers	X	X	X
Switchboard Operators	X	X	

Employee Type	Exempt from Overtime	Exempt from Minimum Wage	Exempt from Child Labor
Taxi Drivers	X		
Truck and Trailer Sales	X		
Young Actors/Performers			X

FLSA Record Keeping Requirements

The FLSA requires employers to keep accurate records of hours worked and wages paid to employees.[28] The FLSA requires no particular form for the records, but does require that the records include certain identifying information about the employee and data about the hours worked and the wages earned. The following is a listing of the basic records that an employer must maintain:[29]

- Employee's full name and Social Security number;
- Employee's address, including zip code;
- Employee's birth date, if younger than 19;
- Employee's sex and occupation;
- Time and day of week when employee's workweek begins;
- Hours employee worked each day;
- Total hours employee worked each workweek;
- Basis on which employee's wages are paid (e.g., "$6 an hour," "$220 a week," "piecework");
- Employee's regular hourly pay rate;
- Employee's total daily or weekly straight-time earnings;
- Employee's total overtime earnings for the workweek;
- All additions to or deductions from the employee's wages;
- Total wages paid to employee each pay period; and
- Date of payment and the pay period covered by the payment.

Posting Requirements

Every employer of employees subject to the FLSA's minimum wage provisions must post, and keep posted, a notice explaining the FLSA in a conspicuous place in all of the employer's establishments so as to permit employees to readily read the notice. The content of the notice is prescribed by the Wage and Hour Division of the DOL. An approved copy of the minimum wage poster is made available on the DOL's website at www.dol.gov for informational purposes or for employers to use as posters.

What Does the FLSA Not Require?

While the FLSA has several significant requirements, there are some common misconceptions about the FLSA, so it is important to examine some things the FLSA does *not* require:[30]

- If employers comply with the minimum wage, the FLSA does not require pay raises;
- The FLSA does not require extra pay for weekend or night work;
- There is no requirement in the FLSA for severance pay;
- The FLSA does not require breaks or meal periods be given to workers (but Colorado state law does require breaks or meal periods be given to workers under certain circumstances—see below);[31]
- The FLSA does not require performance evaluations;
- The FLSA does not limit the number of hours per day or per week that employees aged 16 years and older can work;
- Because the FLSA has no provisions regarding the scheduling of employees (with the exception of certain child labor provisions), an employer may change an employee's work hours without giving prior notice or obtaining the employee's consent (unless there is a prior agreement to the contrary). However, under Colorado law a change in hours may entitle the employee to unemployment insurance benefits;[32]
- The FLSA has no requirement for double-time pay; and
- The FLSA does not require an employer to provide employees pay stubs (but Colorado law does—see below)[33]

Enforcement of the Overtime Laws

The United States Department of Labor may recover back wages, either administratively or through court action, for employees that have been underpaid in violation of the FLSA.[34] Violations of the FLSA may result in civil or criminal action. Fines of up to $1,000 per violation apply to employers who willfully or repeatedly violate the minimum wage or overtime pay provisions. The FLSA prohibits discriminating against or discharging workers who file a complaint or participate in any proceedings under the FLSA.[35]

WORDS OF WISDOM: Both the FLSA[36] and Colorado Minimum Wage Order Number 22[37] contain anti-discrimination and anti-retaliation provisions.

Colorado Minimum Wage Order Number 22

As stated above, Colorado Minimum Wage Order Number 22[38] has many provisions similar to the FLSA, including minimum wage and overtime requirements. Additionally, Colorado Minimum Wage Order Number 22 sets forth requirements for tips, exemptions (such as for ski area workers), and posting requirements. The Colorado Minimum Wage poster can be obtained at the Colorado Department of Labor's website at http://www.coworkforce.com/LAB/wageposter.html.

Two provisions of note that are required by Colorado Minimum Wage Order Number 22 that are *not* provided in the FLSA are requirements for meal and rest periods.[39]

Meal Periods

Generally, employees shall be entitled to an uninterrupted and "duty free" meal period of at least a thirty-minute duration when the scheduled work shift exceeds five consecutive hours of work. The employees must be completely relieved of all duties and be permitted to pursue personal activities to qualify as a non-work, uncompensated period of time. When the nature of the business activity or other circumstances exist that makes an uninterrupted meal period impractical, the employee shall be permitted to consume an "on-duty" meal while performing duties. Employees shall be permitted to fully consume a meal of choice "on the job" and be fully compensated for the "on-duty" meal period without any loss of time or compensation.

Rest Periods

Every employer shall authorize and permit rest periods, which, insofar as practicable, shall be in the middle of each four hour work period. A compensated ten minute rest period for each four hours or major fractions thereof shall be permitted for all employees. Such rest periods shall not be deducted from the employee's wages. It is not necessary that the employee leave the premises for the rest period.

Colorado Wage Act

Pay Day

Under Colorado law, all wages or compensation earned by any employee in any employment (other than profit-sharing, pension, or other deferred compensation plans), shall be due and payable for regular pay periods of no greater duration than one calendar month or thirty days, whichever is longer, and on regular paydays no later than ten days following the close of each pay period unless the employer and the employee mutually agree on any other alternative period of wage or salary payments.[40]

In agricultural and horticultural pursuits and in stock or poultry raising, when the employee is boarded and lodged by the employer, all wages or compensation earned by any employee shall be due and payable for regular periods of no greater duration than one month and on paydays no later than ten days following the close of each pay period.[41]

Pay Stubs

According to Colorado law, every employer shall at least monthly, or at the time of each payment of wages or compensation, furnish to each employee an itemized pay statement in writing showing the following:[42]
- Gross wages earned;
- All withholdings and deductions;
- Net wages earned;
- The inclusive dates of the pay period;
- The name of the employee or the employee's Social Security number; and
- The name and address of the employer.

Hiring Kids: The Minimum Employers Should Know About Child Labor Laws

Employment laws generally try to protect children from unsafe working environments, as well as from long work hours. Employees under the age of 18 have special protections under both state and federal laws. The FLSA[43] is the federal law that applies to young employees, and the DOL enforces the FSLA. In Colorado, the Colorado Youth Employment Opportunity Act[44] is the state law, and the Colorado Department of Labor and Employment enforces that law. There are additional regulations regarding the employment of minors, which are not discussed here (e.g. agriculture and theatrical). For detailed information on the employment of minors in Colorado, employers can contact the Colorado Department of Labor. The following section is a synopsis of the basic employment rules applying to children.

Permissible Jobs for Kids

Generally children under the age of 14 are not permitted to work in Colorado.[45] According to the Colorado Department of Labor, minors aged 9 or older may work *only* in the following non-hazardous occupations:[46]
- Delivery of handbills;
- Delivery of advertising and advertising samples;

- Shoe shining;
- Gardening and lawn care involving no power driven lawn equipment;
- Cleaning of walks involving no power-driven equipment;
- Casual work in the home of the employer not prohibited; and
- Caddying; and
- Other specified occupations.

Individuals aged 12 and older may work in the following non-hazardous occupations:[47]

- Sale and delivery of periodicals and door-to-door selling of merchandise and delivery thereof;
- Baby-sitting;
- Gardening and lawn care, including use of power-driven machines if approved by the division or the minor has received training;
- Cleaning walks, including the use of power-driven snow removal equipment;
- Agricultural work except that declared hazardous by the FLSA; and
- Other approved occupations.

For children aged 14 and older, permissible occupations include:[48]

- Non-hazardous manufacturing;
- Public messenger service and errands by foot, bicycle, and public transportation;
- Operation of closed automatic freight and passenger elevators;
- Janitorial/custodial services;
- Office and clerical work;
- Warehousing and storage, including unloading and loading;
- Non-hazardous construction and repair work;
- Retail food service;
- Gas service stations (dispensing gas, oil, courtesy service, washing/polishing, etc.);
- Retail stores (selling, modeling, cashiering, window trimming, etc.);
- Restaurants, hotels, and motels—except the operation of power slicers; and
- Certain occupations related to parks and recreation.

Work Hours for Kids

The following chart sets forth the limitations under federal and state laws for the work hours for children under the age of 18 (to the extent that state and federal law vary, employers should follow the more restrictive requirements listed in the chart):[49]

Law	Age	Number of Hours	Time Restrictions
Federal	18-older	Unlimited	None
Federal	16-17	Unlimited	None
Federal	14-15	No more than 3 hours on a school day; No more than 18 hours in a school week; No more than 8 hours on a non-school day; No more than 40 hours in a non-school week.	Not before 7 a.m. or after 7 p.m. during the school year; From June 1 through Labor Day, evening hours extended to 9 p.m.
Colorado	Under 16	No more than 8 hours on a non-school day; No more than 40 hours in a non-school week.	Except babysitters, not between the hours of 9:30 p.m. and 5:00 a.m., unless the next day is not a school day.

In seasonal employment for the culture, harvest, or care of perishable products where wages are paid on a piece basis, a minor 14 years of age or older may be permitted to work hours in excess of the limitations; but in no case is the minor permitted to work more than 12 hours in any 24-hour period nor more than 30 hours in any 72-hour period, except that a minor 14 or 15 years of age may work more than 8 hours per day in only 10 days in any 30-day period.[50]

WORDS OF WISDOM: Violations of child labor laws can be costly. The DOL's Wage and Hour Division has fined a Utah based theater chain $22,230 in civil money penalties for allegedly employing minors in violation of federal child labor hours standards.[51] A total of 24 youths ages 14 and 15 were allegedly employed in violation of the hours and time-of-day standards of the FLSA. The alleged violations included employment of minors in the theatres later than 7:00 p.m. during the school year and later than 9:00 p.m. from June 1st to Labor Day. Youngsters also allegedly worked more than three hours on school days and more than 18 hours during school weeks, with work schedules allegedly exceeding the 7:00 p.m. standard by more than three hours on a routine basis. One minor was found working as late as 12:30 a.m. In this case, the penalty assessments were increased, because this employer had identical violations in a 1996 investigation.

Unsafe Working Environments for Kids

The U.S. and Colorado Departments of Labor have set forth a number of hazardous jobs workers 18 or younger can *never* perform:[52]

• Manufacturing, transporting or storing explosives;
• Driving a motor vehicle and being an outside helper on a motor vehicle;

- Coal or other mining;
- Oil drilling or quarrying;
- Logging and sawmilling;
- Anything involving exposure to radioactive substances and exposure to ionizing radiations;
- Anything involving power-driven hoisting equipment;
- Anything involving metal-forming, punching, and shearing machines;*
- Meat packing or processing (including anything involving power-driven meat slicing machines);
- Slaughtering/rendering of meat;
- Anything involving bakery machines;
- Anything involving paper-products machines;*
- Anything involving wood-working machines;*
- Manufacturing brick or other clay construction products or of silica refractory products, tile, and related products;
- Anything involving power-driven circular saws, band saws, and guillotine shears;*
- Anything involving automatic pin setting machines;
- Operation of a high pressure steam boiler or high temperature water boiler;
- Roofing operations;*
- Work involving the risk of falling from a height greater than 10 feet or more above the ground (except agriculture which is 20 feet or less);
- Excavation operations;*
- Wrecking/ demolition, and ship-breaking operations; and
- Wrecking/demolition, but not manual auto wrecking.

* The DOL makes limited exceptions in these types of jobs for apprentices and students. Additionally, special rules apply to farms and other types of agricultural businesses.

Enforcement of Child Labor Laws

The United States Department of Labor may recover back wages, either administratively or through court action, for employees that have been underpaid in violation of the FSLA.[53] Violations of the FLSA may result in civil or criminal action. Fines of up to $10,000 per violation may be assessed against employers who violate the child labor provisions of the FLSA. The FLSA also prohibits discriminating against or discharging workers who file a complaint or participate in any proceedings under the FLSA.[54]

FOOTNOTES

[1] 29 U.S.C. §§ 201 to 219.

[2] Colorado Minimum Wage Order No. 22, Aug. 1, 1998.

[3] 29 U.S.C. § 203(s)(1)(A)(ii).

[4] 29 U.S.C. § 207.

[5] Department of Labor, Fact Sheet #13, Employment Relationship Under the Fair Labor Standards Act, http://www.dol.gov/esa/regs/compliance/whd/whdfs13.htm

[6] *Id.*

[7] 29 U.S.C. § 206(f); 29 C.F.R. § 552.2(b).

[8] 29 U.S.C. § 206(a)(1).

[9] 29 U.S.C. § 206(g); 29 U.S.C. § 214(a), (b), (c); 29 U.S.C. § 203(m).

[10] 29 U.S.C. § 203(m); 29 C.F.R. § 531.3(d); *See also* Department of Labor E-Laws Advisor at http://www.dol.gov/elaws/esa/flsa/screen5.asp

[11] 29 U.S.C. § 207(a)(1).

[12] 29 U.S.C. § 207(j), (k).

[13] Precision Cleaning Services of Colorado Pays $409, 954 in Back Overtime to 621 Workers in Ten States, Department of Labor Press Release, 4/9/2003, http://www.dol.gov/esa/media/press/whd/whdpressVB.asp?pressdoc=denver/2003017

[14] 29 U.S.C. § 213.

[15] *Id.*

[16] 29 C.F.R. § 541.118; 29 C.F.R. § 541.212; 29 C.F.R. § 541.312.

[17] 29 C.F.R. § 541.1.

[18] 29 C.F.R. § 541.2.

[19] 29 C.F.R. § 541.3.

[20] 29 C.F.R. § 541.5.

[21] *Senate Votes to Block Changes to Overtime Rules,* HR Next, http:// www2.hrnext.com/, Sept. 12, 2003.

[22] *Statement of Labor Secretary Elaine L. Chao on U.S. Senate Vote to Block Proposal Updating White-Collar Overtime Rules,* OPA News Release: 09/10/2003, http://www.dol.gov/opa/media/press/opa/OPA2003480.htm

[23] Department of Labor, Fact Sheet # 17, Exemption for Executive, Administrative, Professional and Outside Sales Employees Under the Fair Labor Standards Act (FLSA) http://www.dol.gov/esa/regs/compliance/whd/whdfs17.htm

[24] 29 U.S.C. § 213(a)(17).

[25] Department of Labor, Handy Reference Guide to the FLSA, http://www.dol.gov/esa/regs/compliance/whd/hrg.htm

[26] *Id.*

[27] *Id.*

[28] 29 U.S.C. § 211(c).

[29] Department of Labor, Handy Reference Guide to the FLSA, http://www.dol.gov/esa/regs/compliance/whd/hrg.htm

[30] *Id.*

[31] Colorado Minimum Wage Order No. 22.

[32] C.R.S. § 8-73-103 (benefits for partial unemployment).

[33] C.R.S. § 8-4-105(4).

[34] *See* Department of Labor, Handy Reference Guide to the FLSA, http://www.dol.gov/esa/regs/compliance/whd/hrg.htm

[35] *Id.*

[36] 29 U.S.C. §§ 201, *et seq.*

[37] Colorado Minimum Wage Order No. 22.

[38] *Id.*

[39] *Id.*

[40] C.R.S. § 8-4-105(1).

[41] C.R.S. § 8-4-105(2).

[42] C.R.S. § 8-4-105(4).

[43] 29 U.S.C. §§ 201-219.

[44] C.R.S. §§ 8-12-101 to 8-12-117.

[45] C.R.S. § 8-12-105(1).

[46] C.R.S. § 8-12-106.

[47] C.R.S. § 8-12-107.

[48] C.R.S. § 8-12-108.

[49] *Id., See also,* 29 U.S.C. §§ 201, *et seq.*

[50] *Id.*

[51] Utah Theater Chain Fined $22230 for Child Labor Violations, News Release, 3/4/03, http://www.dol.gov/esa/media/press/whd/whdpressVB.asp?pressdoc=denver/2003009

[52] *See* Department of Labor, Youth and Labor, Hazardous Jobs, http://www.dol.gov/dol/topic/youthlabor/hazardousjobs.htm

[53] *See* Department of Labor, Handy Reference Guide to the FLSA, http://www.dol.gov/esa/regs/compliance/whd/hrg.htm

[54] *Id.*

CHAPTER 14:
Employee Privacy—Legally Healthy Boundaries in the Information Age

Overview of Employee Privacy

One of the fundamental values shared throughout the United States is the right to be free from intrusion into personal matters. From the beginnings of this country, the founders enacted strong protections for individual privacy rights. The right to privacy arguably is even more important today—in the information age of computers, video and audio surveillance, advanced medical technologies, voice mail, and e-mail.

Nevertheless, employers may have valid, legal reasons—justified by business necessity—to monitor some communications or find out specific information about their employees. However, the laws, including statutes and judicial cases, protect workers' reasonable expectations of privacy. Employees may have a legitimate expectation that employers will not intrude into employees' communications, especially if employers have not told their employees otherwise. The employees' expectation of privacy means that employers should plan in advance why and how the employer may legally obtain business related personal information from and about their employees.

WORDS OF WISDOM: The field of employee privacy is another area to consider for employee training (see Chapter 8). Managers and supervisors can easily make mistakes regarding employee privacy. Before problems arise, employers should be sure to take all preventive measures possible, including contacting legal counsel for information about employee privacy.

What are Employees' Reasonable Expectations of Privacy?

It depends. Privacy is such a broad concept, that it can be difficult to even define. The federal appeals court in Colorado has defined privacy this way:

"The concept of privacy is multi-faceted. Indeed, one can apply the moniker of a privacy interest to several understandings of privacy, such as the right to have sufficient moral freedom to exercise full individual autonomy, the right of an individual to define who he or she is by controlling access to information about him or herself, and the right of an individual to solitude, secrecy, and anonymity."[1]

If employers do not say anything about privacy, employees may have a stronger expectation of privacy, especially in places traditionally considered private, such as desks, lockers, phone calls, computers, restrooms, or anywhere a person would not expect someone to be watching or searching.

However, within limits, employers can designate certain areas as non-private, and if employers communicate that some areas are non-private to their employees, the employees challenging a search or monitoring in a non-private area would have a harder time proving that the employee's expectation of privacy was "reasonable."

WORDS OF WISDOM: People have a high expectation of privacy in employee restrooms or changing areas, particularly if the employer has not warned workers that these areas might be monitored, and particularly if there is no legitimate business reason for such monitoring!

Some laws provide employees with a "reasonable expectation of privacy" by giving legal protection to certain information. For example, the ADA[2] protects the privacy of certain medical information (see Chapter 12). Colorado laws[3] protect the privacy of certain arrest records (see Chapter 3). (See Appendix 1 for a list of other laws that may protect employee privacy interests.)

Employers May Need to Obtain Certain Information

Before embarking on activities that could be considered violations of privacy, employers should analyze *why* they need the information they are seeking. Two things employers should evaluate before obtaining personal information are:

1. Business necessity; and
2. Job relatedness.

Business Necessity

Before obtaining private information, employers should consider carefully whether the information is necessary for business reasons. Depending on the circumstances, examples of possible valid business reasons include the following:

- Making sure employees are doing their jobs (e.g., preventing personal internet-surfing on company time);
- Preventing harassment via company e-mail, phones, computers, etc. (See Chapter 6);
- Protecting company trade secrets and confidential information;
- Making sure employees can safely perform their jobs (e.g., medical testing; see Chapter 3);
- Applicant background checks and testing (see Chapter 3);
- Keeping track of productivity;
- Monitoring customer service;
- Addressing threats of violence (see Chapter 16); and
- Investigating reasonable suspicions of theft.

Job Relatedness

Another question employers should ask before obtaining certain employee information is whether the information sought relates to the job, especially the essential functions of the job (discussed more fully in Chapter 3). If the information relates to the job, ask how it relates and make sure it is necessary to obtain the information.

How Employers May Legally Obtain Business Related Information

Employers may obtain information about employees in a number of ways, including monitoring communications, searching the workplace, accessing certain documents, and testing employees. With the exception of employment testing, which is addressed in Chapter 3, each of these areas is discussed briefly below.

Monitoring Communications

Telephone Calls and E-Mail

Employers generally may monitor telephone calls and e-mail messages under two circumstances:

1. If the employer monitors telephone calls and e-mail messages in the "ordinary course of business," such as monitoring business calls for quality control; or
2. If the employer gets consent from their employees.

WORDS OF WISDOM: At least two federal laws and one Colorado law are important regarding monitoring communications. The Federal Wiretapping Act[4] and the Electronic Communications Privacy Act[5] provide criminal and civil penalties for the unlawful interception of telephone calls and e-mails, as well as the use of information gathered from an unlawful interception. Colorado law makes wiretapping and eavesdropping illegal and no exceptions are made for employers.[6] However, employers can protect themselves by: (1) getting consent from employees; (2) limiting employees' expectations of privacy by stating that all company property is subject to monitoring (including phones and computers); (3) only monitoring for business related reasons; and, (4) keeping out of personal phone calls and e-mails.

If an employer monitors calls in the ordinary course of business, it is a good idea for the employer to give advance notice, either through a recorded statement or written policy. Also, employers can obtain consent from their employees to monitor calls by providing a written policy. It is best to have employees sign off on the receipt of the policy, since some employees have won lawsuits by demonstrating that they never received a copy of the monitoring policy or the company handbook. (See Chapter 2 for more information on handbooks.)

WORDS OF WISDOM: Under federal law, once an employer realizes that a call is personal, the employer must immediately stop monitoring the call.[7] If the employer has warned employees pursuant to a written policy not to make personal calls from certain phones, the employer may have a better chance of winning a privacy dispute.[8]

Unless employers' policies tell workers that employee e-mail messages will remain private, employers generally have the right to read employee e-mail messages if there is a business purpose to do so. Again, employers make the most of their protections by advising employees in advance if employers intend to monitor e-mail.

Voicemail Messages

Although the question of monitoring voicemail messages has not been completely resolved, employers may have the right to monitor their employees' voicemail if there is a work related reason for doing so, as well as a policy stating that voicemail messages are not private. However, in the absence of such a policy, employers who provide private pass codes and allow personal calls may be creating a legitimate reasonable expectation of privacy regarding voicemail messages.

Internet Use

Employers may monitor internet use by implementing a policy stating that company computers and internet accounts are to be used only for business related purposes and notifying employees that the company reserves the right to search and monitor internet use at any time.

Workplace Searches and Surveillance

Employers have some latitude conducting workplace searches and surveillance for legitimate business reasons. However, workplace searches and surveillance is another area in which employers can strengthen their ability to search without running into legal claims by communicating in advance their policies. In the absence of such policies, employers may actually *create* an expectation of privacy by providing employees with lockers and allowing employees to provide their own locks and keys. Similarly, employers may create a legitimate expectation of privacy by providing desks with locks.

Employers may minimize the risks of liability regarding searching locked desks or lockers by communicating a policy allowing employers to search lockers, desks, purses, briefcases, and papers at any time deemed necessary. The policy should state the legitimate business reasons for such searches, and employers should avoid "random" searches.

WORDS OF WISDOM: Silent videotaping is permissible if it is for a legitimate business purpose. However, videotaping restrooms and changing areas would likely draw claims of invasion of privacy.

Accessing and Disclosure of Certain Documents

Medical Records

The ADA protects applicants and employees from requirements that they disclose certain medical records.[8] (For more information see Chapters 3 and 12.) When employers have obtained medical records consistent with the ADA, the employers must limit access to and disclosure of such information. Employers should always keep medical records in a file separate from the employee's personnel file.

WORDS OF WISDOM: Employers may not require employees to obtain employer approval to take prescription drugs at work. Such a requirement violates the ADA[10] and may violate Colorado common law (judge-made law through court decisions).[11]

Genetic Information

Under Colorado law, genetic information is protected from disclosure and use for non-therapeutic purposes.[12]

Financial Information

Employers may not collect employee financial information unless for a specific business reason. Additionally, employers must get consent from the employees and make certain disclosures to employees before collecting employee financial information. (See Chapter 3.)

Personnel Records

Employers should not disclose information in employee personnel records to any individual who does not have a legitimate business purpose for being included in such a disclosure. For example, while a supervisor may have a need to see personnel files to plan for a coaching session, a fellow employee should not be allowed access to personnel files. It is a good idea to keep personnel files in a locked cabinet.

Other Privacy Considerations

Under Colorado common law, there are other privacy considerations employers should know, including:

- Intrusion;
- Public disclosure of private facts;
- False light; and
- Appropriation.

In general, the employment related privacy issues under Colorado common law involve intrusion and the dissemination of information about the employees to third parties without a need to know such information.

Intrusion

A person who intentionally intrudes on the solitude of another or into another's private affairs may be subject to liability for invasion of privacy if the intrusion would be highly offensive to the reasonable person. For example, an intrusion may occur if an employer opens an employee's personal mail.

Public Disclosure of Private Facts

There are five elements to the claim of public disclosure of private facts, including:

1. The fact(s) disclosed must be of a private nature;
2. The disclosure must be made to the public;
3. The disclosure must be one which would be highly offensive to a reasonable person;
4. The fact(s) disclosed is not of a legitimate public concern; and
5. The person disclosing the fact(s) acted with reckless disregard of the private nature of the fact(s) disclosed.

False Light

A person who publicizes something about an individual that puts the individual in a false light may be liable for invasion of privacy if:

- The false light in which the individual was depicted would be highly offensive to a reasonable person; and
- The person who published the information had knowledge of falsity or acted recklessly.

Importantly, placing someone in a false light in the presence of a few co-workers is not enough to establish liability. The false impression must be conveyed to the public at large or to enough people that it would be certain to become public.

Appropriation

Generally an appropriation claim arises when a person's likeness (usually a picture) is used in company materials (such as advertising or marketing materials) without that person's consent. The best practice is to receive written consent in advance and possibly pay compensation for the use of the likeness.

Practical Steps Regarding Employee Privacy

The following are helpful steps for employers regarding employee privacy:
- Plan in advance—adopt a privacy policy based on sound legal advice;
- Communicate the policy to employees;
- Follow the privacy policy;
- Apply the privacy policy in a consistent way;
- Before taking steps that might invade an employee's privacy, consider whether it is possible to take less intrusive steps and get the information needed;
- Do not conduct "body searches." If an employer thinks a body search is absolutely necessary, based on a reasonable suspicion, call the police;
- Do not monitor personal calls. Once an employer realizes they are hearing a personal call, the employer must stop monitoring; and
- Do not conduct "random" searches of employees unless prepared to defend against a lawsuit.

FOOTNOTES

[1] *U.S. West, Inc. v. Federal Communications Comm'n,* 182 F.3d 1224 (10th Cir. 1999), *cert denied* 120 S. Ct. 2215 (2000).

[2] *See* EEOC, The ADA: A Primer for Small Business, http://www.eeoc.gov/ada/adahandbook.html#confidentiality

[3] C.R.S. § 24-72-308.

[4] The Omnibus Crime Control and Safe Streets Act of 1968 (—the Federal Wiretapping Act"), 18 U.S.C. §§ 2510 *et seq.*

[5] Electronic Communications Privacy Act of 1986 ("ECPA"), 18 U.S.C. § 2701, *et seq.*

[6] C.R.S. § 18-9-305(1).

[7] *See e.g. Watkins v. L.M. Berry & Co.,* 704 F.2d 577 (11th Cir. 1983).

[8] *See e.g. Simmons v. Southwestern Bell Telephone Co.,* 452 F. Supp. 392 (W.D. Okla. 1978).

[9] *See* 42 U.S.C. § 12112(d).

[10] *See Id.*

[11] *See Roe v. Cheyenne Mountain Conference Resort, Inc.,* No. 96-1086 (10th Cir. 1997) *available* at www.law.emory.edu/10circuit/sept97/96-1086.wpd.html

[12] C.R.S. § 10-3-1104.7.

CHAPTER 15:
How and Why to Give Employees Positive (and Negative) Feedback

Developing a Communications Plan

Wise employers know that communication is an important part of developing a legally healthy work environment. Yet communication can be one of the hardest things in the world sometimes. It can be difficult to figure out *what* to say, let alone *how* and *when* to say it. Some people slip into the trap of waiting too long to say something (or not saying anything) in hopes of avoiding confrontation or embarrassment. Other people say the first thing that comes to mind (or blast out an e-mail), sometimes without fully thinking through the possible outcomes.

WORDS OF WISDOM: E-mails can be extremely damaging evidence against employers. Think "evidence" before hitting the "send" key.

Without a plan for communicating with employees, employers may miss outstanding opportunities to cultivate the very people who are working to achieve the goals of their businesses. Three elements of a good communications plan include:
1. Employee performance evaluations;
2. Ongoing coaching and training; and
3. Corrective action.

Consistent Communication

Consistent communication with employees is important for at least two reasons. First, the right messages can inspire employees to do their best and fix things when they go wrong, giving the company a competitive edge in achieving its goals. Because communication is a two-way street, employers can learn from employees and utilize the expertise of their employees. Employers also can guide employees in the direction that best serves the business's goals by helping employees identify positive actions and correct negative behaviors. Second, when employers follow a good plan for communicating with employees, employers can minimize the risks of lawsuits by being proactive in solving problems as they arise.

How to Communicate With Employees

In addition to casual conversations with employees, there are at least three other elements of a good communications plan, including performance reviews, ongoing coaching and training, and corrective action. The key to effectively using any of these options is planning. By planning in advance what to say, and how and when to say it, employers can avoid hasty decisions that often lead to trouble.

Giving Employees Performance Evaluations

Every communications plan should include consistent and objective performance evaluations, keeping in mind the following:
- Goals of performance evaluations;
- What to say; and
- How and when to say it.

Goals for Performance Evaluations

Employers can use performance evaluations to achieve the following goals:
- Treat employees in an evenhanded manner when making personnel decisions;
- Identify employee strengths and communicate the strengths to the employee;
- Document specific examples of employee strengths;
- Identify areas for employee improvement and develop a plan to help the employee improve;
- Document specific examples of areas for employee improvement;
- Give employees notice of areas that must be improved;
- Identify training opportunities;
- Develop employees for advancement within the company; and
- Support personnel actions, such as pay raises or corrective actions.

WORDS OF WISDOM: Provide a written performance evaluation to employees as part of the company's orientation package (see Chapter 4). A written performance evaluation will help establish positive goals from day one and give employees notice of what is expected from them.

The Written Performance Evaluation: What to Say

Written performance evaluations may take many forms, including numerical ratings, charts with guidelines for rating employees, narratives, and checklists. Written performance evaluations are another place that job descriptions come in handy (see Chapter 3). Employers should tailor employee evaluations to the essential functions of the job as described in the written job descriptions, and include general areas of development. While entire books have been written on effective performance evaluations, and while performance evaluations may vary depending on the company and the position, the following is a checklist of potential elements that should be included in a written performance evaluation (in addition to the core functions of the job):

1. Job knowledge:
   - Knowledge of position and essential functions,
   - Knowledge of company procedures,
   - Knowledge of company anti-discrimination and anti-harassment policies,
   - Grasps new job requirements,
   - Acquires new skills to improve effectiveness;
2. Quality of work:
   - Accuracy,
   - Thoroughness,
   - Follow-through,
   - Takes on more demanding tasks as appropriate;
3. Planning and organizing:
   - Sets realistic timetables,
   - Meets deadlines,
   - Prioritizes work,
   - Adjusts to unforeseen events,
   - Monitors and reports work in progress,
   - Anticipates problems,
   - Plans for future requirements;

4. Productivity (based on requirements of job):
   - Volume of work,
   - Quality of work,
   - Timeliness of work;
5. Initiative/problem solving/decision making:
   - Anticipates, identifies, and defines problems,
   - Evaluates and weighs alternatives,
   - Works with others to resolve issues,
   - Implements appropriate, timely solutions;
6. Communication:
   - Expresses ideas and presents information clearly, written and oral,
   - Persuades and establishes rapport in an understandable and respectful manner,
   - Demonstrates good listening skills (attentiveness, responsiveness, understanding);
7. Teamwork/working relationships:
   - Cooperates positively as a team member with members of employee's own department and other departments,
   - Follows company anti-harassment and anti-discrimination policies,
   - Negotiates with respect for others,
   - Resolves conflict,
   - Reaches agreement,
   - Seeks and incorporates the ideas of others,
   - Works effectively and positively with individuals of diverse backgrounds, abilities, and motivation,
   - Customer service skills;
8. Personal skills:
   - Dedication/reliability/attitude,
   - Judgment and common sense,
   - Flexibility,
   - Attendance/punctuality;
9. Company values:
   - Respect for the rights, differences, and dignity of others,
   - Honesty and integrity in all dealings,
   - Conscientious pursuit of excellence in one's work,
   - Accountability for actions and conduct in the workplace;
10. Leadership:
    - Sets realistic standards,
    - Provides good example,
    - Inspires enthusiasm,

- Acts in evenhanded manner with employees;
11. Development of subordinates (for supervisors):
    - Provides career development resources,
    - Offers guidance,
    - Communicates goals, priorities, objectives,
    - Gives clear task instructions,
    - Completes performance evaluations for staff in a timely fashion,
    - Delegation, follow up, and recognition of employees,
    - Monitors company policies, including anti-retaliation and anti-harassment,
    - Provides information,
    - Encourages and mentors employees for growth,
    - Provides training opportunities,
    - Gives constructive performance feedback,
    - Takes corrective measures when required,
    - Praises and recognizes positive performance,
    - Works effectively with individuals of diverse style, ability, background, and motivation, and
    - Encourages team efforts.

Use specific examples to support the evaluation of the employee's performance in these categories whenever possible. Avoid conclusory statements that lack specific support. Keep the comments job-related, and only rate an employee's performance of tasks and abilities that relate to the position at hand.

WORDS OF WISDOM: Avoid the temptation to "inflate" the employee's job performance. Use the evaluation as an opportunity to document areas for improvement. Careful assessment helps employers monitor the employee's work. Also, by reviewing prior performance evaluations before the meeting with the employee, an employer can identify trends, and if corrective action is necessary, the employer will have documented support for any actions. If an employee later decides to sue the company, the employer will have proof that the employer based their decision on legitimate performance issues.

In addition to specific categories, the performance evaluation also should include questions for general feedback including:

- What are the employee's significant strengths or contributions?
- In what area(s) can and/or must the employee make improvement(s)?
- What types of future assignments/projects/training would the employer recommend for this employee?

Since communication is a two-way street, provide a space for employee comments, such as:

- What my supervisor did to help my work;
- What my supervisor could do to help my work;
- Concerns about the workplace in general, including any concerns relating to discrimination and harassment; and
- Things I like about this company.

Not only will a section for employee comments provide helpful feedback for the company, but it may help to shield the company from liability should the employee try to claim later that there are problems that were unaddressed. Be sure to include the date and spaces for the employee and evaluator to sign the evaluation. Include a statement next to the employee's signature, stating that the employee acknowledges receipt of the evaluation, but that the signature does not necessarily indicate agreement with the contents.

> **WORDS OF WISDOM:** If an employer has not had the company's written performance evaluations reviewed by legal counsel within the past year, consider an annual "check up" for the evaluations.

When and How to Give Employee Performance Evaluations: The Six-Month Review Meeting

To make the most effective use of employee performance evaluations, make them a priority and schedule them twice a year. Avoid the temptation of "fitting them in," or rescheduling them for a "more convenient" time. Consistent communication with employees is essential, and it is not something that should be put off.

Before the meeting, plan what will be said during the evaluation by completing the written performance evaluation. Plan when the evaluation will occur by scheduling the meeting in advance. The following are tips on how to conduct an effective six-month review meeting:

1. Prepare for the evaluation prior to the date and time arranged with the employee and plan an agenda for the meeting;
2. Prepare to discuss both positive and negative aspects of the employee's performance;
3. Set the tone of the meeting by:
    - Providing a comfortable atmosphere,
    - Putting the employee at ease,
    - Ensuring that no interruptions take place,
    - Eliminating physical barriers;

4. Lay the foundation and begin the conversation:
   - Begin on a positive note, explaining the goals of the performance evaluation process,
   - Be friendly, and be sincere,
   - Point out any recent significant positive performances,
   - Address areas for improvement, providing specific examples from the evaluation form,
   - Plan specific action steps and provide timeframes and ways to measure success,
   - Stress the desire for two-way communication;
5. Ask for feedback from the employee:
   - Encourage the employee to point out any accomplishments of which the employer may not be aware,
   - Have the employee list any areas in which improvement is needed,
   - Clarify what the employee has stated;

WORDS OF WISDOM: Self evaluation forms may be useful tools in obtaining relevant information from employees.

---

6. Make any additions, corrections, and deletions to the ratings or comments on the performance evaluation document;
7. Discuss the employee's career goals and objectives and the company's needs:
   - Plan specific job assignments or activities which support the employee's objectives as consistent with business needs,
   - Plan opportunities for training or education that will assist the employee;

WORDS OF WISDOM: Because employers can create contracts with employees in documents such as performance evaluations (especially if the documents set forth future plans and goals), be sure to include disclaimer language on the employee evaluation form, disclaiming any intent to enter into a contract and reaffirming the at-will nature of the employment as appropriate. (See Chapter 2.)

---

8. Reaffirm the company's commitment to anti-discrimination, anti-harassment, and equal employment opportunity; and
9. Provide the employee with a copy of the evaluation, and plan for the next evaluation by providing a new form with goals for the next review period.

By taking these steps, employers can take advantage of an excellent opportunity to lay the foundation for a legally healthy relationship and work environment.

Ongoing Coaching and Training: Cultivating Employees

The second element of an effective communications plan is ongoing coaching and training.

Coaching for Effective Performance

A coach is someone who provides tools for instruction, enlightenment, motivation, inspiration, guidance, goals, objectives, self-discipline, self-discovery, and, when necessary, correction. Sound like too big a task to handle when faced with the day-to-day pressures of the job? Coaching can take place on an informal level through discussions as issues arise, or it can be more formalized, such as through a mentoring program. While time pressures can lead to frustration when employees have questions or do not perform to the level expected, many times five or ten minutes of a supervisor's time can prevent further frustration, both for the supervisor and the employee. Coaching can be an effective tool in handling problems when they are big enough to see, yet small enough to solve.

What makes a good coach? Although coaching styles vary from person to person, here are a few common traits to consider:

- Respect — Demonstrate courtesy and recognition of the value of the employee as more than a "warm body" filling a position;
- Energy — Project a positive spirit and endurance in good times and bad;
- Enthusiasm — Show interest and concern both for the company and the individuals who make it run;
- Patience — Exhibit commitment to a positive outcome during times of stress;
- Humor — Use humor when appropriate (never make the employee the target of the humor, however);
- Lead by example — Employers should hold themselves to the same (if not higher) standards;
- Inclusion — Coach even the less-well-liked employees (or especially those employees);
- Encourage learning — Recognize that mistakes can be positive learning experiences if handled well;
- Ask questions — Find out what employees need to achieve their highest potential;
- Recognize the human side of employees.

By seizing opportunities to develop employees on a day-to-day basis through communicating with them as coaches, employers can minimize problems before they lead to costly and more time consuming issues. Of course, coaching takes practice and training, even for the coach. This is where training and education comes in.

Training and Education

Training is an investment in the workforce. Investments are only good when they pay off, right? In a tight economy, training often is the first thing slashed from the budget (if it was included in the budget to begin with). Deleting training from the budged is often a costly mistake. As discussed in Chapter 8, training employees on employment laws is one important step in shielding companies from liability in the event of discrimination lawsuits. Even more importantly, effective training and implementation of good policies and practices can improve productivity and prevent problems before they arise.

How else can training affect the bottom line? In 1998, the American Society for Training and Development (ASTD) concluded a national study of training in 540 corporations.[1] The study looked at two samples; one sample invested an average of $900 per employee per year, and the other sample invested an average of $275 per employee per year. The researchers found that the companies with the higher investment in training outpaced the other group by achieving 57 percent higher sales per employee and 37 percent higher gross profit per employee. The study also found that the best companies invest up to six percent of payroll on overall workplace training.

If this kind of investment seems out of reach, start with the basics. Topics employers should consider for on-going training include, *at a minimum:*
- Technical and skills training as needed for the specific positions;
- Safety (be sure to consider the Occupational Safety and Health Act requirements for each specific industry);
- Guarding against workplace violence and bullying; and
- Making the most of anti-harassment and anti-discrimination laws.

Other topics promoting a productive workplace include:
- Conflict resolution;
- Dealing with difficult people;
- Making the most of change;
- Effective communications;
- Employee handbook training;
- Time management and organization skills;
- Building a cohesive team;
- Empowering leadership;
- Work/life balance;
- How to lead and succeed;
- How to deal with a difficult boss;

- Mentoring and coaching;
- Conducting effective performance evaluations;
- Conducting effective investigations;
- Counseling and discipline;
- Practical nuts and bolts of employee leave issues;
- Living in an information age: employee privacy;
- Recruiting top notch employees;
- Retaining top notch employees;
- Protecting company information and trade secrets;
- Language skills for employees from abroad;
- Stress management;
- Top ten steps for avoiding lawsuits; and
- Emerging employment laws.

WORDS OF WISDOM: Because new employment laws and interpretations materialize almost every day, it is critical for employers to stay current and to provide training on a consistent basis. For example, employers have new responsibilities under the Sarbanes-Oxley Act of 2002,[2] which protects whistleblowers in publicly traded companies and exposes companies and individuals who do business with publicly traded companies to liability for discrimination or other negative treatment of whistleblowers.

There are many options available to employers for workforce education, including low cost seminars, on-site training, and computer-based education. If an employer has a good relationship with their legal counsel, the legal counsel also can be an excellent resource in keeping the employer updated on current changes in the law.

Corrective Action: Fixing Workplace Problems

From time to time, despite an employer's best efforts at communicating, coaching, and training employees, corrective action is necessary to address poor performance or employee misconduct. Corrective action always should be planned in advance and taken in accordance with the company's policies and procedures. Of course, sometimes corrective action must be taken (almost) immediately, depending on the severity of the conduct (i.e. workplace violence). The possible need for immediate action is why advance planning of policies and procedures is critical, so that when an immediate problem arises, management does not have to try to come up with an answer on the spot.

As discussed in Chapter 8, corrective actions can include coaching, verbal warnings, written warnings, suspension, demotion, transfer, and termination. Managers and supervisors should be trained on how and when to apply effective corrective actions, especially because anti-discrimination laws usually apply to these types of corrective measures.

Whenever employers must take corrective action, they should consider the goals of such measures, including:

- Preventing further negative behavior;
- Replacing the negative behavior with positive conduct;
- Facilitating positive employee attitudes;
- Protecting other employees; and
- Documenting problems for future reference.

While it is never pleasant to confront someone with his or her own misconduct (especially if he or she disputes it), a confrontation is critical. A plan of action can help. When there has been a formal investigation (see Chapter 8), the corrective action will derive from the conclusions and results of the investigation. When the conduct does not warrant a formal investigation, fact gathering is still an important step to take before the corrective action, which may include a discussion with the supervisor, other employees, and the employee at issue. Fact gathering also may include a review of any relevant documents, such as previous warnings, documents evidencing the conduct (for example, absenteeism documentation), and written statements.

When the determination has been made that corrective action is necessary, employers should plan for the meeting. Prepare an agenda, remembering the goals of the corrective action. Ask the employee to the meeting in a private location, and whenever possible, have another neutral employee, such as a human resources representative or an assistant, present to take detailed notes of everything said in the meeting. State the concerns clearly to the employee in an even tone of voice. Ask the employee about his or her perspective and gather additional information from the employee. Stay calm and listen to the employee.

Explain why the conduct must be changed and what positive steps the employee can take to improve. Provide guidelines and timeframes and set a time for follow up. If the corrective action is a verbal warning, be sure to document the verbal warning in the personnel file. If the corrective action is a written warning, have the employee sign a copy of the warning and provide a copy of the warning to the employee for reference.

WORDS OF WISDOM: Written disciplinary warnings may be used as evidence by either the employer or the employee should future litigation arise. Employers should be sure they would want a judge or jury to see what was written and how it was written. If an employer isn't comfortable with their written disciplinary warning, they should run it by their legal counsel.

FOOTNOTES

[1] J. Warkenthein, *Research Shows Training Employees Pays Off With Profits,* San Antonio Business Journal, 2001, http://sanantonio.bizjournals.com/sanantonio/stories/2001/12/03/focus3.html?page=1

[2] Pub. L. No. 107-204, 116 Stat. 745.

CHAPTER 16:
An Overview of Workplace Violence—
Work Zone or War Zone?

Overview of Workplace Violence

Workplace violence has bloodied the headlines in recent times, causing many to question whether the workplace has become a war zone. Consider these still raw wounds reported by CNN in 2003:[1]

- *July 8, 2003: Meridian Mississippi* — Armed with a shotgun and semiautomatic rifle, an employee shot five workers to death and wounded nine others before killing himself at a Lockheed Martin aircraft plant outside Meridian, authorities said.

- *July 2, 2003: Jefferson City, Missouri* — Jonathon Russell shot and killed three co-workers at a manufacturing plant where he worked on the outskirts of Jefferson City, police told The Associated Press. He also wounded five others before shooting himself.

- *February 25, 2003: Huntsville, Alabama* — Emanuel Burl Patterson, 23, allegedly began shooting at Labor Ready Inc., a temporary employment agency near downtown Huntsville. Three people died at the scene, and a 55-year-old victim died later at a Huntsville hospital. A fifth person was wounded.

- *September 16, 2002: New York, New York* — An insurance executive called two co-workers into his office near Times Square, shot them to death and then killed himself, authorities said. The bodies were found in the supervisor's office in the fraud division of Empire Blue Cross and Blue Shield, an official said.
- *September 11, 2001: America* — Terrorist attacks resulted in the deaths of 2,886 workers in New York, Virginia, and Pennsylvania.
- *February 5, 2001: Melrose Park, Illinois* — Former employee William D. Baker, 66, walked into the Navistar engine plant in suburban Chicago and opened fire, killing four people and wounding four others before turning the gun on himself. He was to have begun a five-month prison term for theft of company property the next day.
- *March 8, 2000: Memphis, Tennessee* — Firefighter Frederick Williams was charged with four counts of first-degree murder, one count of aggravated arson, and one count of attempted murder after a shooting following a fire at his home. Police say Williams, who had been on leave from the fire department because of emotional problems, killed his wife inside his home before setting the house on fire. Two firefighters and a sheriff's deputy were shot and killed when they arrived on the scene. A female bystander was wounded, and Williams himself was wounded by police.
- *April 20, 1999: Littleton, Colorado* — In America's worst instance of school violence yet, two teenagers, Dylan Klebold and Eric Harris, open fire on classmates and teachers in their suburban Denver school, killing 15 people including themselves.

Incidents such as these gruesomely confirm statistics that show the dangerous nature of the workplace. Workplace violence continues to be the leading concern for American businesses, according to Pinkerton Consulting & Investigations' Tenth Annual survey of Fortune 1000 corporate security professionals. The total costs associated with workplace violence are estimated at $36 billion annually, and workplace violence affects more than two million Americans every year.

Violence in the workplace has prompted many lawsuits and questions about how to recognize, prevent, and cope with such occurrences. This chapter provides an overview of the workplace violence issues relevant to employers.

Defining Workplace Violence

In view of the enormous costs of workplace violence, defining "workplace violence" generates considerable discussion. Some define the term broadly to include any language or actions that make a person uncomfortable in the workplace, while others define workplace violence as physical assault, threatening behavior, or verbal abuse. According to the National Institute of Occupational Safety and Health

(NIOSH), the spectrum of workplace violence ranges from offensive language to homicide.

Workplace violence generally takes one of three forms:
1. Violence inflicted by unknown third persons (e.g. terrorists, customers);
2. Violence inflicted by co-workers; and
3. Violence inflicted on an employee by someone the employee knows (i.e. domestic violence in the workplace).

According to one study, of all physical attacks occurring on the job:
- 44 percent were by customers or clients;
- 30 percent were by co-workers or former employees;
- 24 percent were by strangers; and
- 2 percent were by someone else, such as domestic violence.

Workplace violence includes fighting, assault, threats of violence, harassment, stalking, rape, and terrorism. Some violent episodes appear to be manifested as a specific attack on the workplace hierarchy, rather than random acts of violence. For example, in July 1995, a Los Angeles Police Department maintenance employee whose performance had been criticized shot and killed four co-workers in his agency. Each of the victims was a carefully selected target, including his supervisor.

Certain kinds of workplace violence incidents are preventable or foreseeable and can lead to employer liability.

Evolving Liability Theories

Occupational Safety and Health Act (OSH Act)

The OSH Act is a federal law under which all employers have a general duty to provide their employees with a workplace free from recognized hazards likely to cause death or serious physical harm. The Occupational Safety and Health Administration (OSHA) can cite employers if there is a recognized hazard of workplace violence in their establishments and the employer does nothing to prevent or abate it. The OSH Act broadly defines the term "employer" to include all persons engaged in a business affecting commerce who have employees, with the exception of the United States or any state or political subdivision of a state.[2]

According to an opinion letter issued by OSHA, the general duty requires employers to take steps necessary to reduce or eliminate the recognized hazards that are present and likely to cause death or serious physical harm to employees, including, in some instances, the violent acts of third parties. Thus, in an employment arena where robbery is a "recognized" hazard, arguably the employer has some obligation to minimize those risks. Failure of a vulnerable employer to implement feasible means of abatement of these hazards could result in a finding of an OSH Act violation. However, occurrences of criminal acts of violence that are not recognized as characteristic of employment, and instead, represent random antisocial acts that may occur anywhere, should not subject employers to a citation for a violation of the OSH Act.

In July 2003, OSHA updated its *Guidelines for Preventing Workplace Violence for Health-Care and Social Service Workers,* where 48 percent of all non-fatal injuries from occupational assaults and violent acts occurred in 2000. OSHA revised the publication by adding updated statistics and new tools for assessing the potential for workplace violence. The guidelines offer assistance and information to employers to aid in establishing effective workplace violence programs.

Additionally, the OSHA Training Institute (OTI) recently was recognized for its innovative on-line course on workplace violence awareness. The OTI course is designed for the general public and provides basic concepts to address the issue of workplace violence. The OTI course addresses situations that fit the definition of workplace violence, risk factors, and prevention programs.

Employers' Potential Civil Liability

In addition to potential exposure under the OSH Act, employers may face liability under Colorado common law for acts of workplace violence. For example, in a case called *Taco Bell v. Lannon,*[3] the Colorado Supreme Court addressed the duty of a proprietor to make its premises reasonably safe for those who enter. The court noted that, depending on the information available to employers, security measures against foreseeable violence may be a duty required of owners and occupiers of land.

Employers are ordinarily under no duty to exercise care until they know, or have reason to know, that the acts of the third person are occurring or are about to occur. However, employers may know, or have reason to know, from past experience, that there is a likelihood of conduct by third persons to endanger the safety of the visitor, even though the employer has no reason to expect it from any particular individual. The court concluded that evidence of ten armed robberies at that particular Taco Bell within the three years prior to the incident was enough to establish that Taco Bell could reasonably foresee harm to customers as a result of criminal acts by third parties. For this reason, Taco Bell had a legal duty to take reasonable steps to protect its customers from the criminal acts of unknown third persons. In addition to foreseeability, the court noted that the imposition of this duty turns on the gravity of the possible harm, as well as the relative burden of imposing the duty when weighed against the benefit to society.

In addition to possible liability for failure to make their premises reasonably safe, employers may face liability for negligent hiring, negligent supervision, and negligent retention. The claims of negligent hiring, negligent supervision, and negligent retention basically arise from allegations that the employer failed to take reasonable steps to investigate potential employees, to adequately supervise employees, or to remove employees that the employer knew or should have known posed an unreasonable risk of harm. Although no case to date has imposed common law liability for failure to conduct a reasonable investigation, recent Supreme Court rulings relating to anti-discrimination laws may signal possible future duties of employers not to be negligent in investigations.

WORDS OF WISDOM: Employers also must be mindful of the rights of the accused. Employers can avoid claims of defamation (or publishing false statements with recklessness as to their falsity), by taking careful steps in the investigatory process. See Chapter 8 for practical steps to conducting investigations.

Agency Recommendations

The U.S. Department of Labor (DOL), NIOSH, and OSHA have issued general recommendations designed to help employers combat violence in the workplace.

DOL suggests that employers take the following steps, if possible:

- Install metal detectors to identify weapons;
- Install alarm systems or panic buttons;
- Use bright and effective lighting systems;
- Use curved mirrors at hallway intersections or concealed areas;
- Allow for more than one exit; and
- Arrange furniture to avoid entrapment.

NIOSH recommends that all workers and employers assess the risk of violence in their workplaces and develop appropriate prevention programs and policies. In addition to the guidelines suggested by DOL, these measures may include the following:

- Locked property safes;
- Physical separation of workers from customers;
- Escort services; and
- Employee training.

Finally, OSHA has articulated several recommendations to employers, including the following:

- Provide safety education for employees. Local police departments can give training on awareness, avoidance, and prevention of mugging, robbery, rape, and other assaults;
- Establish a communication system, such as cellular phones, for employees to use while in the field;

- Instruct employees not to enter any location where they feel unsafe;
- Establish procedures to decrease the risk of robbery (e.g., advise employees not to carry cash bags openly); and
- Require field staff to prepare a daily work plan and keep a contact person informed of their locations throughout the day.

Additionally, employees should take the following steps to avoid violence:
- Learn how to recognize, avoid, or diffuse potentially violent situations by attending personal safety training programs;
- Follow procedures for alerting supervisors to any concerns about safety or security; and
- Report all violent incidents in writing to supervisors, even if there were no injuries.

Successful Workplace Violence Prevention Programs

Elements of a successful workplace violence prevention program include:
- Management commitment and employee involvement;
- Work site analysis;
- Hazard prevention and control; and
- Training and education.

A program with all of the above elements may not only minimize the risks of workplace violence, but it may also strengthen potential legal defenses. For example, in one Colorado case, the court concluded that an employer who had implemented policies relating to workplace violence was relieved of the employer's duty to pay unemployment benefits to an employee discharged for hitting a co-employee.[4] The court noted that the employer had "rigidly adhered" to a policy of summary dismissal for fighting or hitting a co-worker, and the employer had informed the employees of this policy in the employee handbook and employment agreement.

When adopting formal policies regarding workplace violence, employers should examine two types:
1. Preventative policies; and
2. Responsive policies.

Preventative Policies

Preventative policies regarding workplace violence can relate to hiring, workplace conditions, and employee discipline. While engaged in the hiring process, employers should use reasonable care, with consideration given to the type of job and the amount of contact with the public. Reasonable care during the hiring process may involve adopting specific application and background check policies and procedures. Many employers also have adopted "zero tolerance" policies, including work rules prohibiting the possession of guns, firearms, knives, or other types of weapons.

Responsive Policies

To eliminate confusion in the event of a violent incident, employers should establish responsive policies regarding threats and reports of violent behavior. Responsive policies may include:

- Emergency procedures, including the roles of management in certain situations;
- Security to be contacted; and
- A plan for the collection of evidence, managing the flow of information, and when to bring in outside resources.

Additionally, employers should document the actions of workers displaying certain behaviors, including verbal abuse, that are often precursors to violent behavior in the workplace. Without such documentation, employers may miss warning signs and valuable opportunities to take corrective action before violence occurs.

Colorado Statutes Regarding Threats and Violence

Leave for Abuse Victims

A relatively new Colorado law requires all employers with 50 or more employees to allow employees who have been the victim of domestic violence, stalking, sexual assault, or any other crime involving an act of domestic violence, to take up to three days of leave for any one of the following purposes:[5]

- To seek a civil restraining order;
- To obtain medical care or mental health counseling;
- To make their homes secure from attack by the perpetrators; or
- To seek legal assistance.

The law also allows employees to request leave to protect a child who has been the victim of domestic violence, stalking, or sexual assault. However, employees must first use any available vacation, personal leave, and sick leave. Employers must keep confidential all information regarding this leave. Employers that deny this leave, or terminate or discriminate against any employee for requesting leave may be held liable for a violation of the law.

Employer Restraining Orders

Employers may obtain a restraining order for the protection of their employees. In the past, restraining orders could only be issued in the employee's name. If a court finds that an imminent danger exists to the employees of a business entity, a judge may issue an order forbidding contact by the aggressor for the protection of all employees.

Employee Restraining Orders and Criminal Charges

Employees may obtain restraining orders in their own names. Also, employees may pursue criminal charges against alleged stalkers, as well as pursue claims against those who cause or threaten to cause serious bodily injury.

WORDS OF WISDOM. The numbers confirm what the headlines portray—violent acts occur frequently in American workplaces. By addressing the problem proactively, employers may not only pre-empt violent attacks, but may minimize their risk of lawsuits and help transform a potential "war zone" into a safe and productive work zone.

FOOTNOTES

[1] www.cnn.com
[2] 29 U.S.C. § 651(b)
[3] 744 P.2d 43 (Colo. 1987).
[4] *Baca v. Marriott Hotels, Inc.*, 732 P.2d 1252, Colo.App., Dec 31, 1986.
[5] Mandatory Leave for Domestic Violence Act, C.R.S. §§ 24-34-402.7, *et. seq.*

CHAPTER 17:
A Basic Introduction to Labor and Union Issues

The Federal Union Law and the National Labor Relations Board

The National Labor Relations Act (NLRA) is the primary law governing relations between unions and private employers.[1] The law guarantees the right of employees to organize and bargain collectively with their employers (or to refrain from all such activity). The NLRA implements the national labor policy assuring free choice and encouraging collective bargaining as a means of maintaining industrial peace. The NLRA generally applies to all employers involved in interstate commerce other than airlines, railroads, agriculture, and government.

The National Labor Relations Board (NLRB) is an independent federal agency created by Congress in 1935 to administer the National Labor Relations Act. The NLRB has two principal functions:

1. To determine, through secret ballot elections, the free democratic choice by employees whether they wish to be represented by a union in dealing with their employers and if so, by which union;[2] and
2. To prevent and remedy unlawful acts, called unfair labor practices, by either employers or unions.[3]

The NLRB does not act on its own. Instead, the NLRB processes only those charges of unfair labor practices and petitions for employee elections that are filed with the NLRB in one of the 51 regional, sub-regional, or resident NLRB offices.

Exclusions from the NLRA's Coverage

The NLRA specifically excludes the following individuals from coverage:

- Agricultural laborers;
- Domestic service providers for any person or family in a home;
- People employed by a parent or spouse;
- Supervisors;
- Employees of employers subject to the Railway Labor Act;
- Federal, state, or local government employees;
- Any other employees of a person who is not an employer as defined in the NLRA; and
- Individuals having the status of independent contractors.[4]

Unfair Labor Practices: Examples of Employer Conduct Which Violate the NLRA

According to the NLRB, the following conduct violates the NLRA:[5]

- Threatening employees with loss of jobs or benefits if they join or vote for a union or engage in protected concerted activity;
- Threatening to close the plant if employees select a union to represent the employees;
- Questioning employees about their union sympathies or activities in circumstances that tend to interfere with, restrain, or coerce employees in the exercise of their rights under the NLRA;
- Promising benefits to employees to discourage their union support; and
- Transferring, laying off, terminating, or assigning employees more difficult work tasks because they engaged in union or protected concerted activity.

What Happens When a Charge is Filed?

When an unfair labor practice (ULP) charge is filed, the appropriate NLRB field office conducts an investigation to determine whether there is reasonable cause to believe the NLRA has been violated. If the NLRB regional director determines that the charge lacks merit, the charge will be dismissed unless the charging party decides to withdraw the charge. A charge dismissal may be appealed to the NLRB's general counsel's office in Washington, D.C.

If the NLRB regional director finds reasonable cause to believe a violation of the law has been committed, the regional director seeks a voluntary settlement to remedy the alleged violations. If these settlement efforts fail, a formal complaint is issued and the case goes to hearing before an NLRB administrative law judge. The NLRB administrative law judge issues a written decision that may be appealed to the NLRB five-member board in Washington, D.C. for a final agency determination. A U.S. Court of Appeals can review the decision made by the NLRB five-member board.

Depending upon the nature of the case, the NLRB's general counsel's goal is to complete investigations and, where further proceedings are warranted, issue complaints if settlement is not reached within 7 to 15 weeks from the filing of the charge. Of the approximately 30,000 ULP charges filed each year, about one-third are found to have merit. According to the NLRB, ninety percent of these charges are settled.[6]

For more information on the NLRB and the NLRA, check out the NLRB's website at http://www.nlrb.gov. The NLRB's website provides guidance, manuals, and forms, among other helpful information. Additionally, employers can also contact the Denver Regional Office of the NLRB at: NLRB, 600 17th Street 7th Floor, North Tower, Denver, Colorado 80202-5433, Phone: (303) 844-3551.

Colorado Union Law—The Colorado Labor Peace Act

The Colorado Labor Peace Act (CLPA) was enacted in 1943, and it provides a comprehensive labor relations regulatory scheme for Colorado.[7] The CLPA provides, in pertinent part:

> "[A]n employer shall not be prohibited from entering into an all-union agreement with the representatives of his employees ... if such all-union agreement is approved by the affirmative vote of at least a majority of all the employees eligible to vote or three-quarters or more of the employees who actually voted, whichever is greater ... in favor of such all-union agreement...."

According to the Colorado Attorney General's Opinion No 88-10,[8] because the CLPA only regulates, rather than prohibits, union security agreements, Colorado does not technically qualify as a "right to work" state. As commonly understood, a "right to work" state is a state that prohibits contractual terms that condition employment on membership in (or financial support of) a labor organization.

Union Activity in Colorado

The Colorado AFL-CIO is dedicated to organizing working people in the state of Colorado; securing and protecting dignity, equality, rights, and benefits; and raising the standard of living and quality of life for all working people and their families. The stated mission of the Colorado AFL-CIO is to promote organized labor, educate its members and the public about the labor movement, and encourage the active involvement of all of union members in their communities.

The Denver Area Labor Federation (DALF) is the AFL-CIO Central Labor Council for the Denver metro area, and it represents more than 90,000 union members through its political and organizing programs. Founded in 1882, the federation works with local and national labor and community organizations regarding policies and initiatives in support of workers' rights. DALF works closely with the Colorado AFL-CIO. For more information, see http://www.denverlabor.org/.

The following is a reference list of Colorado AFL-CIO affiliated unions employers might encounter:

- AFGE Local 11;
- Amalgamated Transit Union Local 19;
- Amalgamated Transit Union Local 1001;
- American Postal Workers (Denver Chapter);
- Colorado Building and Construction Trades Council;
- Colorado Federation of Public Employees;
- Colorado Postal Workers Union;
- Denver Musicians Association;
- Denver Paramedics IAFF Local 3634;
- Electrical Workers IBEW 113;
- Firefighters IAFF Local 5;
- IBEW Local 111;
- IBEW Local 113;
- International Association of Firefighters;
- International Brotherhood of Teamsters;
- International Union of Operating Engineers Local 9;
- Labor's Community Agency;
- Machinists Local 1886;
- Pipefitters Local 208;
- Teamsters Local 435;
- UA Local 145; and
- UFCW Local 7.

For a list of national AFL-CIO unions, see the AFL-CIO's website at http://coaflcio.org/affiliated_unions.htm.

FOOTNOTES

[1] 29 U.S.C. §§ 151-169.

[2] National Labor Relations Board, Fact Sheet on the National Labor Relations Board, http://www.nlrb.gov/facts.html

[3] 29 U.S.C. § 160(a).

[4] 29 U.S.C. § 152(2), (3).

[5] The National Labor Relations Board and You: Unfair Labor Practices, NLRB, http://www.nlrb.gov/publications/engulp.pdf

[6] Id.

[7] C.R.S. § 8-3-108(1)(c)(I) (emphasis added).

[8] Colorado Attorney General Opinion No 88-10 (Dec. 16, 1988), available at http://www.ago.state.co.us/AGO/ago88/ago8810.htm+%22Colorado+Attorney+General%22+Opinion+%22No+88-10%22&hl=en&ie=UTF-8

CHAPTER 18:
Employee Separations—
Some Good Things Come to an End

Overview of Employee Separations

All employment relationships end at some point. Some endings are more pleasant than others. Sometimes the decision to end employment is mutual, or the employee leaves of his or her own volition. Other times, employers have to make the unpleasant decision to terminate the relationship, for whatever reason.

Because terminating employment can mean the end of a person's livelihood, a loss of identity, a change of friends, and other negative consequences, it can create extremely negative emotions. Sometimes these emotions translate into lawsuits. To understand the risks associated with terminations and ways to minimize those risks, it is helpful to understand the various ways employment relationships can end, the laws governing the final paycheck, and options for minimizing possible claims against the company.

How Does It End?

Employment relationships can end in any number of ways, including:
- Resignation or job abandonment;
- Completion of contract;
- Retirement;
- Downsizing or reductions in force; or
- Termination.

Because the legal consequences and the employers' responsibilities vary depending on the type of job separation, here is a quick discussion regarding the different types of separations.

Resignation or Job Abandonment

Resignation occurs when an employee voluntarily leaves his or her employment. The key word here is "voluntarily." Absent a written contract, an employee generally is under no duty to provide any written notice of resignation. Although some employees give an employer the courtesy of two weeks (or other notice), it is generally not required to give any notice. Sometimes employees abandon their jobs by simply failing to return to work again. This can be considered a voluntary resignation, or employers may have procedures for terminating a worker's employment for failing to appear or call. In these situations, the separation could be either a resignation or a termination. Employers should determine in advance how to classify these situations and treat them consistently.

If there is any way to obtain the employee's written confirmation that the resignation is voluntary, it can be helpful if the employee later decides that he or she wants to bring a claim of wrongful termination against the company or seek unemployment insurance compensation. In any event, the employer should keep detailed records as to the reasons for the separation.

Employers should understand that simply giving the employee the "option" of "voluntarily" resigning, rather than being fired, will not necessarily hold up as a resignation if it is later challenged down the line. This kind of a "choice" is really no choice at all if the employer is telling the worker that the worker will be fired anyway. If the employee later decides to claim that he or she was fired, even a written statement saying that the employment separation was a "voluntary" resignation may not insulate the company from a constructive discharge claim.

> **WORDS OF WISDOM:** Depending on the reasons for an employee's resignation, he or she may still be entitled to unemployment insurance benefits.

Completion of Contract

When employers have written contracts with their employees, the employment relationship may end by virtue of the terms of the contract. If the contract provides for employment through a specified date, the employment may end on that date with no additional liability by either party. The employment also may end for other reasons, such as breach of contract by either party or for "cause," depending on the language of the contract. (See Chapter 2.)

> **WORDS OF WISDOM:** If the employer and employee continue the working relationship after the expiration of the contract, the employment relationship may be converted from a contract for a specific amount of time to an "at-will" contract, terminable at any time, with or without cause or notice.

Retirement

The employment relationship also may end by virtue of voluntary retirement. It is important to note that forced retirement based on age is a violation of the Age Discrimination in Employment Act.[1] However, under Colorado law, an employer may compel the retirement of any employee who is age 65 through 69 and who, for the two year period immediately before retirement, is employed in a bona fide executive or a high policy-making position if such employee is entitled to an immediate non-forfeitable annual retirement benefit of at least $44,000.00.[2]

> **WORDS OF WISDOM:** Nothing in the Colorado age discrimination law prohibits an individual from electing early retirement at a specified age, nor is it unlawful to require early retirement for reasons other than age.[3]

Downsizing or Reduction in Force

It is hard to pick up a newspaper without reading about downsizing or reductions in force. Nationwide, employers initiated 2,150 mass layoff actions in

November 2002, as measured by new filings for unemployment insurance benefits during the month, according to the U.S. Department of Labor's Bureau of Labor Statistics. For more information on downsizing and resources available to employers, visit the Department of Labor website at www.dol.gov, which provides statistics, summaries of laws, and e-law guidance.

WORDS OF WISDOM: Under certain conditions, the Worker Adjustment and Retraining Notification Act (WARN) requires employers to give their workers 60 days notice before a plant closing or mass layoff.[4] All employers are encouraged to provide notice to the State Dislocated Worker Unit as quickly as possible.

Termination

Firing employees can be one of the most difficult parts of running a company. It can be stressful for both the person conducting the termination and the employee. It definitely is not the time for an employer to lose their cool. However, it is the time for an employer to ensure that they understand the steps they can take to make sure their company follows the law. First, it is important to understand the two types of terminations:

1. Actual or express termination; and
2. Constructive discharge.

Actual or Express Termination

Actual or express terminations are somewhat easy to spot. The employer tells the employee that the employee's services are no longer needed. Express terminations may come in many forms, from the phrase, "you're fired," to the comment, "it's just not working out—please turn in your keys." Express terminations may be verbal or in the form of a termination letter.

Constructive Discharge

Constructive discharge may be more difficult to spot, because the formal words of firing are not required, and sometimes there is a question as to whether there was a voluntary resignation. Constructive discharge means an employee was forced out because the employer allowed the working conditions to become so objectively difficult or intolerable that the employee had no choice but to resign. A successful argument for constructive discharge depends on whether a reasonable person under the same or similar circumstances would view the working conditions as intolerable.

WORDS OF WISDOM: Cumulative events can cause working conditions to deteriorate to an intolerable level.

Some examples of constructive discharge include the creation and tolerance of a hostile work environment and giving the "quit or be fired" ultimatum. In one Colorado case,[5] the court found constructive discharge where the following actions were taken by the employer: a vice president and sales manager "waged a campaign" to undermine the employee's authority—they painted her as unstable, unethical, incompetent, and lacking in credibility; they humiliated her publicly in the eyes of her subordinates; they eliminated her authority; and they demoted her. Under those circumstances, the court concluded that the company had created an environment that a reasonable person in the same or similar circumstances would view as intolerable. Although constructive discharge does not involve a formal firing, the legal consequences can be the same as an express termination.

WORDS OF WISDOM: Many employment contracts provide specific conditions under which employment may be terminated, such as misconduct, intoxication, dishonesty, insubordination, or excessive absenteeism. When an employment agreement allows termination only for "cause" but does not define "cause," it is unclear under Colorado law what "cause" means or which party has the burden of proving that "cause" did or did not exist.

Law Governing the Final Paycheck

The Colorado Wage Law is the state law governing the employee's final paycheck and other pay provisions. The purpose of the Colorado Wage Law is to assure timely payment of wages and provide legal relief when wages are not paid as required by the law. The law applies only to private employers and does not cover independent contractors. The Colorado Wage Law has different requirements depending upon whether the employee voluntarily resigns or the employer terminates the employment relationship.

Employer Termination

When an employer terminates the employment relationship, the wages or compensation for labor or services earned and unpaid at the time of the discharge is due and payable immediately (i.e., at the time of termination). However, if the employer's accounting unit responsible for drawing the payroll checks is not regularly scheduled to be operational on the date of termination, the employer shall make the wages that are due available to the employee no later than six hours after the start of the employer's next regular workday.[6]

Voluntary Resignation

When an employee quits or resigns, the wages or compensation shall become due on the next regular payday.[7]

Place of Payment

When a separation of employment occurs, the employer shall make the separated employee's check for wages due available at the work site, the employer's office, or by mail to the employee's last known mailing address if requested by the employee.[8]

Authorized Set Offs for Lawful Charges

According to the Colorado Wage Law, an employer has the right to set off any lawful charges or indebtedness owing by the employee to the employer.[9] Under the Colorado Wage Law "lawful charges or indebtedness" includes:

- Deductions mandated by or in accordance with local, state, or federal law, including but not limited to deductions for taxes, Federal Insurance Contributions Act (FICA) requirements, garnishments, or any other court ordered deductions;
- Deductions for loans, advances, goods or services, and equipment or property provided by an employer to an employee pursuant to a written agreement between the employer and employee (so long as the written agreement is enforceable and not in violation of the law);
- Any deduction to cover the replacement cost of a shortage due to theft by an employee if a theft report has been filed with the proper law enforcement agency in conjunction with such a theft, pending final adjudication by a court of competent jurisdiction; and
- Any deduction which is authorized by an employee if such authorization is revocable including but not limited to deductions for hospitalization, medical insurance, other insurance, savings plans, stock purchases, voluntary pension plans, charities, and deposits to financial institutions.[10]

Disputed Amounts

If there is a dispute as to the amount due to the employee, the employer shall pay all wages or parts of wages the employer admits are due, leaving the employee to pursue any remedies the employee might have for the balance due. If the employee accepts the undisputed amount, it is not evidence that the employee has made any agreements to waive the amount in dispute.[11]

Penalties and Damages

If the employer refuses to pay wages or compensation upon termination or resignation as set forth above, the employee may recover the amounts due. In addition, if there was not a good faith legal justification for the employer's refusal to pay wages or compensation upon termination or resignation, the employee may recover a penalty of the greater of: (1) fifty percent of the amount due; or (2) an amount equal to the amount of wages payable per day to the employee, not to exceed ten days.

Nonwaiver of Rights

The Colorado Wage Law specifically states that employers may not require employees to waive or modify the employees' rights under the law, either verbally or in writing.[12]

Civil Relief

The Colorado Wage Law allows any person aggrieved by a violation of any provision of the law to file suit in any court having jurisdiction over the parties, but the action must be brought within two years after the cause of action accrues (except for claims of willful violation, which shall be commenced within three years).[13]

WORDS OF WISDOM: Like many of the other laws, the Colorado Wage Law prohibits discrimination against those who use the law or testify in a proceeding related to the law. Specifically, the Colorado Wage Law states that no employer shall intimidate, threaten, restrain, coerce, blacklist, discharge, or in any manner discriminate against any employee who has filed any complaint or instituted or caused to be instituted any proceeding under this article or related law or who has testified or may testify in any proceeding on behalf of himself or another regarding the afforded protections under this article. There is a misdemeanor criminal penalty for violation of this provision, and upon conviction, the employer shall be punished by a fine of not more than five hundred dollars, or by imprisonment in the county jail for not more than 60 days, or by both fine and imprisonment.[14]

A Good Time to Minimize Possible Claims

Unless an employer has already been contacted by an employee's attorney, the termination meeting may be the employer's last opportunity to avoid a legal claim. Emotions may be flaring on both sides by the time the termination occurs, including feelings of anger, betrayal, disappointment, fear, hopelessness, vulnerability, and powerlessness. It is a good idea to have a plan before the meeting for dealing with these emotions. If the employer doesn't have a plan, the employer may lose track of important goals regarding the termination—to let the employee go without driving the employee straight to a lawyer's office and to move forward without the interruptions caused by a lawsuit. There are steps employers can take to minimize possible claims:

- Review all company policies regarding separations of employment and follow the policies and procedures;
- Treat the employee with respect, regardless of the reasons for termination;
- Stay calm and do not engage in a debate regarding the termination. Have a plan in advance for what will be said (and what won't be said), and stick to it;
- Although no law requires severance for a regular termination, before the meeting, consider offering one in exchange for a separation agreement (formalizing the termination and including a release of any claims the employee may have against the company and its employees and agents).
- Consider including a provision in the separation agreement for alternative dispute resolution, such as an arbitration agreement, to minimize the likelihood of ending up in protracted litigation;
- Ask the employee if the employee wants the employer to provide a limited reference, and if so, have the employee sign a release allowing the employer to do so. Although there is a Colorado law providing employers with qualified immunity to give references, an advance understanding with the employee may help to ease the employer's mind and the employee's. It's scary to be fired (even for someone who deserves it, or possibly *especially* for that person), and clarity on the reference issue can be a great step toward calming an employee who otherwise may want to run to the courthouse;
- Have a neutral and discreet witness with the employer during the meeting to take notes;
- If possible, solicit feedback from the employee and write down everything that is said;
- Try to leave the employee's dignity intact. Minimize the disruption by terminating the employee's employment at the end of the day if possible. Make arrangements with the employee for the gathering of personal belongings; and

- Be discreet in explanations to other employees. Do not tell details to people who have no reason to know. Prepare a neutral statement stating that the employee is no longer with the company and wishing him or her luck in the future.

Potential Provisions in a Separation Agreement

A valid separation and release agreement signed by the employee in exchange for a severance payment can virtually eliminate the odds of ending up in court (especially if it contains an arbitration provision in the event of breach of the separation agreement). Some common separation and release agreement provisions include:

- Name, position, and date of termination;
- Statement that the termination decision is mutual and that neither party admits to any wrongdoing;
- Release by the employee of all potential claims against the employer, known or unknown at the date of the agreement;
- Confidentiality provision, stating that the terms of the separation agreement must not be disclosed to anyone other than the employee's spouse and the employee's legal and tax advisors;
- Non-compete provision, if the situation meets the requirements of the non-compete statute;
- Confidentiality provision, protecting company trade secrets from use or disclosure by the employee;
- Review and revocation period as required by the Older Workers' Benefit Protection Act for a valid release of age discrimination claims;
- Provision advising the employee to consult with legal counsel; and
- Acknowledgment of the informed and voluntary nature of the release.

Other separation and release agreement provisions may be added as necessary. It would be wise for an employer to consult with legal counsel before the agreement is signed, since this is the last time the employer may have any degree of control over the agreement, if there is to be one.

WORDS OF WISDOM: Employers also should take care to evaluate the ramifications of terminations and lay offs on their unemployment insurance rates. Although the Colorado unemployment system is outside the scope of this book, employers can find more information on unemployment insurance by visiting the Colorado Department of Labor website at www.coworkforce.gov.

Even when it comes to employee separations, Colorado employers can take care to make wise decisions, utilize the legal resources available to them, and make separations as easy as possible under the circumstances.

FOOTNOTES

[1] 29 U.S.C. §§ 621 to 634.

[2] C.R.S. § 24-34-402(4)(c).

[3] Commission Rule 40.4, 3 C.C.R. 708-1.

[4] 29 U.S.C. §§ 2101 to 2109.

[5] *See Montemayor v. Jacor Communications, Inc.,* No. 00CA1434 (Colo. App. Oct. 24, 2002).

[6] C.R.S. § 8-4-104(1)(a).

[7] C.R.S. § 8-4-104(1)(b).

[8] C.R.S. § 8-4-104(1).

[9] C.R.S. § 8-4-104(2).

[10] C.R.S. § 8-4-101(7.5).

[11] C.R.S. § 8-4-110.

[12] C.R.S. § 8-4-125.

[13] C.R.S. § 8-4-123.

[14] C.R.S. § 8-4-124.

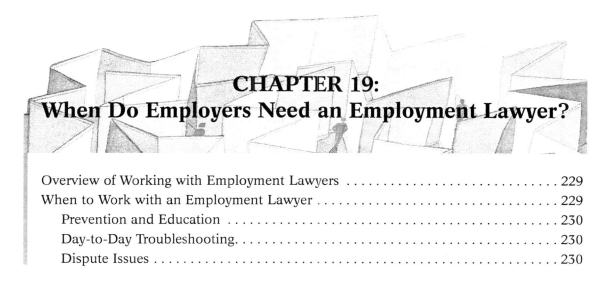

CHAPTER 19:
When Do Employers Need an Employment Lawyer?

Overview of Working with Employment Lawyers

"First let's kill all the lawyers!" — *Shakespeare, Henry VI*

In spite of all of the lawyer jokes and jests to kill the lawyers (hopefully it's said in jest!), like any profession there are good lawyers and bad lawyers. Any good lawyer will tell an employer that employers do not need lawyers for everything—but lawyers are needed for *some* things. How often an employer needs a lawyer depends on the employer's business, the business's goals, the size of the business, changes in the law that may affect the business, and the employees (remember, employers are who they hire).

Hopefully, employers will realize that they should not avoid lawyers, but instead should work *with* lawyers to make the most effective use of their legal counsel. As with employees, an employer's relationship with their lawyer is important. A good lawyer will, among other things, ask an employer about their goals, listen to the employer's concerns and questions, respond to the employer's questions and phone calls in a timely fashion, stay current with the ever-changing employment laws, communicate clearly (in advance) on matters concerning fees and costs (and work efficiently to keep them down for the employer!), get to know the employer and the employer's business, and always watch out for the employer's best interests.

When to Work with an Employment Lawyer

With those goals in mind, there are three broad areas in which employment lawyers can help a business:

    1. Prevention and education;

2. Day-to-day troubleshooting; and
3. Dispute issues.

Prevention and Education

An ounce of prevention . . .

If you knew that a doctor could diagnose cancer in your body in advance and get rid of it, would you go to the doctor before the cancer spread or would you wait until it's too late? Like doctors, lawyers can often diagnose problems in a company when the problems are large enough to see, yet still small enough to solve. Through education, lawyers can even help employers avoid some problems altogether. The following list details some of the preventative measures a good lawyer can discuss with an employer—before the employer receives a dreaded EEOC charge:

- Conduct an annual overall review (check-up) of workforce practices and documentation;
- Create and review policies and documents;
- Draft and review employment and independent contractor contracts;
- Prepare and review handbooks and policies;
- Create enforceable non-compete agreements and trade secrets provisions;
- Draft alternative dispute resolution agreements (i.e. arbitration, mediation, collaberative law, negotiations);
- Prepare severance and release agreements in advance;
- Conduct training of managers, supervisors, and employees.

Day-to-Day Troubleshooting

- Prepare for terminations or layoffs;
- Discuss coaching and discipline concerns;
- Resolve questions regarding leave policies, safety laws, and workplace violence.

Dispute Issues

- Advice on internal resolution ideas;
- Representation in alternative dispute resolution processes (negotiations, mediation, collaborative law, arbitration);
- Representation before the EEOC, CCRD, Colorado Department of Labor, additional state and federal agencies, and in court.

Remember, when Shakespeare's evil murderous character plotted, "first, let's kill all the lawyers," the character was planning an overthrow of the government so he could set up a dictatorship—with himself as king! In fact, the character wanted everyone to "worship" him as "their lord." The character knew that (most) lawyers preserve the law and would work to restore law and order. But the murderous character wanted the people to serve him as an absolute ruler. In other words, the character wanted to get rid of the lawyers to prolong the anarchy after his overthrow of the government.

Prevent anarchy in the workplace—create and maintain a legally healthy working environment. Call an employment lawyer *before* the first signs of trouble.

APPENDIX 1

Summary of Laws
Private Colorado Employers Should Know

While this list is long, it is not all inclusive. The laws change daily, and these charts are intended to provide employers with an overview of the laws with which they should be familiar. Additionally, these laws are quite complex, and the following is simply a general description of some of the laws employers might encounter.

Federal Statutory Laws

Name	Citation	General Description	Coverage	Possible Damages and Penalties
Section 1981	42 U.S.C. § 1981	Protects people from discrimination based on race or national origin in the making of contracts (including making, modification, and termination of employment contracts), and applies to benefits, privileges, terms and conditions of the contract. At-will employment contracts are covered.	All employers.	Economic damages, back pay, front pay, compensatory damages, emotional distress damages, injunctive relief, promotion, restored benefits, punitive damages, attorney fees, reinstatement, costs,no statutory cap on damages (unlike Title VII).
Age Discrimination in Employment Act (ADEA)	29 U.S.C. § 621	Prohibits age discrimination in employment for individuals over the age of 40.	20 or more employees for 20 or more calendar weeks during the current or prior year.	Damages available under FLSA, including legal or equitable relief. Lost wages, liquidated damages, front pay, stock option appreciation. No damages for pain and suffering.
Americans With Disabilities Act of 1990 (ADA)	42 U.S.C. § 12101	Prohibits disability discrimination in employment.	15 or more employees for 20 or more calendar weeks during the current calendar year or the prior year.	Title VII remedies.
Civil Rights Act of 1991	42 U.S.C. § 2981(a), 42 U.S.C. § 1988 (b)	Allows Title VII claimants to recover compensatory and punitive damages.	Private employers in industries affecting commerce with 15 or more employees for 20 or more weeks per year.	Compensatory damages, back pay, front pay, lost benefits, punitive damages, emotional distress damages, attorney fees, costs, interest; injunctive relief.

Name	Citation	General Description	Coverage	Possible Damages and Penalties
Consolidated Omnibus Budget Reconciliation Act of 1985 (COBRA)	29 U.S.C. § 11162	Continuation of group health insurance if discharge or reduction in hours at employees' expense; if discharge up to 18 months, employer must provide notification letter.	20 or more employees and if employer offers a group healthcare plan.	See statute.
Drug Free Workplace Act of 1988	41 U.S.C. § 701	Certification requirements of drug free workplace, policy statement.	Federal contractors and grantees doing substantial government business.	Suspension from doing federal work.
Electronic Communications Privacy Act of 1986	18 U.S.C. § 2510	Prohibits employers from intentionally obtaining unauthorized access to e-mail and voice mail. Does not restrict secret use of silent videotaping.	All private employers.	See statute.
Employee Polygraph Protection Act of 1988	23 U.S.C. §§ 2001 to 2009, 29 C.F.R. § 801	Prohibits requirement of polygraph testing or discipline for refusal, with strict exception.	All private employers.	See statute.
Employee Retirement Income Security Act (ERISA)	29 U.S.C. § 1140	Protects employees' rights to benefits under a covered plan; prohibits discrimination.	Any employee benefit plan by employer engaged in commerce or any industry or activity affecting commerce and/or by any employee organization(s) representing employees engaged in commerce or any industry or activity affecting commerce.	Back pay, restoration of benefits, attorney fees.
Equal Pay Act	29 U.S.C. § 206(d)	Prohibits sex-based wage discrimination; requires equal pay for equal work.	All private employers.	Back pay for up to 3 years before lawsuit, liquidated damages, attorney fees, injunctive relief; criminal penalties for willful violations.
Fair Credit Reporting Act	15 U.S.C. § 1681	Governs disclosure of certain credit and financial information.	All private employers.	See statute.
Fair Labor Standards Act (FLSA) (wage and hour laws)	29 U.S.C. § 201	Minimum wages, overtime pay, equal pay, record keeping; sets forth exemptions; prohibits retaliation.	All private employers.	Back pay, liquidated damages, attorney fees, injunction.

Name	Citation	General Description	Coverage	Possible Damages and Penalties
False Claims Act/ Qui Tam Claims	31 U.S.C. §§ 3729 to 3733	Provides civil remedies for employees who report fraud on government by government contractors.	Employers with contracts with federal government.	Civil remedies, sanctions of double damages, penalties.
Family and Medical Leave Act (FMLA)	29 U.S.C. § 2612	Governs leave to attend to serious health condition of oneself or immediate family or for birth or adoption of child; provides 12 weeks unpaid leave, may be taken intermittently under some circumstances.	50 or more employees for each working day during 20 or more calendar weeks in the current or prior calendar year.	Reinstatement, front pay, back pay, liquidated damages.
Federal Anti-Wire Tap Act	18 U.S.C. §§ 2510 to 2521	Prohibits intentional interception of any wire, oral, or electronic communication or intentionally discloses the contents of the interception; prohibits tape recording of employees' phone calls without their knowledge or consent; provides exceptions.	All private employers.	See statute.
Federal Arbitration Act	9 U.S.C. § 1	Governs arbitration agreements, with exceptions.	Per agreement.	N/A
Federal Jury Service	28 U.S.C. § 1875	Employees are protected from discharge, intimidation, coercion because of federal jury service; leave of absence must be reinstated; must provide benefits and insurance as normal.	All private employers.	See statute.
Federal Uniformed Services Employment and Reemployment Rights Act of 1994 (USERRA)	38 U.S.C. § 4301	Protection of rights of private and public employees called to active duty and reserves.	All private employers.	Back pay, reinstatement, liquidated damages, attorney fees, expert witness fees, litigation costs.
Gramm-Leach-Bliley Act	15 U.S.C. § 6801	Protects certain financial information.	See statute.	See statute.

Name	Citation	General Description	Coverage	Possible Damages and Penalties
Health Insurance Portability and Accountability Act (HIPAA)	Pub. L. No. 104-191, 110 Stat. 1936	Privacy rules, protected health, personal, personnel data.	All employers.	See statute.
Immigration Reform and Control Act of 1986 (IRCA)	8 U.S.C. § 1324a	Governs employment of non-citizen workers; prohibits employers from knowingly hiring or retaining anyone not authorized to work legally in the U.S.	All private employers.	See statute.
IRCA – anti-discrimination provisions- Section 102	8 U.S.C. § 1324b	Prohibits unfair immigration-related employment practices, including citizenship status discrimination, national origin discrimination, document abuse.	4 to 14 employees.	Back pay up to 2 years, civil fines, attorney fees, special orders.
National Labor Relations Act (NLRA)	29 U.S.C. §§ 141 to 187	Protects right to unionize; right to bargain collectively; right to engage in concerted protected activity.	All private employers.	Back pay, interest, reinstatement.
Occupational Safety and Health Act (OSHA)	29 U.S.C. § 651	Regulates safe and healthful working conditions.	All private employers; special requirements for employers with 11 or more employees.	Civil remedies and criminal penalties.
Older Workers Benefit Protection Act/part of ADEA	29 U.S.C. § 623	Sets forth requirements for valid release of age discrimination claims.	20 or more employees for 20 or more calendar weeks during the current or prior year.	Invalid release.
Pregnancy Discrimination Act of 1968	92 U.S.C. § 2076 (amendment to Title VII)	Prohibits pregnancy discrimination in employment.	15 or more employees for 20 or more weeks per year.	Title VII remedies.
Racketeer Influenced and Corrupt Organizations (RICO)	18 U.S.C. §§ 1961 to 1968	Conspiracy.	See statute.	See statute.
Rehabilitation Act	29 U.S.C. §§ 791 to 794	Prohibits disability discrimination in employment.	Private employers who receive federal funds and federal employers.	No statutory remedy stated; courts may award compensatory damages; possibly punitive damages; any appropriate relief.

Name	Citation	General Description	Coverage	Possible Damages and Penalties
Sarbanes-Oxley Act	Pub. L. No. 107-204, 116 Stat. 745	Requires complaint procedure for employers; provides protections for employees who report violations of SEC laws.	Publicly traded companies.	See statute.
Title VII of the Civil Rights Act of 1964	42 U.S.C. §§ 2000e to 2000e-17	Prohibits discrimination and harassment based on sex, race, color, national origin, religion; prohibits retaliation.	Private employers in industries affecting commerce with 15 or more employees for 20 or more weeks per year.	Compensatory damages, back pay, front pay, lost benefits, punitive damages, emotional distress damages, attorney fees, costs, interest, injunctive relief.
Weingarten Rights	*NLRB V. WEINGARTEN, INC.,* 420 U.S. 251	Right to have co-worker present at investigatory interviews or meetings that the employee believes will result in disciplinary action from their employer.	All employees.	Damages if termination.
Worker Adjustment and Retraining Notification Act (WARN Act)	29 U.S.C. § 2101	Requires notice before mass layoff or plant closing, with exceptions.	100 full-time employees or 100 or more employees, including part-time, who work at least 4,000 hours per week.	Lost wages and benefits up to 60 days, attorney fees, and civil penalties.

Colorado Statutory Laws

Name/Topic	Citation	General Description	Coverage	Possible Penalties
Access to Personnel Files	No statute	N/A	N/A	N/A
Adoption	C.R.S. § 19-5-211(1.5)	Employer must treat adoptive parents like biological parents/ i.e. equal maternity/ paternity leave if provided by employer.	All employers who provide such benefits.	No specific statutory remedy.
Child Support Obligations	C.R.S. § 14-14-105(2)	Unlawful to punish employee for child support collection on employer.	All private employers.	Contempt of court; reinstatement; damages up to 6 weeks lost wages; attorney fees, costs.
Colorado Anti-Discrimination Act/ Colorado Civil Rights Act	C.R.S. § 24-34-402, C.R.S. § 24-34-402.5	Discrimination based on marital status, off duty lawful activities.	2 or more employees.	Reinstatement; back pay.

Name/Topic	Citation	General Description	Coverage	Possible Penalties
Colorado Employment Security Act - (Unemployment benefits)	C.R.S. § 8-70-103	(Unemployment benefits) Employee qualifies for benefits if unemployed through his or her own.	All private sector employers employing one or more persons in covered employment; nonprofits and charitable if 4 or more employees in 20 weeks of current or prior year; there are exceptions.	Unemployment benefits; see statute.
Colorado Minimum Wage Order Number 22	Wage Order	Meals – 30 minutes unpaid within 5 hours of starting work. Rest – 10 minutes per 4 hours paid.	Retail, service, commercial support service, food and beverage and health industries.	Civil penalties; lost wages.
Colorado Uniform Arbitration Act	C.R.S. § 13-22-201	Provides statutory procedures for arbitration; expressly includes employment contracts.	Per contract.	N/A
Colorado Uniform Trade Secrets Act	C.R.S. § 7-74-101	Protects employer trade secrets; sets forth standards for trade secrets.	All private employers.	Monetary damages; injunctive relief.
Colorado Wage Claim Act	C.R.S. § 8-4-104	Sets forth requirements for pay upon job separation.	Private sector employers.	Wages due; plus penalties of 50% of amount proven to be due, amount payable per day up to 10 days; mandatory attorney fees to prevailing party.
Colorado Workers' Compensation Act	C.R.S. § 8-14.5-101	Governs on the job injuries.	All private employers with 1 or more employees.	See statute.
Defamation Mitigation	C.R.S. § 13-25-125	Permits defendant in defamation case to present evidence that tends to mitigate damages.	N/A	N/A
Employer Liability	C.R.S. § 8-2-201	Sets forth negligence claim for injuries.	All private employers.	Damages.

Appendix 1: Summary of Laws

Name/Topic	Citation	General Description	Coverage	Possible Penalties
Employer Reference Immunity	C.R.S. § 8-2-114	Employers are immune from civil liability and not liable in civil damages for disclosure, unless information disclosed was false and the employer knew or reasonably should have known it was false; upon request of employee, employer must send written information to last known address, or at place of business.	All private employers.	N/A
Equal Pay Requirement	C.R.S. § 8-5-101	Prohibits compensation discrimination on basis of sex.	All employers.	Lost wages.
Freedom of Association/ Unions, Societies, Political Parties	C.R.S. § 8-2-102	Making it unlawful for any employer to prevent employees from forming, joining, or belonging to any lawful labor organization, union, society or political party.	All private employers.	Misdemeanor, punishable by fine of $100-$500, and imprisonment for 6 months to a year.
Garnishment	C.R.S. § 5-5-106, C.R.S. § 13-54.5-110	Unlawful to discharge employee based on garnishment by creditors.	All private employers.	Lost wages not to exceed 6 weeks; reinstatement.
Genetic Information	C.R.S. §§ 10-3-1104.5 to 1104.7	Limits use and disclosure of HIV and genetic testing information by insurance companies. Requires informed consent prior to testing or disclosure of results to 3rd parties, such as employers.	All private employers.	Legal and equitable remedies; attorney fees.
Jury Duty	C.R.S. § 13-71-134(1), C.R.S. § 13-71-126	Cannot interfere with jury duty requirements, must pay regular wages, up to $50 day to regular employees for first 3 days of service.	All private employers.	Civil action, treble damages, attorney fees.

Colorado Employment Law

Name/Topic	Citation	General Description	Coverage	Possible Penalties
Military duty	C.R.S. § 28-3-506, C.R.S. § 28-3-601, C.R.S. § 28-3-602, C.R.S. § 28-3-609	Prohibits discrimination due to service or intended service in national guard or state militia. Entitled to unpaid leave of absence for up to 15 days a year. Leave without pay must be granted for additional periods of military service where compelled. Reinstatement rights.	All private employers.	Misdemeanor, fine up to $500. Private right of action for damages.
Non-Compete Statute	C.R.S. § 8.2.113	Prohibits non-compete agreements except for sale of business, trade secrets, training expense, executive and management personnel and their professional staff.	All private employers.	Damages; equitable remedies; injunctive relief.
Protection of Political Activities	C.R.S. § 8-2-108	Making it unlawful for employer to prevent any employee from participating in politics, becoming a candidate, or being elected.	See statute.	Misdemeanor, punishable by fine of $2,000 and up to one year of imprisonment/ and private right of action for damages.
Protection for Required Testimony	C.R.S. § 8-2.5-101	Making it unlawful to prevent an employee from testifying before a committee of general assembly, court, or speaking to a member of the general assembly, if so requested by committee, court, or member.	All private employers.	Misdemeanor, punishable by fine of up to $1,000/ and private right of action for damages, plus attorney fees.
Regulating Youth Employment	C.R.S. § 8-12-101	Regulates youth employment.	All private employers.	See statute.
Sealed Criminal Records	C.R.S. § 24-72-308	May not require disclosure of sealed arrest records if employee was acquitted, no charges were filed, or case was dismissed. Does not apply to pleas or convictions, DUI, DWI, sexual assault, indecent exposure, incest, or child prostitution.	All private employers.	Misdemeanor/fine up to $100 and imprisonment up to 90 days.

Appendix 1: Summary of Laws

Name/Topic	Citation	General Description	Coverage	Possible Penalties
State drug and alcohol testing laws	No statute	N/A	N/A	N/A
State Health Insurance Continuation Law	C.R.S. § 10-16-108	Employees and dependents who had been covered for at least 6 months by group health insurance have continuation right for 18 months; notice to be given within 10 days after termination.	Employers with group insurance.	See statute.
State Minimum Wage Law	C.R.S. § 8-6-109	$5.15 by order of the Colorado Department of Labor & Employment.	See statute.	See statute.
Statutory Fraud	C.R.S. § 8-2-107	Fraudulent inducement.	All private employers.	Damages.
Termination of Pregnancy	C.R.S. § 18-6-104	Employee not required to participate in termination of pregnancy if employee objects on moral or religious grounds; protection from discipline.	See statute.	See statute.
Volunteer Firefighters	C.R.S. § 31-30-1131	No termination of volunteer fire fighter failing to report to work due to emergency fire.	All private employers.	See statute.
Voting	C.R.S. § 31-10-603, C.R.S. § 31-10-1522, C.R.S. § 1-7-102(1), C.R.S. § 31-10-603	Cannot interfere with voting; 2 hours off with pay, but employee must apply before day of election; employer may specify hours, but if employee asks, must be at beginning or end of shift.	All employers.	See statute.
Whistleblowing	C.R.S. § 24-50-101, C.R.S. § 24-114-102	Protects state employees and employees of private enterprises under contract with a state agency from retaliation for whistleblowing reports.	State employers and employers with state contracts.	See statute.
Wiretapping Law	C.R.S. § 18-9-301	Prohibits wiretapping.	All private employers.	Criminal.

APPENDIX 2
Guidelines for Selected Statutes and
Record Keeping Requirements

NOTE: The following is not an exhaustive list of record keeping requirements under these listed statutes. This list is only intended to give employers an idea of some of the major record keeping requirements. For example, there are specific requirements for keeping tax records, records regarding benefit plans, and other important records that are not listed. For specific advice concerning the record keeping requirements of various statutes, consult legal counsel and the appropriate governmental agencies.

Age Discrimination in Employment Act (ADEA)

Maintain for at least three years:
- Date of birth;
- Occupation/job title.

Maintain for at least one year:
- All advertisements relating to job openings;
- Records of changes in positions (such as promotions, transfers, demotions, lay-offs, terminations);
- Resumes or other forms of employment history;
- Test papers for a position if the documents disclose test results;
- Training or apprenticeships records.

For more information, see www.eeoc.gov.

Americans with Disabilities Act (ADA)

Maintain for at least one year:
- Completed job application and other hiring information;
- Job orders submitted by employer to employment agencies;
- Results of any physical examination conducted by employer in connection with personnel action;
- Records of changes in positions (such as promotions, transfers, demotions, lay-offs, terminations);
- Training or apprenticeships information;
- Requests for job accommodations.

For more information, see www.eeoc.gov.

Equal Pay Act (EPA)

Maintain for at least three years:
- Gender of all employees;
- Occupation/job titles of employees.

For more information, see www.dol.gov.

Fair Labor Standards Act (FLSA)

Maintain for at least three years:
- Date of birth if employee is under age of 19;
- Occupation/job title of employees.

For more information, see www.dol.gov.

Immigration Reform and Control Act of 1986 (IRCA)

Maintain for at least three years after hiring or date of recruitment or referral:
- Form 1-9.

For more information, see www.bice.gov.

Social Security Act (SSA)

Maintain for at least four years after payment of tax or due date, whichever is later:
- Employee name;
- Any identifying number used in place of a name on any work records (four years from tax due date or payment of tax, whichever is later);
- Social security number (four years from tax due date or payment of tax, whichever is later);
- Employee home address, including zip code.

For more information, see www.ssa.gov.

Title VII

Maintain for at least 1 year:
- Completed job application and other hiring information;
- Records of changes in positions (such as promotions, transfers, demotions, lay-offs, terminations);
- Training or apprenticeships information.

For more information, see www.eeoc.gov.

APPENDIX 3
Employer Posting Requirements and Internet Resources

There are numerous state and federal posting requirements for employers. Some posting requirements may only apply under certain circumstances, but several posting requirements are required in all situations. Posters may be obtained free from the following agencies or may be purchased in combinations from certain publishing companies and business supply companies.

NOTE: For Workers' Compensation Posters, contact the employer's workers' compensation insurance carrier. Employers should prepare and post the following notice in 1/2 inch letters: "If injured on the job, written notice must be given to your employer within four working days of the accident, pursuant to section 8-43-102(1) C.R.S." Employers are also required to post or notify workers in writing regarding when and where they will be paid. For more information see: http://www.state.co.us/oed/guide/7-14.html.

Anti-Discrimination
Colorado Division of Civil Rights
1560 Broadway, Suite 1050
Denver, CO 80202
(303) 894-2997
1-800-262-4845
http://www.dora.state.co.us/civil-rights

Polygraph Protection Act
Federal Minimum Wage
Family & Medical Leave Act
U.S. Dept. of Labor, Wage-Hour Division
1801 California St., Ste. 935
Denver, CO 80202
(303) 844-4405
http://www.dol.gov/elaws

Equal Employment Opportunity
Equal Employment Opportunity Commission (EEOC)
PO Box 12549
Cincinnati, OH 45312
1-800-669-3362
http://www.eeoc.gov

State Minimum Wage
Colorado Division of Labor & Employment
Labor Standards Unit
1515 Arapahoe St., Tower II, Suite 375
Denver, CO 80202
(303) 318-8441
http://www.coworkforce.com

Occupational Safety
Occupation Safety & Health Administration (OSHA)
1999 Broadway, Suite 1690
Denver, CO 80202
(303) 844-1600
http://www.osha.gov

Unemployment Insurance
Division of Employment and Training
U. I. Tax Liability Unit
1515 Arapahoe St., Tower III, Suite 200
Denver, CO 80202
(303) 318-9000
1-800-480-8299, State Wide Only
http://www.coworkforce.com

Colorado Department of Labor and Employment
1515 Arapahoe, Tower II, Suite 400
Denver, CO 80202
(303) 318-8000
http://www.coworkforce.com

INDEX

F

Fair Labor Standards Act. *See* FLSA
False light, 193
Family and Medical Leave Act. *See* FMLA
Faragher/Ellerth defense to harassment, 134
  avoiding harm, 136
  avoiding or limiting effects of harassment, 134-135
  employee's failure to complain, 135-136
  reasonable care, 134
Final paychecks, 223-225
Financial information privacy, 192
FLSA, 172
  administrative exemption, 175
  commissioned sales employee exemption, 177
  computer specialists exemption, 176
  covered employees, 172
  employment relationships, 172-173
  enforcement, 179
  executive exemption, 175
  exemptions, 174, 177-178
    commissioned sales employee exemption, 177
    computer specialists exemption, 176
    white collar employees, 174-176
  independent contractors, 173
  minimum wage, 173
  misconceptions, 179
  outside sales exemption, 176
  overtime pay, 173-174
  posting requirements, 178
  professional exemption, 175
  record keeping, 178
  white collar employee exemptions, 174-176
FMLA
  benefits, 157
  certification, 159-160
  covered employers, 155
  eligible employees, 155
  employee notice, 158
  employer notice, 159
  health benefits, maintenance of, 157
  health care providers, 160
  intermittent leave, 155-156
  job restoration, 158
  "key" employee exception, 158
  life insurance coverage, 157
  protection of employees requesting or taking FMLA leave, 160-161
  provisions of, 154-162
  purposes of, 154
  record keeping, 161-162
  reduced schedule leave, 155-156
  serious health condition, 156
  unpaid leave, entitlement to, 155
"Funny" jokes, 88-89

G

Gays, harassment, 96
Genetic information privacy, 192
Good faith and fair dealing, 30
Green cards, 56-57

H

Handbooks, employee. *See* Employee handbooks
Harassment, 87-88
  age based, 95
  anti-discrimination and harassment-free workplaces. *See* Anti-discrimination and harassment-free workplaces
  color based, 92-95
  disability based, 95-96
  employer liability, 131
    "alter ego" harassment, 133-134
    co-worker harassment, 133
    Faragher/Ellerth defense, 134-136
    manager harassment, 131-133
    supervisor harassment, 131-133
    vicarious liability, 132
  Faragher/Ellerth defense, 134
    avoiding harm, 136
    avoiding or limiting effects of harassment, 134-135
    employee's failure to complain, 135-136
    reasonable care, 134
  "funny" jokes distinguished, 88-89
  hostile work environment, 90
  jurors, 96
  military personnel, 96
  national origin based, 92-95
  nature of, 89-90
  race based, 92-95

Temporary employees, 27
Termination of employees, 222-223
Termination of employment. *See* Employee
   separation
Testing, job-related, 48-49
Training and education, 203-204
Transgender harassment, 96
Transsexual harassment, 96

U

Undue hardship
   disability discrimination, 81-82
   religious discrimination, 79
Unemployment benefits for independent
   contractors, 17
Unintended contracts, 33
Unions
   Colorado Labor Peace Act, 217-218
   National Labor Relations Act, 215-216
   unfair labor charges, 216-217

V

Verbal contracts, 25-26
Vicarious liability
   harassment, 132
   independent contractors, 19
Violence in the workplace. *See* Workplace
   violence
Voicemail message privacy, 191
Voter harassment, 96
Voting, 163-164

W

W-4, 52
Wage Act, Colorado, 180-181
Wage and hour laws, 172
   child labor, 181
     enforcement of laws, 184
     permissible jobs, 181-182
     work environments, 183-184
     work hours, 182-183
   Colorado Minimum Wage Order
     Number 22, 172, 180
   Colorado Wage Act, 180-181
   Fair Labor Standards Act. *See* FLSA
   final paychecks, 223-225
White collar employee exemptions under
   FLSA, 174-176
Workers' compensation for independent
   contractors, 17
Workplace violence, 207-208
   civil liability, 210-211
   criminal charges, 214
   defined, 208-209
   leave for abuse victims, 213
   liability theories, 209-211
   OSHA duties, 209-210
   prevention programs, 212
     preventative policies, 212-213
     responsive policies, 213
   prevention recommendations, 211-212
   restraining orders, 213-214
Written contracts, 27-31